Interventions: New Studies in Medieval Culture
Ethan Knapp, Series Editor

Inventing Womanhood

Gender and Language in Later Middle English Writing

TARA WILLIAMS

THE OHIO STATE UNIVERSITY PRESS / COLUMBUS

A subvention to aid the publication of this volume was provided by the Medieval Academy of America.

Library of Congress Cataloging-in-Publication Data

Williams, Tara, 1975–
    Inventing womanhood : gender and language in later Middle English writing / Tara Williams.
       p. cm. — (Interventions: new studies in medieval culture)
    Includes bibliographical references and index.
    ISBN-13: 978-0-8142-1151-9 (cloth : alk. paper)
    ISBN-10: 0-8142-1151-8 (cloth : alk. paper)
    ISBN-13: 978-0-8142-9252-5 (cd)
1. English literature—Middle English, 1100–1500—History and criticism. 2. Women in literature—History—To 1500. 3. Sex role in literature—History—To 1500. 4. Motherhood in literature—History—To 1500. 5. Women and literature—History—To 1500. I. Title. II. Series: Interventions : new studies in medieval culture.
    PR275.W6W55 2011
    820.9'3522—dc22
                      2010030318

This book is available in the following editions:
Cloth (ISBN 978-0-8142-1151-9)
CD-ROM (ISBN 978-0-8142-9252-5)
Paper (ISBN: 978-0-8142-5763-0)
Cover design by Larry Nozik
Text design by Jennifer Shoffey Forsythe
Type set in Adobe Garamond

CONTENTS

ACKNOWLEDGMENTS

Many thanks to Larry Scanlon, who first showed me how fascinating medieval studies could be. The guidance of Larry and the other members of my dissertation committee—Susan Crane, Chris Chism, and Felicity Riddy—was vital to this project from its earliest phase. In its later phases, the book was much improved by the thoughtful comments of the reviewers for Ohio State University Press, Frank Grady and Rebecca Krug. Thanks are also owed to the people I worked with at the press—especially Malcolm Litchfield, Ethan Knapp, and Eugene O'Connor.

I have been fortunate to have engaged students, wonderful colleagues, and supportive department chairs since I came to Oregon State. As the only medievalist there, I'm also lucky to have been welcomed by a larger community of excellent medieval scholars, including Gail Sherman and Warren Ginsberg. I'm particularly grateful to those OSU colleagues who have read drafts or discussed ideas with me: Kerry Ahearn, Chris Anderson, Richmond Barbour, Vicki Tolar Burton, Neil Davison, Lisa Ede, Evan Gottlieb, Anita Helle, Ted Leeson, Rebecca Olson, David Robinson, and Andrew Valls. Special thanks are due to Peter Betjemann, who valiantly read—and offered insightful suggestions to improve—some of my roughest drafts, and to Betty Campbell, who read the introduction and gave just the right advice at just the right moment (as she so often does).

This work was supported by funding from the Richard III Society and a fellowship at the Oregon State University Center for the Humanities, where I spent a peaceful and productive term. Parts of the introduction and first chapter originally appeared as "'T'assaye in Thee Thy Wommanheede': Griselda Chosen, Translated, and Tried" in *Studies in the Age of Chaucer* 27 (2005): 93–127, and part of Chapter 4 as "Manipulating Mary: Maternal, Sexual, and Textual Authority in *The Book of Margery Kempe*," *Modern Philology* 107.4 (May 2010): 528–55. I gratefully acknowledge permission to reprint the revised versions here.

Thanks to my brother, Ryan, and my parents, Rod and Billie Williams; they always believed I could write a book and celebrated every step along the way. Hugo lived with this project for many years and I simply could not have written it without his interest, support, and understanding.

THE ORIGINS OF WOMANHOOD

I n 1348, a group of beautiful women began appearing at tournaments dressed as men. Henry Knighton, a canon of St. Mary's Abbey in Leicester, mentions in his chronicle these unusual women and the discomfort they provoked. The passage shows Knighton grappling with the problem of describing women who do not conform to established feminine categories, pointing up the limitations of existing models of womanhood:

> In those days a rumour arose and great excitement amongst the people because, when tournaments were held, at almost every place a troop of ladies would appear, as though they were a company of players, dressed in men's clothes of striking richness and variety, to the number of forty or sometimes fifty such damsels, all very eye-catching and beautiful, though hardly of the kingdom's better sort. They were dressed in parti-coloured tunics, of one colour on one side and a different one on the other, with short hoods, and liripipes wound about their heads like strings, with belts of gold and silver clasped about them, and even with the kind of knives commonly called daggers slung low across their bellies, in pouches. And thus they paraded themselves at tournaments on fine chargers and other well-arrayed horses, and consumed and spent their substance, and wantonly and with disgraceful lubricity displayed their bodies, as the rumour ran.
>
> And thus, neither fearing God nor abashed by the voice of popular outrage, they slipped the traces of matrimonial restraint. . . . But God in this as in all things had a marvellous remedy to dispel their wantonness, for at the times and places appointed for those vanities He visited cloudbursts, and thunder and flashing lightning, and tempests of astonishing violence upon them.[1]

The most unsettling aspect of these women seems to be that they have "slipped the traces of matrimonial restraint [laxato matrimonialis pudicie freno]." Because their marital situations are unknown, they cannot be classified as maidens, wives, or widows—the traditional triad of female roles. Those roles take on meaning most fully in a familial context and in relation to men, but Knighton's women appear outside of that framework and so must be dealt with on their own terms. He struggles to do so by likening them to "players [interludii]," suggesting that they are lower class, and, most extensively, by relating them to recognizable masculine models or characteristics. If Knighton cannot connect these women to their fathers or husbands, in other words, he can underscore a different set of connections to maleness: the women's manifestation as a mounted "troop [cohors]" armed with daggers and wearing "men's clothing [apparatu uirili]." However, tension exists between these aspects and the feminine elements of the women's appearance and behavior; these "ladies [dominarum]" remain unambiguously female, neither actors nor men. Rather than condemning this spectacle with the "popular outrage [populi uocem]" that Knighton projects, people react with fascination and "great excitement [ingens clamor]." The new vision of femininity that the women embody intrigues and disturbs Knighton as well as the tournament audiences, partly because the women are never clearly classified (using the available terms and categories) or controlled.

This is the second issue the passage raises: in "slipp[ing] the traces of matrimonial restraint," the women also evade the largely subordinate relationship to masculine authority inherent in maidenhood, wifehood, and—albeit to a lesser extent—widowhood, and therefore raise questions about whether and how women might exercise power in other ways. These questions carry a spiritual undertone, since the Church helped both to limit women's authority as wives and to expand it as virgins or visionaries (most often in the mode of the Virgin Mary, who derived authority from her position as Christ's mother and intercessor for humanity). However, in addition to commanding the attention of the spectators and the chronicler himself, the women seem to possess wealth and independent agency; they even appear prepared to defend themselves with daggers. Their power does not conform to any sanctioned model, secular or spiritual, and instead—in Knighton's portrayal—signifies a lack of respect for God and places the women in direct conflict with him. To resolve the thorny issue of female power, then, the passage turns to deus ex machina. But God's attempts to punish or contain the women are apparently ineffective; because multiple "tempests [tempestatum]" occur, the implication is that these women continue to appear at tournaments and continue to feed the rumor for some time.

If these women have escaped the restraints of matrimony, however, Knighton has not: he strains to understand and describe these women who exceed conventional feminine identities based on marital status but he lacks both precedent and vocabulary. Although Knighton is writing in Latin, the same problem exists in Middle English and, as I will argue below, became more urgent due to a number of cultural changes. In response, from the late fourteenth through the fifteenth century, Middle English writers experimented with new ways of imagining and representing women's lives and experiences. Two especially significant aspects of that experimentation were the coining of a number of new gendered terms, including *womanhood* and *femininity,* and the refashioning of others already in use, such as *motherhood.*[2] This book suggests that Middle English writers used these words with remarkable eagerness to signal moments where the writers are particularly interested or invested in exploring new ideas about femininity.[3] As suggested by the episode of the tournament women, some of the most vital issues are how to develop and define the larger idea of womanhood underlying more specific identities like wife or mother and how to construct women's relationship to different kinds of authority, generally masculine and frequently religious. Such concerns appear most prominently in connection with femininity in this period; *manhood* had already been in recorded use for at least 150 years before the analogous terms relating to women appeared in the written record.

While writers often carry out this linguistic and literary experimentation through or in relation to individual female characters like the Wife of Bath, I am most interested in the general concepts of womanhood formulated during this process. Few scholars have tackled that broader idea directly, although Sarah Salih has considered a specific gendered identity in the form of virginity and Jennifer Summit has traced the development and impact of the "woman writer" as a gendered category.[4] Perhaps the work that most closely parallels this investigation of femininity is the recent research attending to medieval notions of masculinity. Isabel Davis, for instance, takes up representations of male selfhood in life writing and Holly Crocker considers Chaucer's portrayals of masculinity in relation to questions of visibility and agency.[5] Crocker's concern with constructions of manhood roughly resembles mine with constructions of womanhood. While her analysis does not center on language, she does note the importance—and the slipperiness—of gendered vocabulary: "the Middle English *manhed* has several meanings, whose overlapping resonance indicate this identity's potential fluidity."[6]

Although I am interested in the various gendered terms that writers created and adapted, I find *womanhood* to be particularly important, both because it directly invokes the conceptual problem of what defines women collectively, beyond specific experiences or roles, and because it was used so widely and in such interesting ways in the late Middle Ages. The word first appears in the works of Geoffrey Chaucer and John Gower (associated with characters such as Criseyde, Griselda, Hippolyta, and Amans's lady), but the invention of womanhood to which my title refers is a complex diachronic process that incorporated a wide set of usages and influences and that involved innovation at the level of both language and literary representation.[7] This process continued into the 1400s as other writers adopted and adapted gendered terms and the related ideas. More than six centuries later, we tend to think of much of this gendered vocabulary as self-evidently transparent: *womanhood,* for instance, means the condition of being a woman. But what it meant to be a woman—outside the traditional roles of maiden, wife, and widow—was very much an open question in the later Middle Ages and was becoming a more immediate concern after the outbreak of the plague. When Chaucer and Gower employ this new word, then, they do so with surprising precision. It does not mean simply the condition of being a woman but instead signifies particular elements of womanliness, from beauty to an ability to exercise intercessory influence. When later writers pick up *womanhood* and its sister terms to use in their own texts, they do so with a similar sense of the terms' linguistic usefulness—indicating that this language addressed the gap that had developed between social reality and available vocabulary—but often with a different set of personal and poetic aims.

The gendered language that forms the focus of *Inventing Womanhood* occurs across a range of texts, but many of the earliest or most significant usages appear in literary texts, which privileged neologisms and linguistic creativity. Consequently, this book focuses both on literary texts and on the literary aspects of texts generally perceived to fall outside the canon. Most recent studies of medieval gender treat literary texts less often or less centrally than previous scholarship did; Chaucer was especially important for those earlier critics but Mary Erler, Rebecca Krug, Catherine Sanok, Nancy Bradley Warren, Claire Waters, and others have since incorporated other rich sources such as religious texts and documents related to family life.[8] Some scholars focus on less well-known texts that we still consider literary, as in Theresa Coletti's latest book on medieval drama.[9] Nonetheless, while the foundational work by critics such as Susan Crane, Carolyn Dinshaw, Elaine Tuttle Hansen, and Jill Mann has remained influential, canonical literature itself has become more peripheral.[10] This shift in focus has uncovered valuable information about what Krug calls women's "literate practices"—the many different ways in which they influenced the production, circulation, and reception of texts—and expanded our understanding of women's representations in texts and roles in society more broadly.[11] It has also illuminated vital connections between secular and religious texts that this project seeks to extend.[12] Both literary and devotional texts, from Chaucer's *Canterbury Tales* to Julian of Norwich's *Shewings,* include innovative uses of the gendered terms under scrutiny here and influence the much wider spectrum of usage that evolves during the fifteenth century. This attention to the concepts of femininity signified by such language thus sheds new light on canonical literary authors while also participating in the ongoing reevaluation of fifteenth-century texts, which gender-based studies have significantly furthered.[13]

Middle English writers' rising interest in gendered language correlates with several important intellectual and social developments in the later fourteenth century. At the time, two common ways of classifying women were firmly entrenched: the threefold model defined by marital status (maiden, wife, or widow)[14] and the binary model based on religious types (the perfect Virgin Mary versus the sinful Eve). While the latter was most common in antifeminist texts, the former was integral to women's identities in social, legal, and religious contexts. Both models, however, demonstrate the tendency to consider women in categories connected to male figures rather than collectively and autonomously. A number of historical shifts made these traditional ways of thinking inadequate and may have prompted Middle English writers to participate in what became the co-evolution of gender concepts and vocabulary.[15] Medieval British society was changing in profound ways, affected both by key events (such as the plague and the peasants' rebellion) and long-term trends (including the rise of the middle class, the development of affective piety, and increasing lay control over marriage); this confluence leads Judith Bennett to argue that 1350 may be the true watershed of the late Middle Ages.[16] These historical developments had pronounced effects on women's roles that created the need for new ways of thinking about and describing them.

We can see the changes already underway when the women Knighton describes appear in 1348, the same year as the first outbreak of the plague in England.[17] The plague's decimation of the population critically contributes to this historical divide, initiating some changes and intensifying others but, overall, increasing financial and social opportunities for women in ways that move even further beyond the extant paradigm. The high number of deaths meant that, by necessity, more economic prospects were open to women. Social convention still limited which opportunities were available and to whom (wealthy widows, for example, were best positioned to take advantage) and the opportunities began to decrease within a relatively short period of time;[18] despite those caveats, however, these financial opportunities did noticeably affect women's social choices. This same time period saw a move to later, companionate marriages and it appears that women's greater economic prospects allowed them to delay marriage longer and exercise a greater degree of choice in their spouses.

Both married and single women also gained greater access to religious authority with the growing popularity of affective piety in the fourteenth and fifteenth centuries: the emphasis on personal visions and emotional responses to the humanity of Christ allowed women to position themselves as his mother or lover. They did not have to become nuns or anchorites in order to embrace spiritual devotion; the idea of the mixed life demonstrated how women could integrate intensive devotional practice into an otherwise secular lifestyle. The late fourteenth century also witnessed the rise of Lollardy, but research suggests that women found few opportunities there that were unavailable to them through orthodox religion, especially with these developments in lay piety, which allowed women like Julian of Norwich and Margery Kempe to participate in powerful religious vocations (though not without risk).[19]

This combination of factors and their effects on women's experiences has led some historians to identify the period as a kind of "golden age" for medieval women.[20] That position has been sufficiently challenged by other scholars and I do not wish to revive the debate here.[21] But the actual available roles for women outside of marriage and a family substantially increased in the late fourteenth century and ideas about what identities or occupations were appropriate for them underwent an abrupt expansion (before a subsequent contraction). For the purposes of this study, I am most interested in how these historical trends affected ideas about women and their possible roles rather than to what extent those changes were realized in real women's lives.

Historical changes, then, open a gap between existing models for imagining womanhood and the potential roles and experiences of women in late medieval Britain. Not surprisingly, this conceptual gap is marked by a corresponding lexical one: David Burnley explains that linguists use the term "lexical gap" to describe that sociolinguistic condition wherein "radical alterations to [a] society and to its communicative needs . . . may leave a language lacking words for the new circumstances."[22] The use of new gendered vocabulary addresses both gaps and so the linguistic conditions of the period are another important part of the historical framework for this project. While *Inventing Womanhood* is not primarily a linguistic study, I do want to consider briefly the unusual nature of the gendered language that it foregrounds, specifically in relation to Chaucer's linguistic practices since he has the earliest known uses of some of the most critical terms, including *femininity* and *womanhood*.[23] Scholars have subjected Chaucer's language to much more detailed scrutiny than any other medieval writer's and it has been productively examined by Ardis Butterfield, Christopher Cannon, Simon Horobin, and others.[24] Cannon has demonstrated that linguistic innovation was part of Middle English literary culture, often in response to source texts in other languages, and argues that Chaucer was typical in this regard; Cannon has also discovered that Chaucer tended to discard his coinages after a few uses, making room for more new words in his vocabulary and maintaining the performance of novelty.[25] *Womanhood,* however—to take one key example—departs from these general practices. As the following chapter will establish, Chaucer adds the word to his sources rather than taking it from them and he continues to return to it, using it in some of his earliest short poems and many of his longer ones, including the *Legend of Good Women, Troilus and Criseyde,* and the *Canterbury Tales.*

This anomalous usage suggests the significance of the notion of womanhood to Chaucer and indicates an interest in representing women in ways that depart from tradition. The usage is further complicated by, in my interpretation, Gower's role as a co-innovator in developing the meanings of *womanhood* and related terms as well as the long process of inventing the concepts being signified, which includes many adaptations throughout the fifteenth century. Because Chaucer and Gower were thinking about women in new ways (outside the extant identities of maiden, wife, and widow—all terms that were already in use), new abstractions were required.

Womanhood proves to be a popular one because of its ability to mediate different categories, such as secular and sacred, wife and mother, or female saint and courtly lady. The later uses of this and related terms by Thomas Hoccleve, John Lydgate, the York dramatist, Osbern Bokenham, Margaret of Anjou, Robert Henryson, William Dunbar, John Capgrave, the Digby dramatist, and many anonymous writers, confirm that these abstractions were useful for talking about women. *Womanhood* is one central manifestation of what appear to be more general preoccupations with how to represent women and with what qualities or opportunities they should or could have (including, perhaps most urgently, their access to authority).

Womanhood offered a way to investigate forms of feminine power, such as intercession and mediation, that can occur in a secular context, but the most established avenues to authority for women were spiritual. Both Warren and Coletti have demonstrated that religious traditions offered useful models and ample material for women to fashion claims not only to authority but also to political and social significance, while Carolyn Collette's work on Anglo-French texts has shown that secular female agency depended on contemporary religious as well as political ideologies.[26] Reexamining those models, some Middle English writers turned to another key term, *motherhood*. While *womanhood* was secular and human from the outset, *motherhood* originated as an explicitly sacred term, as did *manhood* and *fatherhood*; this pattern underscores that the concept of motherhood, particularly as embodied by the Virgin Mary, offered women their primary access to the divine. The first known occurrences of *manhood* in the 1200s and early 1300s, on the other hand, were theological and it was often paired with *godhood* or *godhead* to denote the two aspects of Christ's nature. *Motherhood* and *fatherhood* came into use later, appearing in the fourteenth century. In both cases, the earliest uses of the terms were religious: *fatherhood* described God's relationship to man or the relationship of male religious authority figures to those for whom they were responsible, while *motherhood* applied only to descriptions of Mary. More secular uses of *motherhood* (i.e., uses that involve human women) begin with Gower and Julian of Norwich.[27] Particularly for women writers, this reimagined concept of motherhood with its connection to the most powerful female spiritual figure provides a model for authority that can be tweaked in fruitful ways.

Inventing Womanhood begins with the earliest appearances of the gendered language that strove to capture new concepts of femininity, reading womanhood as an interpretive key for two of Chaucer's *Canterbury Tales*. In contrast to scholars who have seen gender as a minor issue in the *Knight's Tale* and as either highly individual or fundamentally universal in the *Clerk's Tale,* I argue that Chaucer reshapes both stories around the notion of womanhood and its connection to social power in the forms of intercession and submission. In the first narrative, Theseus brings his Amazon queen and her sister into Athenian courtly society, where the sister becomes an object of disruptive desire. In the latter, the marquis Walter marries the lower-class

Griselda and tests her by pretending to murder their children. Both tales radically transform the female characters—from Amazon warriors to Athenian ladies and from peasant maiden to marchioness—and they must verify that they possess the virtues of womanhood proper to their post-transformation roles. I identify submission as the crucial quality but confirm that Chaucer also considers the potential for feminine authority that can coexist with such deference. He further revises his sources to intensify the internal and generic contradictions that these characters represent. Although Walter's motivations have puzzled critics, I propose that he tries Griselda's womanhood by assessing her ability to reconcile her duties as a wife and mother; her behavior similarly incorporates elements from romance and hagiographic traditions. The *Knight's Tale* probes the capability of Hippolyta and Emelye to subsume their Amazon natures within the Athenian model of womanhood and, by extension, to combine mythical legends with courtly literature. In Chaucer's versions, Griselda negotiates these layered paradoxes successfully but the Amazons are never satisfactorily assimilated into royal society nor into womanhood itself.

While Chaucer may have the first recorded uses of many gendered terms, he is not the sole determiner of their meanings; my second chapter treats Gower's equally influential explorations of these ideas through narratives of transformation in the *Confessio Amantis.* Critics have emphasized morality and aesthetics in Gower, but his representation of gender is innovative and in some ways more radical than Chaucer's: Gower considers the multiplicity of human nature—which, in the *Confessio,* encompasses manhood, womanhood, and beastliness—and particularly figures or moments where those aspects overlap. This reading challenges early feminist readings of Gower as insensitive to women's concerns and extends the work of Diane Watt, who has argued for his embrace of amorality and ambiguity. I show that Gower's portrayals of beastly women in the tales of Florent, Tereus, Cornix, and Calistona reveal the unreliability of external evidence as a signifier of womanhood and that his portrayals of womanly men in the stories of Achilles and Deidamia, Sardanapalus, and Iphis indicate that feminine behaviors and desires are not innate but can be learned or feigned. The chapter then turns to the frame of the *Confessio* to posit that its traditionally recognized emphases on morality and politics are mediated through a third concern: gender. I contend that the lady for whom Amans harbors unrequited love is not, as critics have assumed, a conventional romance exemplar but instead the moral center of the text. Amans must learn how to balance the multiple facets of his own nature and then apply that knowledge by conceding his lady's authority to refuse him; this requires him to use the lessons from the tales to resolve the disjunction between romance conventions and reality in interpreting both his own manhood and his lady's womanhood.

The third chapter maintains that Lydgate and Henryson create their own significant versions of femininity, as signaled by their use of gendered language. The *Temple of Glas,* which has received little critical attention despite a recent rise of interest in Lydgate's poetry, describes a love affair between a lady and a knight brought together by Venus. I demonstrate that Lydgate imagines womanhood as a constraint on the lady that dictates her response to the knight's advances as well as her behavior after marriage. Henryson's *Testament of Cresseid* continues the story of Chaucer's *Troilus and Criseyde,* tracing Cresseid's descent into poverty, illness, and finally death after leaving Troilus. I argue that Henryson portrays Cresseid's womanhood as a condition of physical vulnerability; exploiting the etymological generality of womanhood, he expands it from a set of virtuous qualities or behaviors into an existential condition and thus approaches our modern usage. Countering the prevailing interpretation of this text as antifeminist, I show that Henryson critiques Chaucer's portrayal of Criseyde, which claims to be sympathetic yet finally fails to offer any justification for her betrayal of Troilus. Even more directly than Chaucer and Gower, Lydgate illuminates the shortcomings of social models of gender while Henryson moves beyond those models entirely and approaches the modern conception of womanhood.

Turning to the women writing inside this intersection of gender and language (and also from poetic to devotional texts), my fourth chapter argues that Margery Kempe and Julian of Norwich participated in the creation of new ideas about femininity associated with manipulations of gendered language but that, rather than creating or adopting a new term, they remake motherhood. This tactic allows them to take advantage of the existing model of womanhood that offers the strongest foundation for constructing a feminine form of power. Both writers selectively utilize the Virgin Mary as the spiritual and literary paragon of womanhood and exploit the slippage between biological and metaphorical motherhood in religious discourse to authorize women. Julian's *Shewings* describes and interprets her visions, which inspire her theology of Jesus as mother. Although scholars have treated her mother imagery as primarily figurative, I show that she works to broaden the definition of motherhood and link the religious image more closely with human women. This expanded idea authorizes her text as a mothering gesture. Margery Kempe, wife and mother of fourteen children, chronicles her life and travels as a controversial spiritual figure in her *Book*. Critics have dismissed her motherhood as immaterial to her religious adventures; I demonstrate, however, that she combines Marian maternal imagery with the sexual imagery of affective piety to create herself as an unparalleled intimate of Christ. These women writers are an integral part of the social and literary culture from which the new gendered terms emerged and which they influenced, but Julian and Margery also mark out an alternate path through the Middle English possibilities for addressing the post-plague changes to ideas about womanhood.

The use of gendered terms rapidly expanded throughout the fifteenth century. While *womanhood,* for instance, first occurred in fourteenth-century canonical literature, it quickly spread to a wide variety of texts, including the *Secretum Secreto-*

rum, rolls of Parliament, royal correspondence, hagiography, drama, romance, and courtly love lyrics—where its usage became so common as to be almost *de rigueur.* The conclusion considers this final stage in the medieval evolution of woman-hood, looking at how the gendered terms that appeared in the fourteenth century became crucial to fifteenth-century Middle English literary culture while the con-cepts denoted by those terms continued to change. It might be said that medieval women—like those in Knighton's chronicle—invented womanhood, since their actions pushed the cultural boundaries that historical forces had begun to desta-bilize. If the invention of womanhood began as a social development, however, it quickly became a textual phenomenon for Middle English writers, who were able to experiment with radically new ways of imagining and representing women's lives and identities.

CHAPTER 1

AMAZONS AND SAINTS

Chaucer's Tales of Womanhood

Since the earliest work on gender in late medieval literature, there has been a great deal of attention to Chaucer's representations of women and whether those reveal a sly antifeminism or a sympathetic proto-feminism. Many scholars, including Elaine Tuttle Hansen, Jill Mann, and Priscilla Martin, have approached this issue by studying Chaucer's female characters; others, such as Susan Crane, Sheila Delany, and Carolyn Dinshaw, have considered the feminine as a system of meaning or value.[1] Studies of gender have engaged deeply with history and recent work extends that approach, examining Chaucer's texts for evidence of cultural attitudes or representations of social concerns or trends.[2] In this context, Chaucer takes a place as one source among many, often positioned alongside non-literary or less canonical texts; in fact, much current scholarship on gender focuses exclusively on the latter (as will later parts of this study). I want to build here on the critical work that emphasizes Chaucer's texts as literary as well as cultural documents in order to argue that those texts still have significant contributions to make to medieval gender studies, and especially regarding the relationship between gender and language.[3] My argument draws on both character- and value-based approaches, contending that Chaucer explores his interest in representing women not only through well-known figures such as the Wife of Bath and Griselda but also at the level of language itself.

Chaucer coins and employs gendered vocabulary in order to explore some of the ways in which cultural conventions about gender prove inadequate. *Womanhood* serves this purpose particularly well because it can span various female roles and identities—in other words, it offers a unifying foundation for more specific categories such as wifehood and widowhood while also applying to women's experiences outside such categories. Although the *Wife of Bath's Prologue* may be Chaucer's most famous meditation on representations of the feminine, his richest explorations of womanhood occur in the *Knight's Tale* and the *Clerk's Tale,* where he uses gendered language to examine how characters reconcile feminine virtue and social power.

Womanhood only appears once in the first tale and twice in the second, but the concept it invokes functions centrally in both. For Hippolyta and her sister Emelye, the question is whether they can conform to the feminine ideals the tale associates with ancient Greece (underscoring the communal, if class-specific, nature of womanhood), while for Griselda, the question is whether she can distinguish herself from the stereotypes to which most women are subject (emphasizing the exemplary nature of womanhood). The narratives explore the processes and effects of the momentous transformations that raise those questions: Hippolyta changes from Amazonian warrior leader to Athenian courtly queen and Griselda, in addition to moving from peasant maiden to marchioness and mother, exhibits aspects of hagiographical heroine and courtly love object. Chaucer plays up the ways in which these transformations cross or blur the boundaries between different ideals of femininity and thus demand a new way of thinking about gender; the addition of *womanhood* to his sources addresses that demand.

In both tales, the female characters' transformations uncover problematic relationships to power. Chaucer begins with a model of submission and then complicates it as each narrative unfolds, showing how one submissive woman can exert power through intercession in the *Knight's Tale* and how another can exploit submission itself as a powerful tool in the *Clerk's Tale*. He interrogates how much power the women can exercise while still functioning as suitable models of femininity. Paul Strohm has demonstrated that intercession, already integral to medieval notions of wifehood and motherhood, became increasingly important in conceptions of queenship during the thirteenth and fourteenth centuries. Although Strohm expresses skepticism about whether intercession "represented a genuinely alternative feminine power," he sees it as often most efficacious in texts; Chaucer's depictions of female submission and power test the limits of that efficacy.[4] While the tales show women taking on mediating roles as intercessors, wives, and consorts, then, the narratives also reveal the mediating power of *womanhood* itself, which offers a ground on which to work out different ideas about women, their roles, and their experiences—and thus allows for a more complex relationship between women, virtue, and power.

I. The *Knight's Tale*

Charles Muscatine famously described the theme of the *Knight's Tale* as "the struggle between noble designs and chaos."[5] The true chaos in the tale, however, originates from anxiety over the womanhood of the Amazon sisters: they represent an unusual and potentially threatening form of femininity. Although Chaucer revises his source text, Giovanni Boccaccio's *Teseida,* to emphasize the Amazons as women rather than warriors (renaming their country "Femenye" and eliminating descriptions of their past), he also preserves the impression that they are potentially threatening and that the courtly womanhood they adopt may be a façade. The tale establishes a model of womanhood in the Theban widows, who exhibit the key features of submission, status, and suitability and wield an appropriately feminine form of power: intercession. Hippolyta imitates these widows in her one major scene, the intercession with Theseus for Arcite and Palamon, which also contains the tale's sole use of *womanhood.* This single proof, however, is insufficient to banish the doubt that the text cultivates about the nature of the Amazons.

Such doubt exists from the beginning of the tale; Hippolyta and Emelye have already converted from courageous fighters to courtly ladies, but Chaucer provides no explanation of how Theseus or the sisters themselves effected this metamorphosis. In light of other medieval representations of Amazons as fierce and masculine warriors, the apparent ease and speed of the transformation creates persistent doubt about the sisters' womanhood. They may be like the "smylere with the knyf under the cloke" represented in Mars's temple (1999), with womanhood as the "cloke" they adopt.[6] Chaucer uses metaphors of violence to describe the Amazons' effect on others, keeping alive the possibility that their change of heart is an act. Transplanted to Athens, they are dangerous both as military rivals and as women who are not contained by marriage, an institution alien to them. While unmarried, Emelye remains more warrior than wife and represents a possible excess or absence of sexuality. Although Hippolyta marries, it is uncertain whether marriage will constrain the former Amazon ruler and compel the same submission from her that the tale shows other wives exhibiting toward their husbands. The chaos ends not with the intervention of Theseus or the gods, but with the evidence that marriage safely contains both women: Emelye agrees to wed both suitors in succession (leaving no unsatisfied rival) and Hippolyta displays her submission to Theseus in the intercession scene. Ultimately, however, Chaucer undermines these proofs, suggesting they are incomplete and unreliable.

The trouble arises because Amazons are an enigma of femininity: are they women or not? Their nature (which is foreign, aggressive, and apparently irreconcilable with the courtly ideal) and their narrative tradition (which, contrary to conventions of romance, represents women claiming traditionally male forms of power in direct confrontations with men) challenge womanhood's capacity for mediation.[7] Ilse Kirk describes their peculiar status as "the opposites of the *ideal* Athenian women" and at the same time "*liminal:* they were androgyne (females and warriors); they lived on the borders of the known world; they were neither virgins nor married; they desired men but did not want male babies."[8] In the *Knight's Tale,* the interest comes from trying to fit the "liminal" into the "ideal"—Theseus brings the sisters into a more traditional society and its female roles of love object, wife, and queen. Both the possibility of transformation and the possibility of its failure are titillating; the tale holds the two outcomes in tension. Perhaps as a result of Amazons' questionable natures, narratives about them tend to follow a certain trajectory. Batya Weinbaum notes that often "Amazon tales merely chronicle the imposition of the values of male superiority."[9] The other, untold half of such stories is what is being imposed upon and how that imposition is received. Can masculine authority truly convert Amazon warriors into exemplars of womanhood? And if so, what shape would that ideal womanhood take? Chaucer takes up these issues in the *Knight's Tale.*

READING AMAZON AS WOMAN

Although the nature of the story and its female protagonists signal the importance of womanhood to the *Knight's Tale,* Chaucer's insistence on the Amazons' femininity minimizes it. This very insistence is suspicious and a pattern of later revisions belies it; still, in the beginning, Chaucer's changes highlight the Amazons as women and suggest that their womanhood is not problematic. For instance, he renames the Amazon country "Femenye," a minor change with significant effect. Chaucer apparently invents this term and its two occurrences in the *Knight's Tale* are the first recorded in English.[10] The Knight explains that Theseus, "with his wysdom and his chivalrie, / . . . conquered al the regne of Femenye, / That whilom was ycleped Scithia" (865–67).

"Femenye" substitutes gender for geography. Its usage suggests that Theseus's victory is not only over the Amazons but also over womankind (an ambiguity reinforced by the idea that Theseus accomplished this conquest through "his chivalrie") and, by extension, over Hippolyta and Emelye not only as warriors but also as women. Both sisters are absorbed into a collectivity whose primary feature is its femaleness rather than its foreignness; the Knight does not explicitly refer to either as an Amazon.[11] By making gender the salient characteristic of the Amazons, Chaucer minimizes the distance between them and the women of Athens and underscores their commonality.[12]

Most critics have taken *Femenye* to be a marker of difference. The difference, however, is as much from other representations of Amazons as from other women. Elaine Tuttle Hansen claims that the very word "reminds us . . . that Hippolyta and Emily are not to be seen (yet) as courtly ladies in their initial appearance; they are described as Amazons, mythical, fighting, manlike women who have waged 'grete bataille' with Theseus." They are, Hansen continues, "erstwhile powerful separatists, rivals to the hero who first defeats them with martial violence and then domesticates them through marital union."[13] I would argue, however, that Chaucer has eliminated any references that would allow us to construe the sisters as "manlike women" or as conventional Amazons at all. Hippolyta and Emelye are rather disappointing Amazons and, indeed, depart from other popular medieval depictions.[14] In *The Book of the City of Ladies* by Christine de Pizan, Hippolyta attacks "forcefully" and when she is finally captured, the men "considered themselves so greatly honored by this capture that they would not have preferred the captured wealth of an entire city."[15] Sir John Mandeville describes the "reume of Amazon" as a place where "the women . . . wele not suffere men for to haue the gouernaunce of the reume" and "eueremore the quen is chosyn by eleccioun; here that is doutyest in armys, hyre they chese."[16] In contrast, Chaucer presents the Amazon sisters as womanly rather than warlike.

Rather than distinguishing Hippolyta and Emelye or reminding us of their alien nature, the word *Femenye* prepares us for their assimilation into Greek society. Still, Femenye is threatening—in part because of its overwhelming femaleness and in part because its culture imagines femininity differently. Even renamed, the land of the Amazons remains a place where women rule themselves, living virtually without men, and exercise masculine forms of power, including not only aggression but also articulate speech. They live as an independent rather than subordinate community. Although these characteristics commonly appear in portrayals of Amazons, the *Knight's Tale* barely alludes to them. It separates Hippolyta and Emelye from their Amazon community, isolating them in order to facilitate change and diminish the threat to Theseus's authority and state.[17] By inventing and using *Femenye,* Chaucer draws attention to the identity of the Amazons as women while recalling the unconventional conception of womanliness that they embody. The denial of this difference only generates more interest in its existence and anxiety about its potential irruption into the narrative.

Although the addition of *Femenye* is a relatively small change, a larger alteration works to similar effect. Chaucer excises the first book of Boccaccio's *Teseida,* which contains a description of the Amazons, their battle with Theseus, and his marriage to Hippolyta. Whereas *Femenye* recharacterized Amazons as a group, this revision obscures Hippolyta's and Emelye's individual pasts as warriors and leaders. Boccaccio justifies his inclusion of that information:

[T]he author has written about these things for no other purpose than to show from what place Emilia came to Athens. And because the subject—that is, the behavior of these Amazon women—is rather strange to most people, and therefore more interesting, he wanted to portray it [in] somewhat more detail than was perhaps necessary.[18]

Chaucer, on the other hand, justifies excluding the same material:

And certes, if it nere to long to heere,
I wolde have toold yow fully the manere

How wonnen was the regne of Femenye
By Theseus and by his chivalrye;
And of the grete bataille for the nones
Bitwixen Atthenes and Amazones;
And how asseged was Ypolita,
The faire, hardy queene of Scithia;
And of the feste that was at hir weddynge,
And of the tempest at hir hoom-comynge;
But al that thyng I moot as now forbere. (875–85)

While Boccaccio notes the importance of this information for Emilia's character, Chaucer focuses on its relevance for Hippolyta; this comment points up her nearly complete absence from the rest of the tale. It may seem that Chaucer has taken Boccaccio at his word and determined that this part of the story is not "necessary." But by cutting out the material relating to the Amazons, their nature, and their culture, Chaucer screens from the reader not only the process of transformation but also the baseline from which the transformation must occur. As Elizabeth Fowler points out, the tale emphasizes the political model of conquest over consent but questions about the sisters' consent persist because the narrative skirts the scenes that would resolve those questions.[19]

The elimination of the Amazons' context affects Emelye's character by highlighting her questionable status as a woman, which necessitates convincing proof of her femininity. Never having ruled in her own right or demonstrated a capability for war or leadership, Emelye is defined primarily as the younger sister of both Hippolyta and Theseus. Unlike her older sister, however, Emelye does not marry before coming to Athens and so her position in that society is uncertain; it is unclear whether she will follow the normal course of marrying or even whether she is marriageable. Because she is seen as a sister rather than a warrior, her womanhood is still in doubt—a doubt that her beauty, two suitors, and obedience only partially address. Hansen argues that Emelye threatens Theseus and male authority; only her marriage "domesticates the dangerous female excess that an Amazon sister-in-law might represent in Theseus's royal household."[20] I read the threat Emelye represents as both subtler and more enduring. Marriage does not "domesticate" her; as I will argue below, she remains threatening at the tale's conclusion. Instead, her marriageability demonstrates her womanhood. In other words, the fact that not one but two noble suitors perceive her as a potential wife rather than a potential foe suggests that she has exchanged Amazonian ideals of femininity for Athenian ones and can now be understood through the traditional categories of maiden, wife, and widow.[21]

Palamon and Arcite's attraction helps validate Emelye's womanhood; she does not exhibit the fearsome beauty of Boccaccio's Hippolyta, which I will discuss

below, but a beauty suitable for a courtly lady. While their rivalry implies that Emelye is still dangerous as a source of conflict, the suitors (and their enduring devotion in the absence of encouragement, following the tradition of courtly love) also
function as an assertion of her womanhood proportional to the reasonable doubt
about it.[22] The multiple suitors further demonstrate her exchangeability, a crucial
proof of her submission to male authority. But this evidence is not conclusive;
Chaucer continues to imply that Emelye is a threat by associating her with violence
and instilling doubt about her transformation in the same scenes that establish her
qualifications as a romance heroine.

The violent associations begin with Emelye's first appearance in the narrative
action, when she wanders into the garden in view of Palamon and Arcite and they
immediately desire her. Their attraction renders her a valid love object but raises the
issue of how well she will conform to this and other feminine roles. Her beauty, at
least, seems conventional; before the men see Emelye, the Knight assimilates her to
the courtly model and establishes her as eligible for their desire by comparing her to
a lily, a rose, and the month of May (1035–39). However, the repeated emphasis on
Emelye's "freshness" (1037, 1048, 1068, 1118) underscores that she is demonstrating
a fresh identity: beloved maiden instead of Amazon. Her beauty provokes Palamon
to wonder whether she "be womman or goddesse" (1101), which reminds us of the
possibility that she is truly neither but something else altogether. If this passage
is a critique of romance, as some critics have suggested, it might also be read as a
critique of the traditional, and more limited, ways of understanding womanhood:
there is something more to Emelye's character and experience than extant terms can
express. Arcite claims that "be she mayde, or wydwe, or elles wyf" (1171), Emelye is
unavailable to them because they are imprisoned. How she fits into womanhood is
in question here, and Arcite lists the three traditional roles as the only options. The
tale works within this frame even while interrogating it, setting up Emelye's identity as "mayde" before she comes to occupy the latter categories.

Emelye's trip to the temple of Diana affirms her status as maiden, incorporating
Amazon characteristics into that more typical identity. She goes to the temple with
a group of "Hir maydens" (2275). Praying to Diana, Emelye addresses her as "Goddesse of maydens" and asks to be "a mayden al my lyf" rather than a "wyf" (2300,
2305–6). This wish is less Amazonian—since Amazons were not necessarily virgins
and were often described, as in Mandeville's *Travels,* as having sex in order to satisfy
their desires or produce daughters[23]—than practical. In Athens, Emelye can be a
maiden, wife, or widow, and she chooses the first. Establishing her maidenhood
locates her within this society and makes her later roles as near-widow (when Arcite
dies before their marriage) and wife (to Palamon) more credible. Some characteristics of maidens dedicated to chastity resemble those of Amazons—hunting and
living together in female groups, for instance—but in a form Athenians can more
easily recognize and accept. By identifying herself as a maiden, Emelye chooses

the feminine role in Athenian society most comfortable for her.[24] This move also refocuses the interest of the tale on the less complex issue of her "maydenhede" rather than her womanhood (2329). Maidenhood requires a physical intactness and conventional beauty that others judge Emelye to possess, whereas Chaucer depicts womanhood as a condition with more subjective ties to virtue and moral behavior.

When it becomes clear that she must exchange the role of maiden for that of wife, however, Emelye seems to adapt easily. Courtly society, like other patriarchal systems, is partly predicated on the exchange of women between men; Emelye is exchanged between Theseus and a suitor and then again between suitors. Chaucer highlights her exchangeability and makes Emelye more amenable to it than Boccaccio's Emilia. Chaucer also facilitates it in practical terms by eliminating her first wedding; although Arcite will later refer to Emelye as his wife (2775), they do not marry in this version of the story as they do in Boccaccio's. The Knight comments on this characteristic of Emelye's, noting that she, like all women, is changeable in her affections: "For wommen, as to speken in comune, / Thei folwen alle the favour of Fortune" (2681–82).

The narrative suggests that, instead of being a failing, this characteristic positions Emelye firmly within an imagined community of women. It also makes her yield more easily to Theseus's command that she marry Arcite, and then to Arcite's wish that she marry Palamon. When Theseus suggests this second marriage to Emelye, he appeals to her as a woman to take "hym for housbonde and for lord. / Lene me youre hond, for this is oure accord. / Lat se now of youre wommanly pitee" (3081–83). Emelye offers no protest—indeed, no words at all—to this proposition, but marries Palamon "with alle blisse and melodye" and "hym loveth so tendrely" (3097, 3103). The narrator implies that her "wommanly" nature makes her agree to the exchange: the marriage to Palamon, like the engagement to Arcite, is an act of submission to Theseus, the incarnation of male authority.

In Boccaccio, Emilia does speak at this moment and her speech reveals a stronger attachment to Arcita; she mourns him more vocally and at greater length and expresses reluctance to wed Palemone.[25] When Emilia appears before Theseus for his last speech (the equivalent of the "first mover" speech of the *Knight's Tale*), she is "still weeping."[26] In her objection to Theseus's proposal, Emilia claims that Arcita may have died due to Diana's displeasure, suggesting not only a reluctance to marry again but also that she should never have married. Boccaccio's Emilia resists being exchanged and holds more firmly to her maidenhood, undergoing a more visibly difficult transformation than Chaucer's Emelye and giving voice to that difficulty.

Even as Chaucer fits Emelye into more traditional femininity, however, he hints at the inexact and awkward nature of that fit. Through localized changes to the men's first sight of Emelye and Arcite's deathbed scene, Chaucer evokes the danger involved in loving an Amazon and hints at the implausibility of her transformation, contributing to what Muscatine described as the chaos in the tale. Chaucer first uses violent language to describe Emelye's effect on Arcite and Palamon. Immediately upon seeing her, Palamon "bleynte and cride, 'A!' / As though he stongen were unto the herte" (1078–79). Here the narrator rather than Palamon applies the simile (suggesting that the image surpasses a lover's convention), although Palamon echoes the language within a few lines. Arcite experiences a similar effect: "And with that sighte hir beautee hurte hym so, / That, if that Palamon was wounded sore, / Arcite is hurt as muche as he, or moore" (1114–16).[27] Susan Crane posits that such language helps to transition Emelye from warrior to woman;[28] at the same time, however, it draws attention to the fact that such a transition is necessary and reminds us that Emelye is a very different kind of woman from the traditional love object of romance.

Although medieval poets commonly employ metaphors of violence to describe the effects of love, here Chaucer changes the subject of these metaphors from the god of love to the beloved. Emelye acts both as the object of desire and the perpetrator of violence: the men's gaze upon her becomes a weapon that she turns on them. In the *Teseida,* the scene plays out quite differently; the two men feel "joy" and "delight" as they gaze with "rapt attention" at "a celestial beauty."[29] After a time, Arcita sees the god of love "and in his hands he holds two gilded arrows. . . . Yes, he has given me such a wound that I shall be racked with pain."[30] While Arcita sees this vision in Emilia's eyes, she merely reflects it back to him: the god of love rather than Emilia inflicts the wound. The distinction between the god of love, "that fierce archer [who] has lodged within my heart something that is draining away my life," and Emilia, whose "form is so engraved upon my heart and so delights my spirit," is clear, leaving Emilia unimplicated in and untouched by the violence the men experience from Emelye in the *Knight's Tale.*[31] In Boccaccio, the violence conforms to traditional love imagery and so we can read Emilia as a romantic heroine, successfully transformed from her Amazon identity. Chaucer ties the violent imagery to Emelye herself as the perpetrator, reminding us that she is not a traditional love object but was and still may be a warrior; she exercises a power over her suitors that sometimes resembles and sometimes inverts ideals of courtly femininity.

The violent effect of Emelye on her suitors extends beyond her first encounter with them; even the language Arcite uses as he dies, when we might assume that their engagement has sealed her transition from warrior to lady, reminds the reader that Emelye is an Amazon. Once again, this language revises Boccaccio. As Arcite speaks to Emelye from his deathbed in the *Knight's Tale,* he addresses her with a mixture of epithets that mark her contradictory status as lover and enemy: "Allas, myn hertes queene! Allas, my wyf, / Myn hertes lady, endere of my lyf! / . . . / Fare wel, my sweete foo, myn Emelye!" (2775–76, 2780). At the moment of his death he speaks his last words, "Mercy, Emelye!" (2808), again indicating that she somehow endangers him. Though differing only by a single word, this final speech conveys an opposite message from Arcita's speech in the *Teseida,* in which he says only,

"Farewell, Emilia."[32] Before his death, Arcita addresses Emilia with less ambiguous epithets, calling her "my heart's desire," "my only love," and "my own dear heart."[33] Boccaccio's Emilia, in short, is more foreign and more overtly threatening at the outset but Chaucer's Emelye, while not emphasized as foreign or threatening, remains a source of tension and chaos throughout the tale.

MODELING AMAZON AS QUEEN

The *Knight's Tale* ends with Emelye's marriage, leaving the couple "Lyvynge in blisse, in richesse, and in heele" (3102). Even the trace of linguistic violence disappears; the Knight's final comment is that "nevere was ther no word hem bitwene / Of jalousie or any oother teene. / Thus endeth Palamon and Emelye" (3105–7). However, this conclusion does not erase the doubts about the Amazons' womanhood. Hippolyta's marriage, which occurs at the outset of the tale, sets up an exploration of wifehood, the phase of womanhood that generally follows maidenhood. In leaving many questions about Hippolyta unsettled, Chaucer implies that Emelye's wedding may not be the resolution that it seems to be. Although Hippolyta demonstrates womanhood through her intercession for Palamon and Arcite, following the example of the Theban widows and their submission, status, and suitability, she largely disappears from the narrative after this early scene and concerns about the authenticity of her transformation go unanswered.

The first reference to Hippolyta in the *Knight's Tale* is a brief narrative of events rather than a delineation of character. After defeating the Amazons, Theseus "weddede the queene Ypolita, / And broghte hire hoom with hym in his contree / With muchel glorie and greet solempnytee, / And eek hir yonge suster Emelye" (868–71). Hippolyta's passivity (in grammar as well as action) signals that she has been brought under male authority. A few lines earlier, her country was renamed *Femenye,* a sign that her power has been taken from her by the Knight as well as Theseus. Following this beginning, the tale continues to restrict the development of Hippolyta's character; she becomes almost completely silent and passive. As David Wallace notes, "Given Chaucer's lifelong dedication to female eloquence, Hippolita's speechlessness seems strange and anomalous."[34] While Emelye is the focus of and impetus for the plot—at times participating in the speech-making as well as the action—Hippolyta fades into the background, effaced through a few key changes.

The first and most dramatic of these changes is, again, Chaucer's elimination of Boccaccio's first book, which shows Hippolyta as a fiercely beautiful and courageous ruler. She is not only a leader but also an aggressor, maltreating the Greeks who land on her shores. She engages in military battles, leading her troops as their "duchess" (and thereby, as Wallace notes, holding a rank equal to Theseus's)[35] and negotiating the surrender of her forces in defeat and of herself in marriage. At this point Boccaccio offers a description of Hippolyta that pays homage to her beauty as well as her prowess in war:

> Hippolita was marvellously beautiful
> and aflame with fearless courage;
> she was like a morning star
> or a fresh rose in the month of May;
> very young and still a maiden,
> rich in possessions, and of royal lineage,
> wise and well-mannered, and by nature
> passionate in arms and fierce beyond measure.[36]

Like the Knight's description of Hippolyta as the "faire, hardy queene of Scithia" (882), this more extended portrayal balances references to her beauty and courage. Boccaccio's description, however, is more complimentary and detailed, mentioning Hippolyta's qualifications as a warrior-leader as well as her other qualities. Her lineage and wisdom equip her to be the wife of Theseus but also to be a ruler in her own right. Beauty forms an important part of womanhood for Emelye (and later for Griselda), but Hippolyta's beauty is extraordinary—rather than certifying her femininity, it indicates her foreignness. The Knight's more limited description of Hippolyta occurs in the passage that describes what he will not tell us about her story (875–92). He summarizes her character in much the same way that he summarizes the events of Book I of the *Teseida*—we are denied full access to both.[37]

What is not said about Hippolyta is significant. Chaucer carries out her conversion from Amazon leader to ladylike consort by identifying her only as the latter from the beginning of the tale. The Knight never refers to her as the "ruler" of the Amazons; in both early references, he designates her "queene." In the first instance, when the Knight explains that Theseus "weddede the queene Ypolita" (868), her status as queen seems due to her marriage. She has become Theseus's queen, the queen of Athens, rather than the queen of her own people. Within the tale, she holds that latter position only retrospectively. In the second instance, which is part of a brief look back at the events preceding the narrative, the Knight does call her the "queene of Scithia" (882). This title describes her status as ruler of the Amazons, but by identifying this earlier and more powerful position as that of a "queene" (rather than using "duchess," as Boccaccio does, or another title that would suggest only "leader" and not "consort"), Chaucer renders Hippolyta's role less authoritative and less foreign; he eases the disjunction between her positions in Scithia and Athens.

Much as *Femenye* encouraged us to see the Amazons as women rather than enemies, this use of "queene" prepares us to see Hippolyta as a possible and future consort rather than a rival (a connotation that terms like "ruler," "sovereign," or "king" might evoke). Chaucer's language makes it seem as if Hippolyta has been absorbed seamlessly into Athenian culture under the structure of Theseus's authority. As Crane points out, "marriage is consequent on military defeat with no intervening movement of consensual subordination or self-transformation on the part of the Amazons."[38] Such a transformation, however, cannot be as quick or painless as it seems in hindsight at the opening of the *Knight's Tale.* The "tempest at hir hoom-comynge" that the Knight describes likely refers to the reaction of Athens as well as the weather (884) and by glossing over the stormy transition of Hippolyta, Chaucer invites the reader's suspicions.

The identification of Hippolyta as queen and the slippage of her queenship between Scithia and Athens provoke the question of whether her previous status will translate appropriately into her new environment. Class is as perplexing an issue here as it will be in the *Clerk's Tale,* where Griselda's rapid elevation to the upper class necessitates proof of her womanhood. The importance of class to womanhood is an intriguing issue, since the term seems to designate a category based solely on gender while its usage frequently suggests an association with status. Class and gender are in tension as factors determining identity; neither is complete alone but it is unclear whether one overrides the other. Within the *Canterbury Tales,* womanhood is not a condition common to all women, but neither is it restricted purely by class. Chaucer suggests that women can lay claim to womanhood on the basis of their virtue; virtue is often related to social class but the former overrides the latter (as the example of Griselda illustrates).[39] If womanhood were a simpler matter of class or gender, then the test/demonstration dynamic in the *Knight's Tale* and the *Clerk's Tale* would be obviated or at least altered. In Hippolyta's case, the problem of her status parallels that of her womanhood: Amazon society defines both in ways significantly different from Athenian society. In addition, the establishment of her womanhood is a vital prerequisite to establishing her suitability as queen. She has no firm ground for Athenian identity in either class or gender, but the latter must be settled before the question of the former can be entertained.

If the status of the Amazons' womanhood is in doubt, the tale does present a definitive model of womanhood: the Theban widows. Untroubled by any questions about class, the widows exemplify what virtuous women should be and how they should behave. Chaucer promotes the widows from plot mechanism (justifying the war that brings Arcite and Palamon under Theseus's authority) to feminine ideal. He accomplishes this through revisions, making the Amazons clearly present for the widows' scene and interpolating a parallel intercession scene featuring Hippolyta modeling her behavior after the widows. Their appeal to Theseus demonstrates womanhood in the three areas most important for Hippolyta to prove her own: deferring to male authority (specifically Theseus's), possessing high status and acting accordingly, and demonstrating suitability for wifehood and motherhood. For Emelye, her beauty established her status, her suitors established her suitability for wifehood, and her exchangeability established her submission to male authority. These elements are more directly relevant to Hippolyta and the need to pin them down is more imperative because of her position as queen. She emulates the widows but her disappearance after that single moment allows doubt about her womanhood to linger for the remainder of the tale.

Chaucer makes the Amazons witness the plea to Theseus, thereby elevating the widows to overt paragons of womanhood. The presence or absence of the Amazons is uncertain during the scene in Boccaccio, while they are undoubtedly present (though as silent observers only) in Chaucer. When the scene begins, the Knight mentions only Theseus and it seems possible here, as in Boccaccio, that he may be encountering the widows alone:

> This duc, of whom I make mencioun,
> Whan he was come almoost unto the toun,
>
> . . .
>
> He was war, as he caste his eye aside,
> Where that ther kneled in the heighe weye
> A compaignye of ladyes. (893–94, 896–98)

The narrative reveals that Hippolyta and Emelye witnessed the scene only when Theseus dismisses them from it, after the widows' appeal and his response: "And [he] sente anon Ypolita the queene, / And Emelye, hir yonge suster sheene, / . . . / And forth he rit" (971–72, 974). This reference clarifies the role of the Amazons in their new society: they are sent home just as the action begins. More importantly, Theseus's encounter with the widows and its result demonstrate how women are expected to behave—and how they can legitimately exercise power—in Greek society and in relation to Theseus.[40] This "compaignye of ladyes" understands how to appeal to Theseus through both their physical and verbal performances. Their appearance, which affects Theseus before a word is spoken, testifies to their womanhood, similar to the ways in which Griselda's appearance will signal her womanhood to Walter from a distance. Through speech, the widows present themselves as intercessors—a traditional female role and relation to male authority—and so function as models of womanly power.

The Knight begins by carefully describing what the Amazons must have seen, the visual aspect of the widows' performance for Theseus. They are kneeling

> . . . tweye and tweye,
> Ech after oother clad in clothes blake;
> But swich a cry and swich a wo they make
> That in this world nys creature lyvynge
> That herde swich another waymentynge;
> And of this cry they nolde nevere stenten
> Til they the reynes of his brydel henten. (898–904)

The widows' appearance illustrates their womanhood. Their identity as a "compaignye" exemplifies its communal nature, though it is communal only within this exceptional group of women. The black clothing and ceaseless wailing signify devotion to their dead husbands and powerlessness in the face of male authority. While its very excess marks their grief as a performance, it is caused by one male power figure and designed to enlist another on their behalf. Their kneeling position is one of submission, indicating that they are both acknowledging Theseus's authority and asking for his mercy. They are intimating that they are subject to him.

Theseus initially responds impatiently, asking why the women "Perturben so my feste" (906). Once they have his attention, however, the widows expand their performance into a speech emphasizing the same themes: his authority and their submission. Throughout her address, their spokesperson stresses more generally the widows' miserable condition. Before speaking, she swoons (913). Near the beginning of her speech, she asks, "Som drope of pitee, thurgh thy gentillesse, / Upon us wrecched wommen lat thou falle" (920–21). At the conclusion, the other women join her in echoing, "Have on us wrecched wommen som mercy, / And lat oure sorwe synken in thyn herte" (950–51). More specifically (and more effectively), the eldest widow appeals to Theseus on several counts: his prestige, their own high class, and their devotion to their (dead) husbands.

The primary ground for the widows' appeal is their submission to Theseus, which they first demonstrated physically and now express verbally. Their appearance and actions testify to their complete deference to his authority; in addition, the first word spoken by the eldest widow is "Lord" (915). She puts off answering Theseus's questions (905–11) in favor of acknowledging his power. This move occupies the first fifteen lines of her speech and within that span she addresses Theseus as "lord" four times, beginning and ending with the epithet (915, 922, 927, 930). She applies the same word to Creon and to their dead husbands, suggesting that it is less a precise title than a general signifier of male authority. She also refers to Theseus as a "conqueror" and acclaims his "glorie," "honour," and "myght" (916, 917, 930). The speaker emphasizes that they "han ben waitynge al this fourtenyght" to see him (929). Only after establishing the widows' relation to Theseus as one of powerlessness to absolute power does she embark upon her story.

But if acknowledging Theseus's position as a male authority figure is an essential element of their petition, the widows' own status is equally important in defining them as the rightful objects of his mercy and, by implication, as proper figures of womanhood. After her first appeal to Theseus as one of the "wrecched wommen" in need of his "gentillesse," the eldest widow justifies her plea: "For, certes, lord, ther is noon of us alle / That she ne hath been a duchesse or a queene" (922–23). At least some of these women are equivalent in rank to Hippolyta, whom the Knight consistently describes as "queene." In the intercession scene—in which Hippolyta models her behavior on the widows' and thereby demonstrates her womanhood—

the Knight will refer to her not by name but by rank. Similarly, he identifies the eldest widow only by her marital state (widowed) and rank ("wyf to kyng Cappaneus," 932). The status of the widows conditions Theseus's response: "Hym thoughte that his herte wolde breke, / Whan he saugh hem so pitous and so maat, / That whilom weren of so greet estaat" (954–56). While their change in fortune itself seems pitiful, such a change is possible only for those of the upper class. The status of the widows adds credibility and force to their appeal, particularly because it is connected to their virtuous natures.

The fact that these women were married to the powerful men of Thebes illustrates their suitability as wives. That they remain devoted to their late husbands further demonstrates that they performed (and continue to perform) their wifely duties. Because this submission to their husbands occurs after the women have gained a certain measure of autonomy through the men's deaths, their actions make them admirable models of womanhood even outside the bounds of wifehood. The widows are paragons of womanhood: they are untainted by sexuality and they demonstrate obedience even though they are no longer bound by marriage, the institution that usually compelled such submission. Their model of womanhood can be recommended to and imitated by other women with minimal potential for subversion; it is perfect for a troubling figure like Hippolyta.

While my analysis has stressed the widows' subordinate position, they do exercise power in their interaction with Theseus and this point is important to understanding Hippolyta's later intercession. The widows base their appeal on their role as intercessors for their dead husbands; they approach Theseus on behalf of "alle oure lordes whiche that been yslawe" (943). Intercession was an accepted mode of power—or at least influence—for women. The crucial point about the widows' plea is that it works: they enlist Theseus in their cause and instigate a battle. Although they accomplish their objective indirectly, these women exercise power while still embodying the ideals of womanhood. Submission may be a crucial quality of womanhood, but powerlessness is not. If, in the Greece Chaucer portrays, women cannot fight battles and lead warriors, they can speak eloquently and affect the course of events. If women lack the authority to make and enforce their own decisions, they can nonetheless influence the decisions that are made.[41]

It seems unlikely that Hippolyta, the former ruler of a realm, could be satisfied with this limited power. Even if she could, however, the tale has offered no evidence that she possesses the foundation for it, the elements of womanhood demonstrated by the Theban widows. Her wedding is prefaced not by courtship but by battle and marriage makes her a trophy of war as much as a wife. In the narrative, she is still an unknown quantity. Her intercession on behalf of Arcite and Palamon proves that the question of Hippolyta's womanhood is inextricable from the problem of feminine power and, while pretending to settle both, resolves neither.[42] Hippolyta's intercession is Chaucer's invention, mirroring the widows' earlier scene and exhibiting her conformity to that same set of behaviors and values. Chaucer puts her womanhood directly at stake: "The queene anon, for verray wommanhede, / Gan for to wepe" (1748–49). It is difficult to imagine applying this description to an Amazon warrior but that very difficulty works paradoxically to reassure and to preserve doubt. While a similar course of action unfolds in both texts, Boccaccio does not include either Hippolyta or an intercession. In the *Teseida,* Emilia discovers the two lovers fighting and brings Theseus to the duel. When he asks their names, Arcita offers to reveal them on the condition that they are granted pardon and Theseus agrees. The negotiation occurs entirely between the men, with Emilia serving as the mechanism that brings them together as well as the source of the fighting. No other women appear. In Chaucer, on the other hand, Hippolyta is the central figure and the scene is pivotal in determining her status as woman and queen.

As the hunt begins, Chaucer sets up the intercession scene first by reminding the reader of Hippolyta's peculiar position and then by increasing Theseus's cruelty. The tale describes the hunting party: "Theseus with alle joye and blis, / With his Ypolita, the faire queene, / And Emelye, clothed al in grene, / On huntyng be they riden roially" (1684–87). This language reiterates that Hippolyta is no longer a ruler; she is the "queene" who accompanies Theseus, "*his* Ypolita." She is no longer "faire" and "hardy," as at the beginning of the tale, but only "faire"; perhaps she is also no longer a woman and a warrior but only the former. Theseus discovers the fighters on his own and reacts not by gazing at them in wonder, as he does in Boccaccio's version, but by immediately pulling his own sword and demanding, "Namoore, up peyne of lesynge of youre heed" (1707)—a more violent version of his initial impatient response to the Theban widows. No negotiations take place between the men; Palamon reveals their identities and the reason for their conflict without hesitation or bargaining. He concludes his speech, as in the *Teseida,* by asking to be put to death but again Chaucer alters Theseus's response. Boccaccio's Theseus replies, "God forbid that it should be as you ask, even though through your folly you have deserved it."[43] In the *Knight's Tale,* however, Theseus answers, "Youre owene mouth, by youre confessioun, / Hath dampned yow . . . / ye shal be deed" (1744–45, 1747). This more extreme reaction makes the intercession necessary; similarly, in the *Clerk's Tale,* Walter's cruelty will create the conditions for Griselda to demonstrate her virtuous womanhood.

The intercession begins immediately as the women react to Theseus's proclaimed death sentence:

> The queene anon, for verray wommanhede,
> Gan for to wepe, and so dide Emelye,
> And alle the ladyes in the compaignye.
> Greet pitee was it, as it thoughte hem alle,
> That evere swich a chaunce sholde falle,

For gentil men they were of greet estaat,
And no thyng but for love was this debaat;
And saugh hir blody woundes wyde and soore,
And alle crieden, bothe lasse and moore,
"Have mercy, Lord, upon us wommen alle!"
And on hir bare knees adoun they falle
And wolde have kist his feet ther as he stood;
Til at the laste aslaked was his mood,
For pitee renneth soone in gentil herte. (1748–61)

This passage contains the sole occurrence of *womanhood* in the tale. It suggests that Hippolyta has transformed from an Amazon ruler to an exemplar of Greek womanhood suitable to serve as Theseus's consort. If their marriage represents the final stage of Theseus's conquest of the Amazons, then this moment seems proof that the conquest is complete: Hippolyta behaves not as a captive warrior but as an Athenian queen. She does not act on her own power but appeals and submits to the authority of her husband.

There are important structural parallels between this intercession and its earlier counterpart. Like the widows, these women take a deferential posture: "And on hir bare knees adoun they falle / And wolde have kist his feet ther as he stood" (1758–59). Submission is again the keynote. Both scenes also emphasize the presence of a company of women led by a queen. As Wallace points out, the intercession scene marks "the assimilation of Hippolita into generic 'wommanhede.'"[44] This "assimilation" is significant because one of Hippolyta's most threatening aspects is her history of thinking and acting for herself; she stood out even among women who were wildly unusual by traditional standards. That she can act as a part of this Greek female community suggests that she is not threatening as an individual. She is no longer a military rival but one of many Athenian women and her most distinguishing feature is not a battle scar or amputated breast but her rank as queen. The intercession recontextualizes Hippolyta within her new culture and establishes her on the spectrum of womanhood in Greek society. She now relates to Theseus and to a female community as an Athenian woman rather than as an Amazon or a creature completely of another kind. Here she appears in a revised version of Femenye—one in line with new ideals of womanhood.

However, a striking difference between the parallel scenes hints at the cost of this assimilation: rather than speaking eloquently and at length as the eldest Theban widow did, Hippolyta remains virtually silent. She is not completely speechless—this is the single moment in which we may be hearing her voice, but it is subsumed in the communal voice of the women. Although she leads their actions, she does not speak for them. And while the eldest widow gave a thirty-two-line speech, Hippolyta speaks only in the chorus, which echoes the communal plea by the widows ("Have on us wrecched wommen som mercy" [950]): "Have mercy, Lord, upon us wommen alle!" (1757). Like the widows, the queen and her women address Theseus as "Lord" and ask for his "mercy," indicating that he holds the power and they have only the right of appeal. Also like the widows, the queen and her women characterize themselves collectively. The beginning of the tale implied that Hippolyta could lead and speak for the Amazons; now she must demonstrate that she can act in concert with Athenian women and their ideology as the tale represents it. That she leads in the crying shows that she feels pity, an important feminine (and queenly) quality. That she does not speak for the women shows that she exercises only intercessory power, deferring to Theseus rather than presuming to make suggestions herself. The women intercede by asking for mercy for them- selves, not for the two lovers—they do not suggest a solution to the problem or articulate their feelings, unlike the widow who movingly described her commu- nity's suffering. The general and even tentative nature of Hippolyta's intercession confirms her womanhood more broadly. She intercedes out of pity to avert fight- ing and bloodshed, reflecting a system of values that differ fundamentally from those she acted on as an Amazon.

While Hippolyta exercises power, it is not the direct power of a ruler but the indirect influence of a supplicant. Acting as an intercessor in this scene testifies to her womanhood since intercession was often seen as the traditional role of the mother. David Herlihy notes that in medieval families the mother "was ideally placed to serve as intermediary between the often conflicting male generations."[45] In this intermediary role, human mothers became analogous to the Virgin Mary, to whom many appealed to intercede with Christ or God. Here Hippolyta, though not acting as a mother, does intercede between two male generations. Although intercession is a wifely role, it carries particular significance for a queen due to her husband's authority. Paul Strohm notes that the model of queen as intercessor dominated the thirteenth and fourteenth centuries, a "reconception" based on "a reassertion of their familial roles as wives and mothers." He continues: "This new form of queenly influence was *petitionary,* in the sense that it cast the queen as one seeking redress rather than one able to institute redress in her own right, and *intercessory,* in that it limited its objectives to the modification of a previously deter- mined male resolve."[46] For Hippolyta, intercession demonstrates her suitability as a queen but also hints at her suitability as a wife and future mother. In the end, she is exercising the only form of power that the tale makes available to her.

As an intercessor, however, Hippolyta's skill does not equal the widows'. The- seus's different reactions to the two groups of women derive from the differences in their verbal approaches. The widows' speech instantly affects him: "This gentil duc doun from his courser sterte / With herte pitous, whan he herde hem speke. / Hym thoughte that his herte wolde breke" (952–54). Theseus cites the particular reason for his pity: their words. After remarking on the widows' bad fortune, he "swoor his ooth, as he was trewe knyght, / He wolde doon so ferforthly his myght / Upon the tiraunt Creon hem to wreke" (959–61). Since the queen and her women speak only a single line, they cannot elicit the same emotional reaction. Instead of reacting immediately to the women, Theseus reconsiders the situation and reasons to himself:

> And though he first for ire quook and sterte,
> He hath considered shortly, in a clause,
> The trespas of hem bothe, and eek the cause,
> And although that his ire hir gilt accused,
> Yet in his resoun he hem bothe excused,
> As thus: he thoghte wel that every man
> Wol helpe hymself in love, if that he kan,
> And eek delivere hymself out of prisoun.
> And eek his herte hadde compassioun
> Of wommen, for they wepen evere in oon. (1762–71)

After their tearful appeal, the women are forgotten by Theseus and finally appear only as a secondary consideration ("And eek his herte hadde compassioun / Of wommen"). After this brief reference, Theseus embarks on a speech about love expanding on the ideas he worked through during his soliloquy. Once again the women disappear from the situation.

The women reappear some forty lines later when it is clear that Theseus has made his decision based on his own reflections rather than on the women's intervention. Theseus himself draws this distinction. While he raised the widows up and embraced them after their plea (957–58), he leaves the queen and her company kneeling:

> And therfore, syn I knowe of loves peyne
> And woot hou soore it kan a man distreyne,
> As he that hath ben caught ofte in his laas,
> I yow foryeve al hoolly this trespaas,
> At requeste of the queene, that kneleth heere,
> And eek of Emelye, my suster deere. (1815–20)

Theseus defines both Amazons in relation to himself, as his "queene" and "suster"—they not only have little personal power but also little individual identity. He also underscores Hippolyta's submissive kneeling, signaling its symbolic importance to him. Still, these women—like the widows—exercise power through intercession: the outcome of the situation is what they desire. Although Theseus only faintly credits their "requeste," that moment intervened between the death sentence and forgiveness.

If, as I have argued, Hippolyta exhibits womanhood here, then it is significant that there is no stamp of approval like that Walter will give to Griselda's womanhood. Rather than acclaiming his wife's womanhood, Theseus stresses her submission to him; the enduring image is of the pleading queen "that kneleth here." Because Hippolyta is virtually absent from the rest of the narrative, no subsequent image replaces that one. This single intercession cannot prove her womanhood. Hippolyta poses a direct threat to masculine authority that a moment of submission—and this is the only interaction between Hippolyta and Theseus that the tale describes—cannot dismiss. In other words, the transformation that the tale initially glossed over continues to be glossed over but continues to be troublesome. Theseus's reaction to Hippolyta's intercession reinforces rather than resolves any misgivings; his continued emphasis on her subordination suggests that he, at least, is not convinced. Hippolyta demonstrates womanhood in this scene, but an isolated act cannot certify her transformation. More rigorous testing and more convincing proofs would be required, which is what we find with Griselda in the *Clerk's Tale*. Walter's doubt and curiosity are aggressive reflections of the sublimated attitudes toward the Amazons in the *Knight's Tale* and Chaucer foregrounds Griselda's womanhood through Walter's repeated testing of it, making her the center of the tale in a way the Amazons were not.

II. The *Clerk's Tale*

Gender issues in the *Clerk's Tale* have attracted more critical attention than in the *Knight's Tale* but scholarly views of Chaucer's Griselda remain split. More traditional readings stress her passivity or submission in support of the *Clerk's Tale*'s allegorical or exemplary significance.[47] Newer feminist or historicist interpretations stress her assertiveness, even if only ironically.[48] In this fuller picture, Griselda's identity itself becomes a crucial focus of Chaucer's interest. As Carolyn Dinshaw suggests, the interpretive puzzle of the relationship between Walter and Griselda raises "the question of the feminine."[49] This section suggests that for Chaucer the question of the feminine is literally a question of *womanhood*. I will argue Chaucer offers Griselda as a mediating figure: in an essentially ironic strategy, he intensifies the extremes already present in the tale in order to intensify her mediation.[50]

Walter, largely a cipher in most previous accounts of the tale, plays a central role in Chaucer's irony.[51] However inexplicable his cruelty or mysterious his motives, in testing Griselda he seeks to answer the same question as Chaucer: whether her femininity can successfully combine apparently contradictory elements (such as her incompatible duties as wife and mother: to submit to her husband and, in doing so, allow the killing of her children). As we will see, Chaucer's morally ambiguous deployment of Walter also enables him to project the question of Griselda's womanhood onto a larger scale, as a juxtaposition of the courtly and the hagiographic. I will consider womanhood's close relation to Griselda's "translation" and her trials, two issues that have occupied much previous scholarship. The word *womanhood* appears twice in the *Clerk's Tale:* when Walter first sees Griselda and when he ends the tests and offers an explanation. The concept is also significant in several other passages where Chaucer does not directly invoke the term, including the marriage contract, Griselda's "translation" and its subsequent reversal, and the three trials.

As a term mediating between the secular and the sacred, *womanhood's* appearance in the *Clerk's Tale* may draw on two contemporary, if divergent, versions of female sanctity: the maternal martyr and the virgin saint. Barbara Newman has identified as the "hagiographic ideal [of] the maternal martyr" as an important hagiographic tradition.[52] This motif was popular in the thirteenth and fourteenth centuries and used child-sacrifice plots as a strategy by which mothers could become saints. A woman who gave up her children "no longer did so to attain a virile or gender-neutral state of equality with men. By a peculiar paradox, it was precisely this renunciation of her children that set a holy seal on her motherhood, reconciling it as far as possible with the ideal of sexless, sacrificial maternity embodied in the Virgin."[53] Griselda does not become a saint, but she does achieve this superior form of motherhood by sacrificing her children; then, by relinquishing her husband, she achieves a similarly superior kind of wifehood. What is ultimately validated in both cases, however, is her womanhood: it is the ground on which these priorities play out (wifehood over motherhood) and it remains when these other roles have been stripped away. Newman compares the maternal martyrs of hagiography to the "cruel mothers" of romance (among whom she numbers Griselda) and argues that the rising popularity of child-sacrifice plots in the later fourteenth century "seems to be correlated with a shift toward the alternative consensual model of marriage . . . [in which] the indissoluble loyalty of the wedded pair . . . takes precedence over their fertility."[54] If Newman is right, then this change could have provided another impetus for fourteenth-century writers' interest in womanhood.

We can illustrate the richness Chaucer found in the notion of womanhood by briefly comparing Griselda and her mixed spirituality with Cecilia, a virgin saint and his one authentic hagiographic protagonist. Noting that "virgin martyr legends of the fourteenth century focus on conflict and emphasize the saint's antisocial behavior," Karen Winstead goes on to argue that such legends "distanced the saints from the rank-and-file faithful by emphasizing their miraculous powers, their virginity, and their contempt for the institutions of marriage, family, and state."[55] As the author of the *Second Nun's Tale,* Chaucer actively participated in this trend.[56] He presents Cecilia not as a passive sufferer but as a powerful figure who controls and changes her circumstances. However, even here he demonstrates his interest in Cecilia as a woman. Rephrasing his sources, he makes Almachius's first question to her, "What maner womman artow?" (424). The sources make the question more simply about Cecilia's condition, and Chaucer allows her answer to retain that simpler focus: she answers by identifying her class status as a woman.[57] Still, the question itself points to a deeper concern with the nature of women and how they can behave and encourages readers to wonder what kind of woman acts as Cecilia does and how her actions are womanly.

As the author of the *Clerk's Tale,* Chaucer appears less interested in the hagiographic trend described by Winstead. Instead, he seems to want to determine the relationship between these aggressive female saints and other narrative characterizations of women—much as the relationship between Amazon warriors and courtly ladies interested him in the *Knight's Tale.* Griselda's character (submissive but powerful) and her situation (suffering followed by triumph) provide a basis for this investigation. Some critics have read Griselda as the antithesis of the Wife of Bath and an attempt at rehabilitating antifeminist ideas.[58] I would argue instead that Chaucer explores the antifeminist archetype to see whether some of its elements could be productively recuperated. He experiments with the related unruly female saint figure by combining some of its characteristics with the virtuous feminine model, which Griselda often represented and was used to exemplify in conduct books.[59] Can a woman be both powerful and virtuous, both articulate and submissive? If Cecilia and the Wife of Bath are near one end of the spectrum of womanhood and Constance and the Virgin Mary the other, is there a middle ground? In other words, what do you get when you mix Jankyn's *Book of Wikked Wyves* with *Le Ménagier de Paris?*

Using the Griselda story to explore these questions was a departure from its literary origins and from other contemporary versions. Griselda is a twofold exemplar, modeling for wives as well as Christians, but no other writer exploited this status to consider the divergent representations of women in courtly and religious texts. Most writers who used the exemplum acknowledged its dual significance; however, the Clerk's multiple morals amplify this divided tradition rather than attempting to reconcile it. At the conclusion of the tale, he tells us that the story is "nat for . . . wyves" but for "every wight" (1142, 1145); in the envoy, he reworks his advice for "noble wyves" and "archewyves" (1183, 1195; the latter term another invention of Chaucer's). Some scholars have read the Clerk as hedging between Chaucer's sources: Petrarch's version, which asserts the universal moral of the exemplum, and the anonymous French prose translation *Le Livre Griseldis,* which directs its message toward "des femmes mariees."[60] Such interpretations assume that the broader Petrarchan moral is unusual, but this view is too narrow. It is true that, like *Le Livre Griseldis,* Boccaccio's *Decameron,* Philippe de Mézières' *Livre de la Vertue du Sacrement de Mariage, Le Ménagier de Paris,* and the play *Estoire de Griseldis en rimes et par personages* (based on de Mézières' *Livre*) all seem to stress the specifically female nature of Griselda's virtue, and indeed, that the French versions explicitly address wives.[61] Nevertheless, each of these fourteenth-century versions also acknowledges

Griselda as a human exemplar as well as a womanly one. Even Petrarch himself describes her virtue not as inimitable but as capable of being imitated only with difficulty ("vix imitabilis") by women and exhorts his readers to emulate what he specifies as her feminine or womanly constancy ("femine constanciam").[62]

Griselda's identity as a woman is a significant feature of every medieval version of the tale.[63] However, by introducing the concept of womanhood, Chaucer makes this feature a focus of investigation. The adaptation of the story in different genres (conduct books, drama, religious exempla, etc.) and languages (literary Latin as well as various vernaculars) suggests its potential for this kind of use. As Judith Bronfman points out in her history of the Griselda story, "In less than 50 years, Griselda had appeared in virtually all the dominant literary genres of the [fourteenth] century: she had been in a prose cycle tale, an independent prose tale, an epistolary tale, an exemplary tale, a drama, a poetry cycle tale, an independent poem."[64] The Griselda story was adaptable for all of these genres by all of these authors for the same reasons that it was appropriate for Chaucer's examination of womanhood: it provided the basis for multiple interpretations, it was relevant to ideas about and representations of medieval women, and—most significantly—Griselda herself was a nexus of power and submission. As the suffering heroine, she could be cast as exercising a female form of power or enduring in the face of capricious male authority.[65] She could be the submissive, virtuous, and lovely ideal of courtly poetry or the unpredictable, independent saint of contemporary hagiography. The nature of the story and its main character lent themselves to an exploration of what otherwise seemed to be irreconcilable representations of women; Chaucer's addition of *womanhood* to the story introduced the possibility that these representations were not contradictory but could be combined through the new abstraction. *Womanhood* designated a concept that could mediate between these conflicting roles and represented femaleness as a comprehensive spiritual quality.

AT FIRST SIGHT

Griselda is an unlikely paragon of feminine behavior. She transgresses or exceeds the major categories in narrative and social ideals of medieval femininity: maidenhood, wifehood, motherhood, and widowhood. How could a model maiden mortgage her virginity against an upwardly mobile future, presenting it as her dowry in compensation for her peasant status? How could a model mother agree to her children's murders? And how could a model wife be "widowed" not by her husband's death but by his replacement of her with a younger, prettier, and nobler version of herself? Chaucer mobilizes these paradoxes in order to investigate the ideas of womanliness underlying them. The word "wommanhede" first occurs with Walter's first sight of Griselda and it contravenes an important poetic convention:

Upon Grisilde, this povre creature,
Ful ofte sithe this markys sette his ye
As he on huntyng rood paraventure;
And whan it fil that he myghte hire espye,
He noght with wantown lookyng of folye
His eyen caste on hire, but in sad wyse
Upon hir chiere he wolde hym ofte avyse,

Commendynge in his herte hir wommanhede,
And eek hir vertu, passynge any wight
Of so yong age, as wel in chiere as dede. (232–41)

This passage rewrites one of the most celebrated *topoi* in medieval literature: the first sight of the beloved. In most first sightings—as we saw in Palamon and Arcite's response to Emelye in the *Knight's Tale*—the lover is struck powerfully by the woman's image and wounded by love.

When Dante first sees Beatrice in *La Vita Nuova,* he describes her appearance and then its effect on him: "At that moment I say truly that the spirit of life, which dwells in the most secret chamber of the heart, began to tremble so strongly that it appeared terrifying in its smallest veins; and trembling it said these words: 'Behold a god more powerful than I, who comes to rule over me.'"[66] Petrarch describes the onset of his love for Laura as being "taken," and explains, "I did not defend myself against it, / for your lovely eyes, Lady, bound me."[67] In Boccaccio's *Teseida,* Palemone saw in Emilia's eyes the god of love, fitting an arrow to his bow.[68] In *Troilus and Criseyde,* Chaucer offers his magisterial version of the *topos.* Troilus has "scorned hem that Loves peynes dryen" but "sodeynly hym thoughte he felte dyen, / Right with hire look, the spirit in his herte" (I, 303 and 306–7). When he first sets eyes on Criseyde, his heart speeds up and he appreciates her appearance, including her "wommanhod" (I, 283). In this scene from the *Troilus,* Chaucer uses "wommanhod" in purely erotic terms, associating it with her "lymes" and "the pure wise of hire mevynge" (I, 282 and 285); in the *Clerk's Tale* scene, Chaucer makes "wommanhede" the pivotal term in his annexation of the hagiographic to the erotic. Walter does commend Griselda "in his herte" and, like many objects of courtly love, Griselda is gazed upon but does not respond or appear aware of her effect. There is no mention of love, however. The encounter should be an erotic connection; instead, Walter is struck by her sanctity. He looks "upon hir chiere" but there is no description of her beauty or even her physical appearance, beyond the mention of her womanhood. The attraction is about how Griselda looks—since Walter has no other information—but not in the expected way.

The emphasis is on Griselda's "wommanhede, / And eek hir vertu." The Clerk has already enumerated the unseen virtues that he associates with Griselda's womanhood here; the signal virtue is submission, which is characteristic of womanhood and was also key in the *Knight's Tale*. Her first virtuous quality is that "No likerous lust was thurgh hire herte yronne" (214). This establishes that sensual desire does not motivate her any more than it purportedly does Walter's notice of her. Griselda also drinks little, knows no idleness, and exhibits "rype and sad corage" (220). Her exemplary respect and care for her father, however, overshadow her other virtues. The Clerk explains, "in greet reverence and charitee / Hir olde povre fader fostred shee" (221–22). He reiterates the point more strongly later: "And ay she kepte hir fadres lyf on-lofte / With everich obeisaunce and diligence / That child may doon to fadres reverence" (229–31). In other words, Griselda sustains her father's very existence through her marvelous reverence and obedience to his will. The people also notice this virtue in Griselda: "And wondred hem in how honest manere / And tentifly she kepte hir fader deere" (333–34). These virtues, involving submission to male authority, are specific to womanhood. Patience, the virtue of Griselda's that most readings emphasize, is a form of this chief virtue of womanhood although critics have not directly connected the two.[69]

Chaucer refigures this scene by making Walter's attraction to Griselda an attraction to her womanhood. Chaucer clearly links "wommanhede" with Griselda's physical appearance, indicating that the condition is at least partially visible in a woman's body. The implied connection builds on one made some lines earlier between virtue and physical beauty. Griselda is "fair ynogh to sighte" (209) while not a remarkable beauty until her virtue is taken into account: "But for to speke of vertuous beautee, / Thanne was she oon the faireste under sonne" (211–12). Although the relationship is largely metaphorical, these lines establish an association between beauty and virtue that prepares the way for the hint that Griselda's womanhood manifests itself in her body and catches Walter's eye. His reaction to Griselda is unusual no less by the standards of his established personality than by the tradition of first meeting scenes. The physical nature of her womanhood has attracted Walter's attention but not "with wantown lookyng of folye." Instead, she is the object of his "sad" admiration. This seems out of character for the marquis since one of the first things we learn about him is that "on his lust present was al his thoght" (80). His passion for hunting demonstrates this temperament and he is engaging in that very activity when he sees Griselda. If he has noticed this peasant girl for ostensibly virtuous reasons, then his fascination would seem an exception to his general preoccupation with his own desire.

Chaucer's version of this scene amplifies a more implicit feature of Boccaccio's original treatment, which Petrarch eliminated. In the *Decameron*, Gualtieri finds Griselda "very beautiful" and thinks "a life with her would have much to commend it."[70] He concludes the marriage contract and then gives a speech to his followers, reiterating that he is marrying not because he wants to but because they have requested that he do so; he explains, without identifying Griselda, that he has "found a girl after my own heart" and plans to marry her.[71] Petrarch's account omits this second speech, as do *Le Livre Griseldis* and the *Clerk's Tale.* More crucially, Petrarch also anticipates the scene with the comment that "a mature, manly spirit lay hidden in her virginal breast" and explains the virtue that Walter sees in her as "excellent beyond her age and gender."[72] In Boccaccio, Gualtieri realizes he must marry, remembers the pretty peasant girl he has noticed, and decides they would have a good marriage. In Petrarch and those texts derived from him, Walter sees Griselda and, knowing that he needs a wife, makes a practical choice to marry her based on her virtue, which proceeds from her mature, virile spirit. Chaucer's revision makes Griselda a figure of womanhood, both beautiful peasant, as in Boccaccio, and virtuous exemplar, as in Petrarch. Seeing Griselda as an object of love or a notably beautiful woman places her within the particular tradition of female representation associated with romance and courtly poetry. Depicting her as an embodiment of virtue locates her in a different tradition of saints' lives and exempla. In the *Clerk's Tale,* Griselda is both beautiful and virtuous but the focus of Walter's desire will become her womanhood. By exploiting the peculiar nature of the first sight scene and shifting the focus to Griselda's womanhood, Chaucer opens a space between narrative traditions.

FROM MAID TO WIFE: WOMANHOOD AS TRANSLATION

Chaucer's exploration of the concept in the rest of the tale is no less narrative. On the one hand, Griselda's exemplarity is all excess, ambiguity, and paradox. On the other hand, Chaucer's exposition of this narrative continually returns to the political realities of her gender and class, but only through the refractive fictions of her relation to Walter. The trials of Griselda's womanhood are generally taken to begin with the birth of her first child. In fact, they begin with the marriage contract that sets the terms for her wifehood and motherhood. Although apparently an agreement between the couple to marry, the contract does not focus on whether Griselda will be Walter's wife but on how she will perform that role. This is her first trial and, by engaging in an unusual kind of negotiation, Griselda gives initial proof of her womanhood. Most critical interpretations of the contract focus on the promise of submission that Walter requires; if he is concerned with safeguarding his freedom, then it seems logical for him to seek verbal assurance from Griselda on that issue. He asks her to be "redy . . . / To al my lust" (351–52), echoing the narrator's description of Walter's concern with "his lust present" (80). Walter makes it clear that he addresses Griselda not to seek her assent to the marriage—"As I suppose, ye wol that it so be," he says confidently (347), having already set the date and ordered clothes and jewels made for her (253–60)—but to present his "demandes" regarding her behavior (348). The question is not whether Griselda will consent to marriage; it is about the additional terms on which Walter predicates *his* agreement to marry.

The marriage agreement begins as an exchange between men, father and prospective husband. Walter speaks to Janicula, asking, "If that thou wolt unto that purpos drawe, / To take me as for thy sone-in-lawe" (314–15). Janicula replies, "I wol no thyng, ye be my lord so deere; / Right as yow lust, governeth this mateere" (321–22). Walter's superior social status and his power over Janicula complicate their relationship; Walter is in a position to dictate the terms of the marriage agreement. Still, the agreement is contractual and couched in terms of negotiation: they have a "collacioun" and "tretys" (325, 331). A structure now exists for Griselda to move from being under her father's authority to Walter's. When this happens, Walter can reasonably expect that Griselda will accord him an obedience and reverence similar to that she showed her father.

When Walter approaches Griselda, he makes it clear that an agreement exists between himself and Janicula to which they expect her to accede: "It liketh to youre fader and to me / That I yow wedde" (345–46). Without pausing to hear Griselda's response, Walter gives the provisions of the agreement:

> I seye this: be ye redy with good herte
> To al my lust, and that I frely may,
> As me best thynketh, do yow laughe or smerte,
> And nevere ye to grucche it, nyght ne day?
> And eek when I sey "ye," ne sey nat "nay,"
> Neither by word ne frownyng contenance?
> Swere this, and heere I swere oure alliance. (351–57)

Although Walter presents these as questions, they are clearly the only terms under which he is prepared to conclude the marriage. An impressive amount of patriarchal authority backs them: Janicula's authority as Griselda's father and Walter's authority both as her prospective husband and as the marquis who rules father and daughter as his subjects. Under these circumstances, a refusal is virtually impossible, especially from a woman whose submission to male authority has already been established. The conditions Walter offers Griselda are the first test to which he subjects her, preceding the more frequently recognized trials during the marriage. In all of these tests, her womanhood is at issue; she must agree to (and later demonstrate) its characteristic virtue: submission.[73]

Although the contract is a set of requirements, only Griselda's consent puts it into effect. Walter constructs a model of behavior that she must agree to emulate (or not); however, this model was predetermined. Before seeing Griselda, the Clerk tells us, Walter sat in his "paleys honurable" and "shoop his mariage," considering the kind of wedded life he desired and, presumably, how to achieve that (197–98).

Walter's complete ideal is not yet clear to the audience, but Griselda goes beyond the question of consent by reshaping the model he has proposed. This reaction sharply contrasts with Emelye's silent acquiescence to Theseus's command that she wed Palamon. Griselda's reaction to Walter's offer highlights the importance of her role in the contract by refiguring the terms of the deal: her promise to submit exceeds his request. She swears, "nevere willyngly, / In werk ne thoght, I nyl yow disobeye" (362–63). The remarkable pledge of obedience in thought as well as deed is a testament to her womanhood. Even by raising the demands on herself, Griselda exercises a certain degree of control in the exchange and this, too, is a function of her womanhood. Chaucer uses Griselda's character to explore the contradictions of womanly behavior: she is articulate and exercises a kind of feminine power while not only retaining but even heightening her virtuous submission.

After Walter and Griselda agree to marry but before he gives her the ring, she is "translated." This "translation" renders her transformation from maiden to wife and potential mother in visible and material terms; although it has been a focus of several contemporary studies, most consider the linguistic or literal significance of the phrase rather than the means by which that change is completed.[74] The translation must later be undone (as far as possible) when Walter pretends to dissolve the marriage. As Griselda returns his gifts of clothing and ornaments—the material of her translation—she also describes the dowry gifts she gave, including her "mayden-hede" (837, 866). Along with its indispensable complements, sexual availability and submission, Griselda's maidenhead forms an important part of her womanhood, which serves as a priceless (and irrecoverable) counter-gift in the exchange with Walter.

After she agrees to the marriage terms, Walter presents Griselda to the crowd outside and a group of women "dispoillen hire right theere" (374); they comb her hair, dress her in new clothes, and adorn her with ornaments. The improvement is dramatic: "Unnethe the peple hir knew for hire fairnesse / Whan she translated was in swich richesse" (384–85). She is "another creature" (406). It is only after Walter sees that the translation was successful that he "hire spoused with a ryng" (386). And it is only now that Griselda is loved as she was not upon first sight; everyone "hire lovede that looked on hir face" (413). This change of clothes renders Griselda's womanhood visible to all, whereas before only Walter's keen eye discerned it. His ability to identify this quality in a lower-class maiden distinguishes him from his people, who "have no greet insight / In vertu" (242–43). It is within Walter's power not only to recognize Griselda's womanhood but also to make it apparent to his people through her translation. At the same time, this change of clothes signifies a change in her womanhood. Griselda's finery renders her sexuality visible, transforming her from the object of Walter's admiration to the legitimate object of his sexual desire. In Italy, the setting for the tale, a husband's gift of clothing to his wife in the Middle Ages functioned as "proof of the carnal consummation of the marriage," a sign that the wife was honoring the conjugal debt.[75] Similarly, Griselda's change of clothes signifies simultaneously her change of social status and her new sexual availability to Walter. This in turn is an expression of her womanhood, a state in which the sexual act plays such a large role.

The change of clothes also transforms Griselda from a maiden into a wife and potential mother, two important states of womanhood. Christiane Klapisch-Zuber explains that gifts of clothing were customary in medieval Italy: "During the days or months preceding the marriage and within the year following, the husband provided what was in effect a wardrobe for his wife, a kind of countertrousseau." These gifts were "indispensable symbolic agents in the integration of the wife into another household and another lineage."[76] Susan Crane reads clothing as an important signifier in literary terms as well, arguing that Griselda's "reclothing accomplishes her absorption into Walter's household and her subordination to him in marriage."[77] Walter's translation of Griselda is an acceptance of her into his household and, perhaps most importantly, as the mother of his lineage. As his wife, her appearance functions as a symbol of his wealth and power. He effects the transformation in public so that his people will recognize Griselda as the legitimate mother of his heirs. Making good on the earlier suggestion that the virtues of womanhood can become physical and visible, Griselda's body is the site where her incompatible roles—peasant and marchioness, maiden and wife—are reconciled.

Griselda's translation must be undone when the marriage dissolves. The clothing Walter provided—the mechanism of her metamorphosis—was a marriage gift that she now returns. Although the exchange of gifts originally seemed unequal, the reversal of the translation reveals that it was a mutual exchange involving somewhat unusual commodities. When Walter orders Griselda to return to her father's house, she catalogs both of their contributions: "To yow broghte I noght elles, out of drede, / But feith, and nakednesse, and maydenhede; / And heere agayn your clothyng I restoore, / And eek your weddyng ryng, for everemore" (865–68). Walter's gifts, clothing and a wedding ring, were visible and valuable in economic terms. Klapisch-Zuber identifies such gifts as a counterbalance to the wife's dowry in medieval Italian marriage customs.[78]

But while Walter's gifts are fairly straightforward and typical, Griselda's are not. Because of her lower-class origins, she does not bring the customary cash dowry. She did not come to the marriage empty-handed, however; she brought her husband "feith, and nakednesse, and maydenhede." Klapisch-Zuber carefully notes, "An analysis of the dowry cannot be confined to its economic terms alone."[79] Walter cannot measure Griselda's dowry in economic terms but her womanhood is undeniably valuable to him. She makes the connection between maidenhead and wifehood, saying that she will henceforth live as a widow: "For sith I yaf to yow my maydenhede, / And am youre trewe wyf, it is no drede, / God shilde swich a lordes wyf to take / Another man to housbonde or to make!" (837–40). "Maydenhede" was the dowry she brought as a "trewe wyf" and, having given it, she cannot "take / Another man to housbonde." In Chaucer's usage, maidenhead is part of (though not synonymous with) womanhood, and Griselda's maidenhead is an important part of both her womanhood and the dowry she brings to Walter.

Griselda returns to the importance of her "maydenhede," pointing out that Walter cannot restore it to her as she has restored his dowry gifts. In its place, she requests a "smok"

> . . . in gerdon of my maydenhede,
> Which that I broghte, and noght agayn I bere,
> As voucheth sauf to yeve me, to my meede,
> But swich a smok as I was wont to were,
> That I therwith may wrye the wombe of here
> That was youre wyf. (883–88)

Griselda asks for "a smok" like that she wore before her translation, conflating to some extent her "maydenhede" with her clothing. The smock is symbolic of her former sexual condition in addition to being a sign of her former social condition. Griselda also discloses the purpose behind her request; she wishes to "wrye the wombe of here / That was youre wyf." She associates the fine clothing with her role as a wife and with her womb, or ability to bear children, which we have already seen to be a critical element of womanhood. This second change of clothing is an attempt on Griselda's part to reclaim her former sexual status, at least partially, and she represents this attempt in sartorial terms.[80]

Womanhood is generally a virtuous condition of being, but within the system of gift and counter-gift that comprised marriage, Griselda's womanhood is also a valuable commodity. While the socioeconomic importance of the dowry is undeniable, Griselda brings the most critical elements to marriage in her sexuality and submission. These two related components of womanhood become Griselda's dowry. Her sexuality is made available to her husband through her submission. Marital intercourse is more than a site for the exercise of masculine authority; it justifies the existence of such authority. The sexual act, with its ramifications for noble lineage and inheritance, is perhaps the most important reason for a man to have authority over his wife. Submission to the husband ensured that a wife would render the conjugal debt, remain sexually faithful, and continue to bear and raise children in spite of the physical danger that such rigorous maternity represented in the Middle Ages. The ability to produce suitable or legitimate offspring can thus be seen as a defining feature of womanhood, important enough to the husband to justify murder in his mind, as the stories of several female martyrs attest. Sexual submission is also important synecdochically; if a wife did not submit to her husband sexually, her submission in other areas was irrelevant. Apart from practical considerations of heritability, sexual submission was significant symbolically to the husband and to others outside the marriage. Women were most valuable as the producers of heirs and motherhood was the most critical facet of womanhood. Other feminine virtues relate, directly or indirectly, to this vital role.

WOMANHOOD ON TRIAL

Walter tests Griselda's submission, the focus of her marriage promise and an important component of the womanhood that she brought as her dowry, by pretending to murder their children and take a new wife. These trials are the heart of the *Clerk's Tale* and the focus of the Griselda story in every medieval version; they have inspired a corresponding amount of scholarly interest (and bewilderment). Why does Walter test his wife and why, having begun, does he cease? Elaine Tuttle Hansen suggests that Walter tries Griselda because she demonstrates threatening masculine virtues by ruling well in her husband's absence. Kathryn Lynch argues that Walter is trying to gain knowledge of Griselda empirically since he cannot completely trust his intuitive sense of her virtue. Andrew Sprung, apparently unable to discern any viable motivation for the trials, claims that Griselda is simply a figure of male fantasy.[81] Each of these readings, however, oversimplifies Chaucer's depiction of either Walter or Griselda. Walter's testing is crucial to Griselda's model virtue; his extreme demands create the necessary environment for her to demonstrate convincingly the mediating power of womanhood, but through this demonstration she exceeds his ideal of womanhood as complete submission. Thus both Griselda and her husband contribute to her exemplarity.

The trials demonstrate Griselda's virtue by putting her womanhood doubly at stake. Walter is nervous about Griselda's ability to produce suitable and legitimate heirs (which, for Walter, means heirs that his people will accept), a major function of womanhood. Her lower-class origins give the lineage she mothers questionable status in his mind and he projects this anxiety onto his people, even though they evidence little concern on this point. This is a corollary, however, to Walter's concern about Griselda's suitability as a wife, specifically within the context of the marriage terms he has set. Because he designed those terms to ensure his own authority and freedom within the marriage, Griselda must display that chief virtue of noble womanhood, submission. The anxiety of his people over the lack of heirs motivated Walter's decision to wed, but his own anxiety over marriage as an institution ill-suited for a marquis focused on his present pleasure determined his choice of wife. As a result, it is critical that Griselda's womanhood be tested and proven in both of these ways. Having commended her "wommanhede" at first sight, Walter ends the trials by proclaiming that he has tested Griselda "For no malice, ne for no crueltee, / But for t'assaye in thee thy wommanheede" (1074–75). These two moments frame the tale.

The close association of the trials with the children demonstrates their importance in the tests of Griselda's womanhood. Before the birth of their first child, the couple "In Goddes pees lyveth ful esily" (423) and Griselda "Koude al the feet of wyfly hoomlinesse" (429). Her excellence extends to governance: "The commune profit koude she redresse. / Ther nas discord, rancour, ne hevynesse / In al that land that she ne koude apese" (431–33). Negotiation, mediation, and "juggementz of so greet equitee" are also within the realm of womanhood for Griselda (439). In this early phase of their marriage, Walter shows no inclination to test Griselda; in fact, he congratulates himself on having chosen wisely (425–26). Before long, however, their daughter is born and this birth initiates Walter's desire to test his wife. Although the narrative does not present the two events in a causal relationship, their connection is evident in the action of the story: "Whan that this child had souked but a throwe, / This markys in his herte longeth so / To tempte his wyf" (450–52). The association between the birth of the child and the onset of the testing is also apparent in their close juxtaposition in the text. The daughter's birth occurs in the final stanza of the second section and the third section opens by referring to the child and then immediately describing Walter's wish to test Griselda.

The birth of a daughter is an important proof of Griselda's womanhood because it attests to her fertility and ability to bear children; that is, her ability to fulfill her responsibility as a wife. However, this proof is not completely satisfactory, as the reaction of the people reveals:

> Glad was this markys and the folk therfore,
> For though a mayde child coome al bifore,
> She may unto a knave child atteyne
> By liklihede, syn she nys nat bareyne. (445–48)

The birth of a daughter is an encouraging sign that Griselda "nys nat bareyne" and the primary connotations here are hopeful. However, for the first time in the tale, there is a hint that Griselda may be less than perfect: she has not yet proven that she can produce an heir to perpetuate the line. The Clerk's condemnation of Walter's testing as "Nedelees" (455) follows this passage. The Clerk seems satisfied with Griselda's virtue, saying that Walter "hadde assayed hire ynogh bifore, / And foond hire evere good" (456–57). It is not, however, her goodness that is at issue but her womanhood and specifically her ability to provide an heir. Griselda herself seems to have internalized this perspective; she would "levere have born a knave child" (444). For Griselda, as well as Walter and his people, the birth of a daughter is a positive sign of her fertility but does not finally resolve the issue of the ruling lineage.

Up to this point, Griselda's lower-class origins have not manifested themselves in any negative way, but Walter may see the threat of this possibility in the birth of his daughter. The reason he offers for the first trial intimates this: "They [the people] seyn, to hem it is greet shame and wo / For to be subgetz and been in servage / To thee, that born art of a smal village" (481–83). He offers the daughter's birth as the explanation behind the complaints of his people and proposes her death as the only solution. Walter manufactures this excuse, with no apparent basis in reality. The fact that he chooses this fiction, when he need not have offered any explanation at all—when not providing an explanation might have better served to prove his dominance and authority—is notable and reflects his own anxiety over Griselda's womanhood and lower class.

Four years pass between the removal of the daughter and the birth of their second child, a son. Walter has given Griselda no other trials in this time. But after the birth of this second child, his yearning to test her returns: "Whan it was two yeer old, and fro the brest / Departed of his norice, on a day / This markys caughte yet another lest / To tempte his wyf yet ofter, if he may" (617–20). Here again the onset of a trial is closely associated with a child. In this case, it is not immediately after the child's birth but at another milestone in his early development, the day of his weaning, that Walter desires to test the mother. The birth of a son testifies to Griselda's womanhood and her ability to provide her husband with an heir. As such, it would seem sufficient to end the doubts inspired by the birth of a daughter. Walter does not stop the trials, however, indicating that this proof is inadequate. Griselda's womanhood has been proven because she has produced an heir but, due to her lower-class origins, the suitability of this heir is still in question for Walter.

Womanhood is not simply a question of fecundity; if the people do not accept the line mothered by Griselda, her function as a wife and a woman is unfulfilled. Walter articulates this concern in the justification he offers for the second trial, the apparent murder of their son:

> My peple sikly berth oure mariage;
> And namely sith my sone yboren is,
> Now is it worse than evere in al oure age.
> . . .
> Now sey they thus: "Whan Walter is agon,
> Thanne shal the blood of Janicle succede
> And been oure lord, for oother have we noon."
> Swiche wordes seith my peple, out of drede. (625–27, 631–34)

Again, Walter crafts the excuse without basis, but his choice of fictions is significant; although his people have the heir they wanted, he remains uneasy about the larger question of the children's acceptability. He has also constructed an excuse that would seem particularly plausible to Griselda. Her concerns closely resemble the fictional concerns of the people, as demonstrated by her sense of her own lower-class status and her desire for a "knave child."

After the sergeant takes the son, the Clerk interrupts the tale briefly to ask "of wommen" (696) whether this is not enough: "What koude a sturdy housbonde moore devyse / To preeve hir wyfhod and hir stedefastnesse" (698–99). The birth of her children verified Griselda's motherhood; their simulated murder has tested Griselda's "wyfhod" by requiring her to subjugate her motherly feelings to her wifely loyalty. In fact, her perfect submission does cause Walter a moment of doubt about her motherhood, and "if that he / Ne hadde soothly knowen therbifoore / That parfitly hir children loved she," he would have had grave suspicions (688–90). As the final test, the sham marriage will confirm Griselda's womanhood by demonstrating both the nobility of her children (and thus the viability of her motherhood) and her enduring devotion to serving her husband's "lust" (757, 962) even when she is no longer his wife (and thus the perfection of her wifehood).[82] The sham marriage planned by Walter requires the participation of his children. This choice is more than simply arbitrary or convenient in terms of plot. In addition to being another test of Griselda's submission and, by extension, womanhood, the sham marriage is a demonstration of Walter's control over his daughter and a test of *her* womanhood. This final piece of evidence—the daughter's womanhood—also proves Griselda's womanhood and thus brings the testing to an end.

Timing is as important a consideration in the sham marriage as it was in the two prior trials. Five years have passed since the second test and, once again, the interval between tests has passed peacefully.[83] Walter begins preparations "Whan that his doghter twelve yeer was of age" (736). Twelve is "the age at which a woman allegedly achieved the majority that supposedly corresponded to puberty and marriageability."[84] For practical reasons, Walter could not have carried out his plan until his daughter reached marriageable age. He might have pretended to marry someone else at any point during the five years, but he has waited until his daughter was of an age to play her part. The involvement of the daughter in the charade makes it a double test of Griselda (her motherhood and her wifehood) and a double test of womanhood (Griselda's and her daughter's).

Walter's justification for the third test is the same as for the others: the fictitious complaints of his people about Griselda's lower-class background. He explains that he chose her based on his own desires, but that now he must consider what his people want:

> Certes, Grisilde, I hadde ynogh plesance
> To han yow to my wyf for youre goodnesse,
> As for youre trouthe and for youre obeisance,
> Noght for youre lynage, ne for youre richesse;
> But now knowe I in verray soothfastnesse

That in greet lordshipe, if I wel avyse,
Ther is greet servitute in sondry wyse.

I may nat doon as every plowman may.
My peple me constreyneth for to take
Another wyf, and crien day by day. (792–801)

"Lynage" and "richesse," Walter implies, are what his people would prefer in a marchioness; in choosing Griselda for other reasons, he acted like a "plowman." He
suggests that Griselda's class has tainted his own and perhaps endangered his position as ruler. The irony, of course, is that while Walter equates lower status with
greater freedom, Griselda's lower class has not allowed her to act more freely; she
has experienced "greet servitute" in both of the social classes that she has inhabited and Walter's pretense of submitting to his people's wishes points up Griselda's
submission as not only more sincere but also carrying serious costs. While Walter
is again inventing this excuse, it is true enough that his people have begun to talk
about his marriage; rather than speaking against Griselda, however, "the sclaundre
of his diffame / Made hem that they hym hatede therfore" (730–31).

The opinion of the people quickly changes when they see the proposed new
wife, unaware that she is the daughter of Walter and Griselda. The daughter's submission to her father's plan gives initial evidence of her womanhood but the people's
reaction to her as a prospective wife for their marquis is the crucial validation. The
concerns of the people led to the first marriage and were used by Walter to explain
each of the tests; now the opinion of the people helps to end the trials even as it
seems to undermine Griselda's position.[85] They admire the daughter at first sight:

And thanne at erst amonges hem they seye
That Walter was no fool, thogh that hym leste
To chaunge his wyf, for it was for the beste.

For she is fairer, as they deemen alle,
Than is Grisilde, and moore tendre of age,
And fairer fruyt bitwene hem sholde falle,
And moore plesant, for hire heigh lynage. (985–91)

The people focus on the daughter's beauty and her potential motherhood. It is the
daughter's perceived superior womanhood, in both those senses, that reconciles
them to Walter's ill treatment of his current wife and the murders of his children
(for which they previously "hatede" him). Although this reversal leads to a lamenta-
tion on the people's inconstancy, it is not their fickleness that is important here but
their perception of the daughter. Walter's anxiety over the suitability of the children

borne by Griselda can only be soothed by his people's acceptance of them, so it is absolutely vital that the people recognize and affirm the nobility of the children. Their opinion is later substantiated when Walter marries off his daughter "richely," giving her "Unto a lord, oon of the worthieste / Of al Ytaille" (1130, 1131–32).

The people's reaction to the daughter includes the first explicit reference to the importance of motherhood. Walter did not mention it when he first saw Griselda or in the marriage contract and, although the people noted Griselda's "fairnesse" (384) after her translation, they did not remark on the "fruyt" that might result from that marriage. Within the narrative, this silence about Griselda's motherhood allows Walter to fabricate the reaction of his people to his children. It also heightens the dramatic effect of this scene: the people unconsciously confirm Griselda's motherhood in the act of disparaging it. Still, the people's desire to avoid a "straunge successour" inspired them to ask Walter to marry and continue his line and so the absence of any earlier mention of motherhood seems odd (138). Perhaps the passage of time has made them more anxious on this point, or perhaps Walter's rejection of the children has made his people question their suitability. Most notably, this absence underscores the effectiveness of Walter's translation of Griselda and the effect of its undoing. Walter's translation of Griselda completely convinced the people, if not Walter himself, of her potential motherhood; the retranslation of Griselda's womanhood leaves her in an indeterminate space between maidenhood and widowhood, undercutting her motherhood. The crowd's reaction to the daughter hints that they did not anticipate such beauty and nobility from Griselda's offspring; the daughter herself is "fairer fruyt" than they expected.

The establishment of the daughter's womanhood is also partial evidence of Griselda's womanhood because it speaks to the suitability of the children she has produced. The crowd's recognition of the son as noble completes the proof of the mother's womanhood by legitimating him as an heir. The people credit Walter's good governance for bringing these noble children into his family: "Hir brother eek so fair was of visage / That hem to seen the peple hath caught plesaunce, / Commendynge now the markys governaunce" (992–94). "Commendynge" recalls Walter's original sighting and valuation of Griselda and her virtues. The trials have vindicated Griselda's womanhood: she has demonstrated submission, the salient virtue of womanhood; given birth to two legitimate children, including an heir to perpetuate the line of the marquis; and established her wifehood by relinquishing it. Through the translation, its reversal, and its (forthcoming) reinstatement, her womanhood persists.

Once Griselda's womanhood has been proven, the trials can end. I have already noted that the text explicitly offers this justification for Walter's cruelty. Walter was drawn to Griselda because of her womanhood and then successfully tested it through three trials, all associated with their children and her submission of them to his will. When Walter reveals the sham of the third trial and stops testing Griselda, he says to her:

This is thy doghter, which thou hast supposed
To be my wyf; that oother feithfully
Shal be myn heir, as I have ay disposed;
Thou bare hym in thy body trewely.

. . .

Taak hem agayn, for now maystow nat seye
That thou hast lorn noon of thy children tweye.

And folk that ootherweys han seyd of me,
I warne hem wel that I have doon this deede
For no malice, ne for no crueltee,
But for t'assaye in thee thy wommanheede. (1065–75)

This passage openly identifies Walter's motivation for testing Griselda: "t'assaye in thee thy wommanheede."[86] Now that it has been proven, the roles of mother and wife that were stripped from her are restored. Walter identifies the son as "myn heir," accepting him as noble and suitable to carry on the line and stressing Griselda's role as mother of the heir. The explanation Chaucer offers is an interpolation; in his sources, Walter states, tautologically, that the trials were to test his wife.[87] Here he accompanies his justification with a less credible claim: he has not tried Griselda out of "malice" or "crueltee." The tale contradicts this claim, and the Clerk has bluntly condemned Walter's actions as "yvele" (460). His behavior, however, was necessary for two reasons. First, the malicious and cruel nature of his demands upon Griselda proves his sovereignty in marriage. Second, his malice and cruelty allow Griselda to prove her womanhood completely and effectively.

Walter's concern that he might lose sovereignty through marriage has permeated the tale. In their initial request that he marry, his people ask, "Boweth youre nekke under that blisful yok / Of soveraynetee, noght of servyse, / Which that men clepe spousaille or wedlok" (113–15). As a ruler whose mind is always on his own "lust," however, no "yok" is amenable to Walter. He responds to their petition by saying, "I me rejoysed of my liberte, / That seelde tyme is founde in mariage; / Ther I was free, I moot been in servage" (145–47). His choice of Griselda (when his people asked for a marchioness "Born of the gentilleste and of the meeste / Of al this land" [131–32]), his unreasonable demands within the marriage contract, and his trials of her demonstrate that his "soveraynetee" remains intact. It is rather Griselda who is "bisy in servyse" (603) and "mooste servysable of alle" (979). Walter continues to explain his rationale for the trials by asserting that he took away the children "to kepe hem pryvely and stille, / Til I thy purpos knewe and al thy wille" (1077–78). In truth, however, the trials have taught him nothing about his wife's individual "purpos" and "wille" but instead have reassured him that she has none beyond what he imposes. Only tests excessive in their malice and cruelty could definitively establish—to Walter and his people—that he is not "in servage" but is instead served by the unusual marriage he has constructed.

Perversely, Walter's cruelty also creates the environment necessary for Griselda to prove herself an exemplar of womanhood (without such extreme tests, the womanhood of the Amazons was never proven in the *Knight's Tale*). Like the spouses themselves, the two qualities—cruelty and perfect womanliness—are interdependent: womanhood is most apparent (and possibly most meaningful) in the context of unreasonably demanding male authority, while only that kind of authority would require the type of exemplary womanhood Griselda exhibits. Walter's malice sets up in sharp contrast the conflicts and categories that she must mediate. The need to provide a suitable male heir (a need played upon and exaggerated by Walter) heightens the ordinary demands of motherhood for Griselda as a former peasant. On the other hand, the demands of wifehood are also greater because of the promise of obedience that is the basis of her marriage, inspired by Walter's desire to preserve his sovereignty to the greatest degree. He pits her wifehood against her motherhood and raises the stakes of each.

Walter's malicious demands require excessive virtue to endure, which creates the impression of Griselda's patience as Job-like and saintly, bringing undertones of hagiography to the secular context of the tale. Enduring the cruel trials also requires great love, however, which Griselda also demonstrates. She refers to her love as she reiterates her excessive marriage pledge (and even ups the ante further) in response to the testing (857 and 973). This cultivates the sense of Griselda as a figure of romance; "Deth," she says, "may noght make no comparisoun / Unto youre love" (666–67). Hence Walter sets up the conflicts Griselda must mediate (between the social roles of wifehood and motherhood and the literary categories of hagiography and romance) and it is the "malice" and "crueltee" he denies that make the conflicts extreme enough to warrant and witness an extraordinary response. Walter stages the trials for his own ends but becomes, almost in spite of himself, a crucial participant in the construction of Griselda's exemplary womanhood.[88]

Walter's revelation is followed by a third translation: Griselda is again stripped and reclothed, this time with a "clooth of gold" and a "coroune" (1117–18). Finally "she was honured as hire oghte" (1120); this honor, however, is due as much to her husband's agency as her own—both have contributed to this realization of her excellent womanhood. The moment when Walter first admires Griselda's womanhood and the moment when he ends the trials bracket the tale, providing answers to the puzzling questions of why Walter chooses Griselda and why, having chosen her, he tests her so excessively. However, the ideal of womanhood that Griselda ultimately displays—which exceeds Walter's predetermined model—marks a new conception of what is womanly.

This new conception is admittedly extreme: in order to pass Walter's tests, Griselda must prove herself to be possessed of a womanhood that becomes threatening through its endurance and ultimate triumph. The Clerk concludes the tale with several assurances that most (if not all) other women would fail such tests. Womanhood may have the potential to combine these different ideals of womanhood, but most women would have less of the steadfast saint in their combination. In other words, Griselda's womanhood is so exemplary that it may mark the limit of the mediating power of womanhood. Chaucer employs a two-part strategy at the tale's conclusion to allay any discomfort that might be caused by this new conception: first, he draws on Petrarch to universalize Griselda's example and, second, he reminds the reader of more familiar images of powerful women as manipulative wives rather than secular saints.[89] This recharacterization of womanly power undermines Griselda's authority while, at the same time, preserving the possibility that there are multiple forms of feminine power.

Immediately after ending the story, the Clerk offers the Petrarchan moral:

This storie is seyd nat for that wyves sholde
Folwen Grisilde as in humylitee,
For it were inportable, though they wolde,
But for that every wight, in his degree,
Sholde be constant in adversitee
As was Grisilde; therfore Petrak writeth
This storie, which with heigh stile he enditeth. (1142–48)

Chaucer redirects us to the allegorical level of the poem: Griselda's womanhood is important insofar as it stands in for subjecthood, and so the tale is not for "wyves" but for "every wight." This interpretation makes the "storie" not about Griselda's powerful submission—her "humilytee"—but about the human ability to endure suffering and "be constant in adversitee." Walter's cruelty is muted somewhat, but we are left with serious gaps between his allegorical likeness to God and his behavior as Chaucer represented it and the Clerk judged it.

After invoking and summarizing Petrarch, the Clerk signals a shift in perspective by offering "o word . . . er I go" (1163). This "word" turns out to be the envoy, which, apparently unlike the tale itself, is meant specifically for wives; he addresses it to the Wife of Bath and "al hire secte" (1171).[90] Such women are nearly anti-Griseldas: unable to combine different models of womanhood as successfully as she did, they resemble the traditional overbearing wife of the fabliau. While Walter's excessive exercise of authority enables Griselda's exemplarity to exceed his own ideal, these women are comfortably comic because they can be powerful only in a vacuum, when husbands cannot or do not know how to exercise their own masculine and marital authority.

In the end, Chaucer may be retreating from the new and anxiety-producing model of womanhood that Griselda represents into conventional images of more limited feminine authority, returning the readers to the kind of female characters that can more easily be recognized and enjoyed. Chaucer renames these stereotypes, however, calling such women "archewyves" (1195) and, in the context of Griselda's story, we might read them from a different perspective: as an alternative and more accessible (if less effective or comprehensive) form of feminine authority. In a distinct and fundamental departure from Petrarch, Chaucer uses the tale to question and ultimately to broaden ideas about what is womanly and how women can exercise power, creating womanhood as a category that can encompass "archewyves" as well as Patient Griselda. The addition of *womanhood* reshapes the story and allows Chaucer to use it to explore the new concept and examine new ways of representing women that sought their similarities as a gender beyond traditional social roles or generic archetypes.

Chaucer's texts make vital contributions to the earliest phase in the development of new terms like *womanhood* that allow writers to think about women in new ways. His use of gendered language confirms that questions about how to reconcile womanly virtue with feminine power are among the most pressing raised by figures who somehow transcend or transgress the possibilities that social custom or literary precedent have defined for them. More generally, his work shows that texts offer a space for experimenting not only with new vocabulary but also with new concepts; in these cases, Chaucer explores the potential for female social power by reimagining what might look like a limited form of influence (intercession) or even an absence of authority (submission). He is able to do so by manipulating and combining extant ideas of femininity—primarily literary stereotypes, such as those found in romance, hagiography, and legend, but also cultural identities such as mother and wife; this kind of experiment is more easily performed in texts than in life, but might have social as well as literary ramifications.

Womanhood is a motivating interest of Chaucer's throughout his work, but the *Canterbury Tales* provides its most in-depth and varied exploration. Recognizing this larger interest recasts the economy of the collection; rather than being an anomalous beginning or a dead end, the *Knight's Tale* makes a crucial contribution to our understanding of Chaucerian womanhood. Chaucer advances this project not only through the Knight and the Clerk or even in those tales in which the term appears but also in the many contexts and through the many portrayals of femininity that the collection presents. Nonetheless, the high-stakes transformations of Emelye, Hippolyta, and Griselda offer particularly fruitful circumstances for revisiting common associations between femininity and submission in order to test how much power women can exert while still privileging feminine virtues. While Gower is less focused on issues of power and approaches the relationship between gender and language from a different angle, the next chapter will show that he exhibits a similar interest in how transformation can test or reveal womanhood and its connections to moral behavior.

CHAPTER 2

BEASTLY WOMEN AND WOMANLY MEN

Gower's Confessio Amantis

Gower's idea of womanhood is in some ways more flexible and more radical than Chaucer's and it complements as well as counters the latter.[1] Gower's treatment of women has attracted less attention from critics (with a few notable exceptions such as Diane Watt and Karma Lochrie), perhaps because his interests in politics and morality have overshadowed his other concerns.[2] However, gender and morality prove to be closely linked in the *Confessio Amantis* and that text is crucial to the development of womanhood, providing a version that is at least as influential as Chaucer's for later writers. Throughout the *Confessio,* Gower constructs womanhood as analogous to both manhood and beastliness. He imagines all three identities to be characterized by observable signifiers; as a result, any given identity is not only subject to change but also can be learned or feigned.

In its focus on observable signifiers, Gower's idea of gender resembles Judith Butler's theory of the performative nature of gender. Seeking to clarify her position in the tenth anniversary edition of *Gender Trouble,* Butler offered this summary: "The view that gender is performative sought to show that what we take to be an internal essence of gender is manufactured through a sustained set of acts, posited through the gendered stylization of the body. In this way, it showed that what we take to be an 'internal' feature of ourselves is one that we anticipate and produce through certain bodily acts."[3] The "production" of womanhood fascinates Gower and he considers appearances as well as actions; he is also interested in manhood and beastliness as other identities that are similarly produced and rendered recognizable. On this issue, Gower goes further than Chaucer; to embrace an anachronism, Gowerian gender is performative. "What we take to be 'real,'" writes Butler, "what we invoke as the naturalized knowledge of gender is, in fact, a changeable and revisable reality."[4] This statement resonates with Gower's conception of gender in the *Confessio Amantis.*

The "changeable" nature of identity makes Gower—like Chaucer—interested in what happens when characters undergo transformation. While Chaucer's transformations involve an alteration in a woman's circumstances, however, Gower's transformations are more physical and explore how any figure can combine elements of womanhood, manhood, and beastliness. The intersections of these identities intrigue Gower and he locates them in many figures, including Amans. The loathly lady in the Tale of Florent, for example, is somewhere between a woman and a monster for most of the tale. Other characters, such as Achilles and Iphis, demonstrate the malleability of gender identities as they move from one to another. In order to express this multiplicity, Gower uses ambiguous language; straightforward labels cannot communicate the complex natures of the characters he represents.[5]

Gower—again, like Chaucer—is also interested in the relationship between womanhood and social power. But while Chaucer explored how much power women might exercise through intercession and submission, Gower associates femininity with limited power. He finds more potential in women as the objects rather than the agents of authority, making womanhood serve an important social and narrative function by embodying the effects of moral and immoral actions. The disturbing depiction of the impact of Tereus's behavior on Procne and Philomena, for instance, reinforces and deepens readers' judgment of his dishonorable actions and, in many other tales, Gower's representations of womanhood similarly enable critical reflection on morality. Womanhood itself is generally a virtuous state in the *Confessio*—associated with maidenhead or chastity, for example—but Gower does not spend much time detailing which virtues are involved.[6] Instead, he focuses on how it can act as a register of the morality of others, especially men.

While the observable signifiers that characterize womanhood can also signal the effects of immoral (or, more rarely, moral) behavior, one must be able to interpret those signals accurately. This is the challenge that the frame story presents to Amans. Genius attempts to teach Amans how to be a man and an important element of that is how he should think about and react to women, especially the lady who is the object of his desire. He imagines that his lady should respond as a romance heroine, but she appears to be motivated by more practical concerns; this interplay reveals a gap between romance conventions and reality. In order to teach Amans how to treat women, Genius portrays the effects of sin on female victims, underscoring their sufferings as noteworthy injustices. This approach values women as worthy not only of pity but also of a respect and consideration that would have recognized and honored their virtue. Although Watt has persuasively argued that Gower is "amoral" in the larger context of the *Confessio,* the epithet "moral Gower"—originated by Chaucer—remains apt in reference to Gower's portrayal of women.[7]

Gower uses a complex of related terms—including *womanhood, womanish, womanly, motherhood, wifehood, maidenhead,* and *sisterhood*—to explore women, their natures, and their representations. *Womanhood* occurs twenty-four times in the *Confessio,* appearing in the frame as well as the tales and in every book except Book II, and, as Chaucer did, Gower revises his sources to make womanhood a central issue in a number of tales.[8] This chapter presents a reading of the *Confessio Amantis* in three stages. The first examines some of Gower's "beastly women," female characters who either seem to be or literally become beasts. These characters demonstrate that identities are both unstable and overlapping. They also show that womanhood is vulnerable from within and without: some women lose it by acting wrongly while for others it is damaged by rape. The second section considers "womanly men," men who adopt feminine roles or characteristics. These characters illustrate to what extent gender identities depend on observable signifiers and how womanhood itself can be acquired. Finally, the chapter connects Gower's concept of womanhood in the tales with the figure of Amans's lady in the frame narrative. As part of his attempt to educate Amans on how to be a man and hence how to react to women, Genius persistently interprets his exempla, even those with female protagonists, as lessons about male behavior. Only by understanding and sympathizing with female victims can Amans absorb the morals of the tales, but his continuing insensitivity toward his lady signals his inability to read women's experiences accurately. Ironically, Amans's own womanliness (in allowing himself to be ruled by love) mires him in the conventions of romance, which he improperly attempts to apply to his lady's behavior. Gower undermines these romance ideals and, in the end, Amans is "cured" when another female figure, Venus, bluntly observes the incongruity between his idea of himself as a courtly lover and the reality of his unsuitability for that role. Restored to reason, he undergoes his own transformation by recovering his manhood. His closing vision of love demonstrates a new ability to recognize male misconduct, female suffering, and feminine virtue.

Beastly Women

The Tale of Florent contains the first appearance of *womanhood* in the *Confessio.* This tale considers the possibilities raised by transformation and establishes the importance of moral action. Before Florent's ethical behavior reverses her transformation, the loathly lady's unattractive appearance and aggressive behavior make him unable to tell whether she is an example of womanhood or a monstrous figure. By drawing on Ovidian and other classical traditions in which beastliness often takes the shape of an exaggerated femaleness, Gower reveals the parallel status of womanhood and the monstrous as categories based on the assumption that the exterior represents the interior, but he puts this assumption in question for both. He emphasizes the loathly lady's unstable identity as woman/beast through a recurring pun and romance conventions (sometimes inverted, sometimes straightforward). As the wedding night approaches, this instability becomes more troubling until, in the marriage bed, Genius resolves it by rendering the loathly lady beautiful.

The tales of Tereus, Cornix, and Calistona from Book V reverse this metamorphosis: women become animals. They are transformed when their maidenhead is lost or threatened; while Florent acts ethically and the loathly lady wields some power by providing the answer to his quest, these characters are exposed to abuses of male authority. The tales explore whether and in what ways the initial identity persists in woman-to-beast transformations. In each case, Gower demonstrates that both womanly and beastly identities are enacted rather than essential. Womanhood's tie to maidenhead renders both vulnerable and changeable; they can be lost through no fault of the woman. The female characters are not exemplars but victims; nonetheless, Amans struggles to recognize that the male characters acted wrongly against them. Genius does discuss the virtue of preserving "maidehiede" but, oddly, through a male exemplar.

Gower's exploration of womanhood begins with The Tale of Florent, where the quest to find what all women most desire presents a challenge similar to the conceptual problem of the word *womanhood* itself. Both seek to discover what makes women women across traditional categories of marital and class status. Gower stresses this challenge, noting that Florent receives many individual answers to his question, but cannot discover "such a thing in special, / Which to hem alle in general / Is most plesant, and most desired."[9] In the well-known analogue of the Tale of Florent, the *Wife of Bath's Tale,* Chaucer makes a similar point by appealing to marital categories, noting that representatives of each are present for the knight's response:

> Ful many a noble wyf, and many a mayde,
> And many a wydwe, for that they been wise,
> The queene hirself sittynge as a justise,
> Assembled been, his answere for to heere.[10]

After the knight has given his answer, Chaucer reiterates the varied nature of the women present: "In al the court ne was ther wyf, ne mayde, / Ne wydwe that contraried that he sayde."[11] This agreement among different female groups certifies the truth of the knight's answer. Although revealed by the loathly lady, this answer presumably could have come from any of them. Nevertheless, the word *womanhood* does not appear in Chaucer's tale.[12]

The absence of *womanhood* from the *Wife of Bath's Tale* is one of several notable differences between Chaucer's and Gower's versions of the story; others include the reason for and nature of the knight's quest. In Gower, the quest is punishment not for rape but for killing a man in war and the answer to the question is not sovereignty in general but, more specifically, sovereignty in love. Many of the differences, however, arise in the portrayals of the loathly lady and these differences point up Gower's interest in the performative aspects of womanhood and in its usefulness as a register of how others use their power. In the *Wife of Bath's Tale,* the loathly lady is unattractive but unquestionably female. Describing the knight's first sight of her, the Wife refers to the loathly lady as a "wyf" twice in three lines and the knight himself addresses her as "my leeve mooder."[13] However, Gower's narrator is ambiguous on this point, saying that the knight "syh wher sat a creature, / A lothly wommannysch figure, / That forto speke of fleisch and bon / So foul yit syh he nevere non" (I, 1529–32). Genius does not refer to the loathly lady as a woman throughout this initial encounter; he uses the female pronoun but chooses "wight" as his noun.[14] He does call the figure "wommannysch," but that word can describe a creature like a woman rather than a human woman, as indeed it does in other tales.[15] This adjective contributes to rather than dispels doubt about the loathly lady's nature.

The first direct connection between this creature and womanhood comes only as Florent leaves her. He complains that "if he live, he mot him binde / To such on which of alle kinde / Of wommen is thunsemlieste: / Thus wot he noght what is the beste" (I, 1623–26). This passage reverses the hyperbole used to describe female beauty in romance, and instead places the loathly lady on the border between womanliness and beastliness: she might still be a womanlike creature rather than a woman. This continuing instability depends on the first of several puns in the tale on "beste," a word that can be read as either "best" or "beast."[16] Line 1626 means both that the knight does not know what the best course of action is and that he does not know what the beast is. This second interpretation raises numerous questions, including not simply whether the creature is a woman or a beast but whether she is enchanted, whether she is sexually appropriate and available, and whether she is good or evil. These concerns arise at this early moment because the loathly lady has been clear from the outset that she wants to marry the knight in return for aiding him with his quest. In Chaucer's version, she asks only that he will grant her unspecified future request, deferring any sexual possibilities.

The loathly lady's response to Florent's question—that all women desire sovereignty in love—brings her closer to a womanly identity. Genius first describes her as a woman just before the knight gives the answer she provided, completing his quest and saving his life. He realizes that he must say the words that "the *womman* hath him tawht" (I, 1653; my emphasis). In Chaucer, the queen remains silent after the knight gives the correct answer. In Gower, the grandmother set the quest, and she reacts violently to the successful solution:

Sche seide: 'Ha treson, wo thee be,
That hast thus told the privite,
Which alle wommen most desire!
I wolde that thou were afire.' (I, 1659–62)

There are many reasons for the grandmother to be angry with Florent. He killed her grandson and has now eluded her attempt to bring about his death through an apparently impossible quest. Nevertheless, the language of her answer suggests that she is angry only with the loathly lady and only because she has revealed an answer that a man alone would have been unable to discover.[17]

It is not clear whether the grandmother designed the question to be completely unanswerable or whether she assumed only that the answer would be unavailable to a man. Chaucer's version favors the former, since all of the women at court seem surprised by the knight's answer but unable to refute it. Gower's version leans toward the latter, since the grandmother immediately recognizes the correctness of the answer and realizes just as quickly that a woman must have revealed it to Florent. Her reaction suggests that women are a community unified in keeping this secret from men and raises the possibilities that women may be unified in other ways and may be concealing other secrets about their natures. Supplying the answer certifies the loathly lady's womanhood because it is something that only a woman would know but, paradoxically, it also constitutes a betrayal of her kind and so casts doubt on her womanhood.

As Florent returns to the lady to fulfill his promise, Genius offers an inverted blazon of "this vecke wher sche sat, / Which was the lothlieste what / That evere man caste on his yhe" (I, 1675–77). He notes the ugliness of her body and each feature of her face. The Wife of Bath, by contrast, never spends much time on the loathly lady's appearance; she merely tells us that the lady is "olde" and "foule" without going into the gory details.[18] Genius defines the loathly lady not only in terms of her looks (her cheeks, for instance, are "rivelen as an emty skyn / Hangende doun unto the chin" [I, 1681–82]) but also in terms of her effect on men: her neck and shoulders "myhte a mannes lust destourbe" (I, 1688).[19] This mockery of romance conventions highlights the loathly lady's simultaneous distance from and connection to womanhood. She was most fully a woman when she revealed to Florent the female secret he sought, but as the time comes for him to keep his end of the bargain, the question of her monstrous aspect reasserts itself. The dilemma becomes urgent as the marriage becomes imminent: there is a horror of unnatural marriage (an issue to which Gower will return in the eighth book) but there is also the implied horror of the wedding night, when the nature of this creature must be revealed and faced.

As the loathly lady demands that Florent honor his covenant, "be the bridel sche him seseth" (I, 1697). Although the mixture of the beastly and the womanly in her nature repels him, it also compels him: as a knight, he is bound to be chivalrous and "Thogh sche be the fouleste of alle, / Yet to thonour of wommanhiede / Him thoghte he scholde taken hiede" (I, 1718–20). Florent does not firmly connect the loathly lady to womanhood here. However, the possibility that she can lay claim to that identity—if only from its outermost borders—demands a certain standard of behavior from him. Even here, Gower imagines women as a positively character-ized group. The loathly lady represents the furthest limits of womanhood, but not because of any vicious elements in her character. She is not evil or unfaithful or violent; in fact, she has saved the knight's life. Only her appearance sets her apart. By implication, womanhood is virtuous and desirable and, above all, beautiful.

Romance defines women by a superlative beauty that inspires love, but the women are often passive in courtly love relationships. Florent's bride-to-be vio-lates that norm by aggressively requiring him to marry her: she forces him to agree in spite of rather than because of her appearance. Genius reinforces this impres-sion by a repetition of the beast/best pun: Florent gathers his most trusted men and explains "that he nedes moste / This beste wedde to his wif, / For elles hadde he lost his lif" (I, 1740–42). Here "beste" might mean "beast" or "best woman," but it is barely a pun; "beast" is clearly uppermost.[20] Genius stresses the knight's lack of choice: he must do this thing to save his life. The compulsion is dual; the loathly lady imposed the condition but the knight's manly nature and dedication to courtly behavior oblige him to obey.

In preparation for the promised marriage, Florent attempts a "translation" simi-lar to Griselda's in the *Clerk's Tale.* The bride-to-be is bathed and "arraied to the beste" (I, 1748) but the effort is unsuccessful: "when sche was fulliche arraied / And hire atyr was al assaied, / Tho was sche foulere on to se" (I, 1757–59). She reconfirms her animal nature immediately after the wedding as she says, "My lord, go we to bedde, / For I to that entente wedde" (I, 1769–70) and then "profreth him with that to kisse, / As sche a lusti Lady were" (I, 1772–73). The loathly lady's behavior under-mines rather than proves her claim to womanhood. Although she exhibits female desire, her aggressive sexuality is not feminine. She acts "*as* sche a lusti Lady were," but her "lusti" actions—like her "foul" looks—seem beastly instead.

She becomes a "lady" when her appearance alters. Her new husband finally turns to face her in bed and sees "a lady lay him by / Of eyhtetiene wynter age, / Which was the faireste of visage / That evere in al this world he syh" (I, 1802–5). This appearance of the loathly lady as beautiful is another point of difference between Gower and Chaucer; in the *Wife of Bath's Tale,* she does not become beau-tiful until after he has granted her mastery. In the Tale of Florent, on the brink of consummation, at the very moment when the disjunction between her woman-hood and beastliness seems irreconcilable, Genius firmly resolves it. In the context of the knight's indecision over whether she should be beautiful by day or by night, the beast/best pun reappears, albeit weakly. Florent concludes, "I wol that ye be my maistresse, / For I can noght miselve gesse / Which is the beste unto my chois" (I, 1825–27). Although that final line may hint that he cannot decide whether to have his wife as a beast by day or night, the primary meaning is that he does not know which is the best option. The pun has moved from favoring "beast" to favoring "best" as the loathly lady has moved in the same direction.

The rhetoric of this passage marks a sudden reversal. Up to this point, it has been unclear whether the loathly lady represents a love object to be desired or a monstrous obstacle to be overcome, but now Genius creates a traditional courtly love scene. The language of excess applies to the woman's beauty rather than her foulness. She has vaulted, simply by virtue of the change in her appearance, from the outermost boundary of womanhood (where it was in question whether she was woman or creature) to the heart of that category. She has become a lady whose claim to womanhood is indisputable. She is beautiful and so, by definition, she exhibits womanhood. Although Genius has identified other women as ladies in the course of the tale, this is the first moment when he refers to the loathly lady in that way.

As with almost all of Genius's examples, the point here is not the woman, her choices, or her behavior, but the male actions that affect her; this story illustrates the sin of disobedience for Amans. However, the tale raises the question of the relationship between identity and appearance. Is womanhood purely a function of beauty? Was the loathly lady always a woman, or was she a beast until the knight reinstated her womanhood by granting her mastery, restoring them both to their proper roles in courtly love? Is the outward change in her form matched by an inward change, or is her inner nature the same regardless of her appearance? Susan Crane argues that "the shapeshifter masquerades in both the beautiful and the deformed bodies . . . because both are exaggerated versions of womanhood that solicit a sexual reaction from men. This doubling of the masquerade complicates its challenge to gender categories. If both bodies are female, what are the defining characteristics of femaleness?"[21] In my reading, however, both bodies are not truly female: one is womanish, one womanly. In other words, one body approximates womanhood while the other epitomizes it. The defining physical characteristic of womanhood is beauty, both here and in the romance tradition, but this tale reminds us that such appearances are transitory and it underscores that message by demonstrating that the change can occur in either direction—through the loss of beauty or, less conventionally, its recovery.

Gower explores the transitory nature of womanhood in more detail through characters who transform from women to beasts in the tales of Tereus, Neptune and Cornix, and Calistona. *Womanhood* appears in all three stories.[22] As in the Tale of Florent, the female characters are prominent but their actions are not the moral point of the story; the tales illustrate the sins of rape and robbery. One of Gower's innovations, and one of the characteristics that make the appellation "moral

Gower" appropriate, is his depiction of the effects of sin on others.[23] While Chaucer begins the *Wife of Bath's Tale* with the rape of a maiden who is never named or given a voice and subsequently disappears from the narrative, Gower's unusual approach to reshaping stories affords detailed portrayals of the (usually female) victims of sinful behavior. Chaucer allows women greater agency throughout the *Canterbury Tales,* but Gower underscores their significance in purely human terms.

The Tale of Tereus, the first of the group, begins with Tereus's rape of Philomena, his sister-in-law, and concludes with the transformation of Philomena, Procne, and Tereus into animals.[24] Tereus provides an example of a man in whom human and beastly natures coexist. Genius introduces him as "A worthi king of hih lignage, / A noble kniht eke of his hond" (V, 5566–67). But Tereus "mislooks" and his character changes: "His yhe myhte he noght withholde / . . . / And with the sihte he gan desire" (V, 5619 and 5621). He loses "alle grace" and, Genius explains, "Foryat he was a wedded man" (V, 5630–31). As this last phrase implies, Tereus not only forgot that he was married but also forgot he was a man—indeed, nearly forgot he was human. The animal imagery first appears two lines later, when Tereus is like "a wolf which takth his preie" (V, 5633).[25] The crucial element marking his transition from manly knight to beastly creature is his loss of reason: "he was so wod / That he no reson understod" (V, 5639–40).[26] Foreshadowing Philomena's future transformation, Genius describes the struggle between them: "As if a goshauk hadde sesed / A brid, which dorste noght for fere / Remue" (V, 5644–46).[27] Philomena picks up on this animal imagery in a speech that threatens to reveal Tereus's crimes. She calls him "false man" (again, suggesting not only that he has been false in his actions but also that he is not a real man) and "mor cruel than eny beste" (V, 5676 and 5677). When Philomena concludes, Tereus, "as a Lyon wod," cuts out her tongue (V, 5684).

At the end of the tale, Tereus, Philomena, and Procne become birds. Genius describes Philomena's transformation into a nightingale first, bringing the issue of womanhood to the forefront:

> For after that sche was a brid,
> Hir will was evere to ben hid,
> And forto duelle in prive place,
> That noman scholde sen hir face
> For schame, which mai noght be lassed,
> Of thing that was tofore passed,
> Whan that sche loste hir maidenhiede:
> For evere upon hir wommanhiede,
> Thogh that the goddes wolde hire change,
> Sche thenkth, and is the more strange. (V, 5949–58)

These observations are unique to Gower's version. Rather than overtly condemning

Tereus, this passage represents the effects of his actions on Philomena: her shame, damaged maidenhead, and lost womanhood. Philomena sings a song on these same themes, seeming pleased that "nou I am a brid, / Ha, nou mi face mai ben hid: / Thogh I have lost mi Maidenhede, / Schal noman se my chekes rede" (V, 5985–88).

Carolyn Dinshaw argues that Philomena's song "sounds just like a conventional courtly love song" and thereby "converts the experience of forcible rape into desirable, idealized, elite love."[28] The song does contain courtly conventions; Genius explains that she sings of love as "wofull blisse" and "a lusti fievere" (V, 5993 and 5995). However, the substance of the song—and particularly the part Philomena voices directly—focuses on her feelings, showing the impact of the rape. It demonstrates the destructiveness of the sin by showing the suffering of the victim; this is both a natural outgrowth and a particular payoff of Gower's vision of performative womanhood. Readers can observe the effects of immorality as they are enacted through and alongside gender itself. Gower ironically underlines this strategy in the insensitive reaction of Amans, who affirms his obedience to his lady's will after this tale but later expresses his wish to violate her. By contrast, Chaucer's version of the story restricts Philomela to only a few ineffectual cries for help ("Syster!," "Fader dere!," and "Help me, God in hevene!").[29] Chaucer's Philomela does not threaten to reveal Tereus, nor does she describe her suffering.

Like her voice, Philomena's womanhood is both lost and partially preserved through transformation. Gower collapses the category of maidenhood into the category of womanhood and then womanhood into humanness. After the rape, but before being transformed into a bird, Philomena cries out that she can no longer be a "worldes womman," something "that sche wisseth everemore" (V, 5755–56). Because Tereus has imprisoned her, she cannot participate in the world, but the loss of her maidenhead also suggests that she cannot take on the roles of women in the world as wives and mothers. For Philomena, the loss of her maidenhead cloisters her, making her situation a perversion of a dedicated virgin's. Maidenhead and womanhood are irrevocably linked; a loss of the former necessarily entails the loss of the latter. At the same time, it is clear that maidenhead is not interchangeable with womanhood; it is a part-to-whole relationship. Once Tereus raped her, Philomena was no longer fully a woman. She lost her virginity and, as a result, her potential for wifehood. Ultimately she attempts an inhumane revenge and literally loses her humanity.

Both sisters participate in the revenge against Tereus, revealing that both have lost their claim to a traditional womanly identity.[30] However, Genius connects Procne's loss of womanhood to her loss of motherhood:

This Tereüs be Progne his wif
A Sone hath, which as his lif
He loveth, and Ithis he hihte:
His moder wiste wel sche mihte

Do Tereüs no more grief
Than sle this child, which was so lief.
Thus sche, that was, as who seith, mad
Of wo, which hath hir overlad,
Withoute insihte of moderhede
Foryat pite and loste drede,
And in hir chambre prively
This child withouten noise or cry
Sche slou, and hieu him al to pieces. (V, 5885–97)

Genius first suggests the loss by describing her son as "this child." While not directly from Procne's perspective, the passage represents her thoughts (beginning with the phrase "His moder wiste wel") and so bears the overtones of her voice. Genius names her as "his moder" but not the boy as her son. He is "lief" to Tereus but not (or at least no longer) to Procne. She perverts the motherly and wifely actions of caring for a child and preparing a meal; her behavior is a mockery of true womanliness. In contrast to the loss of reason that led to Tereus's beastliness, the loss of pity—particularly that pity that should be most natural for women, the pity for their own children—causes Procne to lose her womanhood and humanity.[31] Much as Tereus "forgot" that he was a married man, Procne "forgets" pity. She is able to forget it because she is "withoute insihte of moderhede." If maidenhead is the essential characteristic of unmarried womanhood, motherhood is the essential characteristic of married womanhood. However, neither completely defines womanhood for Gower, not least because neither can be simply or completely signified in visible ways.

The Tale of Neptune and Cornix further explores the relationship between maidenhead and womanhood as Genius uses Neptune's attempted rape of Cornix to illustrate the vice of robbery.[32] Neptune's trouble—like Tereus's—begins with his gaze. He realizes that Cornix is not powerful enough to resist him

And hire in bothe hise armes hente,
And putte his hond toward the cofre,
Wher forto robbe he made a profre,
That lusti tresor forto stele,
Which passeth othre goodes fele
And cleped is the maidenhede,
Which is the flour of wommanhede. (V, 6176–82)

This passage characterizes maidenhead in two quite different ways, as a treasure and as a flower. The treasure metaphor, part of Genius's attempt to accommodate the sin of robbery to love, is disquieting. It raises the questions of whether maidenhead is a woman's treasure or one belonging to her father or husband and, if the former, whether it is spent once her virginity is lost. Even as a treasure, it does not seem very valuable; Neptune likens it to "some othre smale thinges" (V, 6174). Later in the tale, we are told that its worth to Cornix was much greater because it is something "That no lif mai restore" (V, 6211).[33]

In order to preserve this treasure, Athena transforms Cornix into a crow before Neptune can violate her:

> Out of hire wommanisshe kinde
> Into a briddes like I finde
> Sche was transformed forth withal,
> So that Neptunus nothing stal
> Of such thing as he wolde have stole. (V, 6199–6203)

Cornix exchanges her "wommanisshe" nature for the likeness of a bird, further evidence that nature is both changeable and multivalent. The word "wommanisshe" suggests that femininity is not necessarily innate to Cornix, nor is it the only possible nature for her.

A few lines later, Genius compares the womanly and avian natures, as if both are costumes that are put on (if not as easily discarded):

> [It] was to hire a more delit,
> To kepe hire maidenhede whit
> Under the wede of fethers blake,
> In Perles whyte than forsake
> That no lif mai restore ayein. (V, 6207–11)

The crow nature is like clothing, a "wede of fethers blake," and parallel to the appropriate attire for a woman (and perhaps suggestive of a bride) "in Perles whyte." The crucial constant is the inner intactness that Cornix has maintained. She does not have the shame of which Philomena sang; instead, Cornix is pleased to have escaped.[34] Maidenhead is so valuable that it is better to be an animal than a woman without her maidenhead. The irony, of course, is that Cornix avoided the loss of her maidenhead but, as a crow, she is no longer truly in possession of it. To be a woman is always to be at risk of losing your womanliness in one way (rape or violence) or another (transformation). Gower is heavily influenced by Ovid's versions of these narratives, but Ovid represents female metamorphosis as a weak mirror of divine transcendence whereas Gower interrogates how it affects human—and especially womanly—identity.

The final story of woman-creature transformation presents a woman who loses her maidenhead but manages to maintain vestiges of motherhood, even as a creature. Calistona's story is also unusual because she is a dedicated virgin and follower of Diana, a maiden who has vowed "To kepe hir maidenhode clene" (V, 6246). The narrative glosses over her rape by Jupiter, unlike the rape and attempted rape in the previous tales. Genius explains that her maidenhead was "priveliche stole away" (V, 6248) and that Jupiter "From hire it tok in such a wise, / That sodeinliche forth withal / Hire wombe aros and sche toswal" (V, 6250–52). Calistona's reaction is not detailed. She feels shame, like Philomena, but Genius describes these feelings only when Calistona must reveal her naked body to Diana and her virgins. Diana sees Calistona's pregnant body and cries, "Awey, thou foule beste" (V, 6275). The violation of her body has made Calistona beastly in Diana's eyes before the physical transformation occurs. As the earlier tales suggested, the loss of maidenhead causes a loss of womanhood and even of humanity. The beastliness becomes literal when, after the birth of Calistona's son, Juno transforms her into a bear. The rape robbed Calistona of her maidenhead, but the metamorphosis takes away her "grete beaute" (V, 6303), another important element of her womanhood.

Calistona's case is atypical because women as well as men act against her. Still, most disturbing is the near-victimization by her unknowing son that provokes a climactic reappearance of her "wommanhiede." Calistona sees her grown son, Archas, hunting in the forest:

> Whan sche under the wodesschawe
> Hire child behield, sche was so glad,
> That sche with bothe hire armes sprad,
> As thogh sche were in wommanhiede,
> Toward him cam, and tok non hiede
> Of that he bar a bowe bent.
> And he with that an Arwe hath hent
> And gan to teise it in his bowe,
> As he that can non other knowe,
> Bot that it was a beste wylde. (V, 6324–33)

The incident represents a clash between her two natures; unlike Procne, Calistona has not completely lost motherhood. On one hand, her outward appearance is completely a bear's and even her son sees her as a "beste wylde." On the other hand, a beast would react instinctively by running from the danger, but Calistona's maternal instincts remain uppermost and so she approaches her son. Her posture—arms spread wide to embrace him—is a human one, suggesting that, even at the physical level, vestiges of humanity remain.

Her emotions are also human; she is happy to see her son. To label this "human" is imprecise, however; the passage explains that she acts "as thogh sche were in wommanhiede." It is not her human nature that endures, but her motherhood and so her womanhood—these transcend the basic human/beast divide. The emphasis on Calistona's womanhood is particular to Gower's version; Ovid states only that "her human feelings remained, though she was now a bear [mens antiqua tamen facta quoque mansit in ursa]."³⁵ The four concluding lines of the tale quickly tell us that Jupiter intervened to save both mother and son, although no specific details are given. While this might seem like an expressive (rather than performative) concept of gender, Gower's notions of how identities develop and change can be extended to suggest that Calistona—and other characters, as we will see with Achilles—acquire and perform even those identities that seem most natural to them. In other words, Calistona's combination of womanhood and beastliness is less a case of a core identity showing through an imposed one than of the imperfect overlay of one identity on top of an earlier, but not necessarily more innate, one.

Calistona's tale is also unusual in depicting the struggle between her womanly and beastly natures after her transformation. Though we hear generally how Procne and Philomena feel as birds and that Cornix is pleased to be a crow, we see nothing that they experience as creatures. This last of the three tales proves that the beastly and the womanly (though they may conflict) can coexist within one self; if the loathly lady in the Tale of Florent proved that both aspects can manifest themselves in a single body, then Calistona's more extreme case shows that they can also act as a dual influence on behavior. The tale suggests that motherhood, at least, can endure through such transformations. By extension, womanhood also persists in observable ways: not in appearance, but actions. Genius explains Calistona's situation: "For thogh sche hadde hire forme lore, / The love was noght lost therfore / Which kinde hath set under his lawe" (V, 6321–23). This adds an additional level to womanhood; it involves specific emotions (although we can only apprehend these emotions when they are enacted). Procne forgot pity for her son and lost her womanhood before becoming a beast, but Calistona continues to love her son and retains an aspect of womanhood even as a beast. Motherhood is not a purely physical phenomenon and, as a result, neither is womanhood. Still, behavior is a significant manifestation of the otherwise invisible elements associated with those conditions.

Because beastliness can result from actions as well as appearances, there are other "beastly women" in Gower's text, including Clytemnestra and Medea. Womanhood exists precariously between enacted violence and experienced violation; both virginity and humanity are at risk. Maidenhead is not exclusive to women, however. At the conclusion of these three tales, Genius illustrates "Hou maidenhod is to commende" (V, 6358) with the example of Phyryns, a man who was so attractive that he gouged out his eyes to prevent women from desiring him. With this action, "his maidehiede he boghte" (V, 6384).³⁶ It is unusual to consider virginity as a male virtue but much more so to apply the etymologically feminine word "maidehiede" to a man. Gower's male-dominated focus in the *Confessio Amantis* and hence his need to establish the virtue as one with universal value may dictate this move, which is broadly similar to Chaucer's Clerk's attempt to universalize the example of Griselda in the tradition of Petrarch. Still, if "maidehiede" can belong to a man, then we must wonder whether womanhood can, as well.

Womanly Men

In other tales involving transformation, Gower demonstrates that men can exhibit womanhood as well as maidenhead. He investigates the connection between womanhood and manhood most deeply in the Tale of Achilles and Deidamia, the Evil Example of Sardanapalus, and the Tale of Iphis. Achilles' experience illustrates that both manhood and womanhood can be acquired or imitated. He takes womanhood as a disguise, learning to dress and act in womanly ways; this parallels an early education that cultivated his manliness. Genius uses Sardanapalus as a negative example of love overcoming reason, an unmanly attitude (and one which, as the final section will discuss, Amans embodies). Sardanapalus loves womanhood rather than an individual woman, even going so far as to learn womanly tasks. Iphis is an unusual case: her parents raise the girl as a boy but when she falls in love with a woman, Cupid makes Iphis male. Watt considers some of these same tales as examples of Gower's "transgressive genders," such as feminine masculinity. I see this model as even more widely applicable; these narratives reveal that any person might show evidence of womanhood or manhood because those conditions are identified by appearance, behavior, and speech—all of which can be adopted by anyone.[37] Even desire, as Iphis's story shows, is not completely natural. Throughout, Gower continues to capitalize on the multiplicity of language to suggest the multiplicity of nature.

The best known and most detailed of the tales of womanly men is the Tale of Achilles and Deidamia. This tale is found in Book V, which also includes the rape and transformation tales and the example of Phrynys's male maidenhead. Achilles' famed masculine behavior makes him a particularly interesting and convincing case; if he can practice womanhood, then any man could. The story begins with Thetis disguising her son as a woman in order to circumvent a prophecy that he would die in the Trojan War. Significantly, she seeks to conceal Achilles' physical appearance, wondering "Hou sche him mihte so desguise / That noman scholde his bodi knowe" (V, 2972–73). This comment reveals the intensely performative nature of Gowerian gender: the biological sex of Achilles' body is a fact, but he can change how that body signifies.[38]

An earlier tale from Book IV reveals how Achilles acquired his manly nature and appearance. He built strength and courage by killing dangerous animals every day:

And thus of that Chiro [the centaur] him tawhte

Achilles such an herte cawhte,
That he nomore a Leon dradde,
Whan he his Dart on honde hadde,
Thanne if a Leon were an asse:
And that hath mad him forto passe
Alle othre knihtes of his dede. (IV, 2005–11)

Gower uses puns in order to make his point. The "herte" that Achilles "cawhte" refers both to a hart, the stereotypical prey, and to his heart, the courage that he learned. The consistent use in the text of *hert* for *hart* and *herte* for *heart* strengthens the latter reading.[39] Achilles is a great warrior not by nature, but by training. His manliness is less the result of an innate essence than of an intensive education in the behaviors of manhood.

The disguise that Thetis devises involves a new education in how to be a woman. It begins with Achilles' outward appearance, specifically his clothing: Thetis "Hire Sone, as he a Maiden were, / Let clothen in the same gere / Which longeth unto wommanhiede" (V, 2983–85). He does not reject the clothes as unnatural or inappropriate; Genius says only that Achilles "tok non hiede" (V, 2986). The education continues when his mother teaches Achilles how he must behave:

For Thetis with gret diligence
Him hath so tawht and so afaited,
That, hou so that it were awaited,
With sobre and goodli contenance
He scholde his wommanhiede avance,
That non the sothe knowe myhte,
Bot that in every mannes syhte
He scholde seme a pure Maide. (V, 3002–9)

In the first occurrence of "wommanhiede," it was distinct from Achilles; here he not only exhibits but also owns it: "his wommanhiede." Gower again plays with ambiguity: "avance" suggests that Achilles can improve or further his womanhood but also that it is something he advances or puts over on others. With womanly clothes and actions, Achilles is a maid to "every mannes syhte"; Genius later underscores this point by clarifying, "He was a womman to beholde" (V, 3021). These descriptions may indicate that Achilles is a woman only at a shallow level or that the change from man to woman involved a virtual loss of voice, but they also indicate that gender is closely identified with appearance, particularly clothing. To be a woman, one must look like a woman. If someone looks like a woman, most people find little reason to suspect that the person has any other identity.

A later passage suggests that both manliness and womanliness are "manners" that can be discarded or adopted, even by this most manly of men. Thetis places

Achilles in the company of King Lichomede's daughters:

> [She] lefte there Achilles feigned,
> As he which hath himself restreigned
> In al that evere he mai and can
> Out of the manere of a man,
> And tok his wommannysshe chiere. (V, 3051–55)

Here again, Genius does not distance Achilles from womanliness but explicitly describes it as part of him. His "wommannysshe chiere" is parallel to the "manere of a man" and both seem based on appearance and replicable actions rather than one being more natural than the other. Karma Lochrie points out that "the fact that . . . gender-passing is so completely successful in the story of Achilles points to the instability of the cultural construction of gender."[40] Gender is unstable because it does not belong to either sex exclusively; however, the "cultural construction" of womanhood involves a stable set of behaviors, and so men as well as women can embody it.[41] Achilles' struggle and need for restraint results from conflicting educations—one manly, one womanly—rather than a conflict between his nature and disguise.

Gower again exploits the ambiguity of language when Achilles' manhood asserts itself through sexual desire:

> The longe nyhtes hem [Achilles and Deidamia] betuene
> Nature, which mai noght forbere,
> Hath mad hem bothe forto stere:
> Thei kessen ferst, and overmore
> The hihe weie of loves lore
> Thei gon, and al was don in dede,
> Wherof lost is the maydenhede. (V, 3062–68)

This passage suggests either that Achilles' sexual desire is naturally masculine or that his inculcated manliness overrides his more recent education in womanliness; the final line supports both readings. It literally signifies that Deidamia has lost her virginity but, because "*the* maydenhede" rather than *her* maidenhead is lost and because we have already seen that maidenhead can apply to men, that line may also indicate that Achilles has lost his virginity. The most interesting possibility is that the line hints at the unmasking of his disguise. He has lost his maidenhead in a metaphorical sense because he no longer exhibits womanhood, at least by night.[42] The following line supports that interpretation: "And that was afterward wel knowe" (V, 3069). What becomes well known in the tale is not Deidamia's loss of virginity but Achilles' identity as a man.[43] Gower's careful construction of the line holds all of these possibilities in tension.

The unmasking of Achilles seems to suggest that nature triumphs over nurture. Because of Gower's ambiguous language, however, the scene may indicate only that the stronger nurturance wins out. When Ulysses goes to find Achilles, Ulysses knows where Achilles will be and that he will be dressed as a woman. Ulysses witnesses the women singing and dancing in a Bacchic ritual, but the Greeks cannot tell Achilles apart: "Thei couden wite which was he, / Ne be his vois, ne be his pas" (V, 3150–51). His voice and appearance make him indistinguishable from "real" women. Ulysses lays out "the moste riche aray, / Wherof a womman mai be gay" (V, 3105–6) and a "knihtes harneis" (V, 3157), allowing every lady to choose whichever gift she most likes. Achilles' choice of apparel reveals him:

> Whan he the bryhte helm behield,
> The swerd, the hauberk and the Schield,
> His herte fell therto anon;
> Of all that othre wolde he non,
> The knihtes gere he underfongeth,
> And thilke aray which that belongeth
> Unto the wommen he forsok. (V, 3169–75)

Because his "herte" leads Achilles to the knightly gear, his "true" nature seems to be asserting itself unconsciously but irresistibly. However, the earlier tale of Achilles' education also allows for the possibility that his education in how to be a man is overcoming his more recent education in how to be a woman.[44] Gower's use of *herte* in both tales strengthens this interpretation. The "herte" that leads Achilles to the armor is the "herte" that he "cawte" through the centaur's instruction. Achilles' rejection of the womanly "aray" rejects womanhood in the form of the clothing and behavior it entails; he embraces manhood on the same superficial level.

In the Evil Example of Sardanapalus, his heart chooses womanhood over manhood and hence leads him into trouble. As its title indicates, the tale is an extreme and notable negative illustration. Genius tells it to demonstrate that, while love is natural, one must not let it overcome reason:

> To sen a man fro his astat
> Thurgh his sotie effeminat,
> And leve that a man schal do,
> It is as Hose above the Scho,
> To man which oghte noght ben used. (VII, 4303–7)

This passage suggests that, rather than women driving men to distraction (the role traditionally given women in romance), men are responsible for letting their love overcome their reason. Courtly poets often portrayed men as feminized by desire;

here, by driving themselves to distraction, men are taking on the conventional woman's role and hence are "effeminat." The hose and shoe image indicates that love is over reason rather than under, or subject to, it. Because the passage discusses men taking on a female role, the image also has a secondary meaning: for men, their manly nature should be over their womanly nature. Genius identifies a lack of manhood as the root of the problem; overtaken by love, "manhode stod behinde" (VII, 4311). This issue is crucial. Genius has already established that a man should not "change for the wommanhede / The worthinesse of his manhede" (VII, 4255–56). Men should display and practice manliness and not the womanliness that results from love overruling reason; indeed, this is Amans's central problem.

Sardanapalus is guilty of womanly behavior in this figurative sense but also in more concrete ways. In his case, the hose is definitely over the shoe:

[He fell] into thilke fyri rage
Of love, which the men assoteth,
Wherof himself he so rioteth,
And wax so forforth womannyssh,
That ayein kinde, as if a fissh
Abide wolde upon the lond. (VII, 4318–23)

Sardanapalus does not fall in love with a particular woman but with all women, effecting a sort of self-transformation; the text tells us that "In wommen such a lust he fond" that he "only wroghte after the wille / Of wommen" (VII, 4324 and 4326–27). Genius does not describe a specific love object: although Sardanapalus experiences the "fyri" love typical of romance, he seems to love womanhood itself. Unreasonable love may make men "womannyssh," but in Sardanapalus's case, his love for womanly things and behaviors leads him dangerously close to demonstrating womanhood.

That love brings Sardanapalus to the women's chamber, and

. . . ther he keste and there he pleide,
Thei tawhten him a Las to breide,
And weve a Pours, and to enfile
A Perle: and fell that ilke while,
On Barbarus the Prince of Mede
Sih hou this king in wommanhede
Was falle fro chivalerie. (VII, 4331–37)

Like Achilles, Sardanapalus exhibits womanhood as the result of an education in how to behave like a woman; here, he learns to perform specific feminine tasks. Unlike Achilles, Sardanapalus seeks out womanhood and therefore becomes a negative example whereas Achilles was absolved from blame. But Sardanapalus's position seems to be the most critical difference; while Achilles shows that one person can accommodate both "chivalerie" and "wommanhede," at least in sequence, Genius presents these as mutually exclusive alternatives for a king. Sardanapalus chooses the latter at the expense of the former and, because kingship in this tale requires masculine chivalric behavior, his choice jeopardizes the kingdom and ultimately leads to his usurpation.

Sardanapalus and Achilles choose their identities, although for different reasons; Iphis has an identity imposed upon him/her. Iphis's tale, which appears in the same book as the Education of Achilles, represents a woman who becomes manly and ultimately undergoes a sexual transformation, showing that manly and womanly natures coexist in women as well as men. In this brief narrative (which, until recently, critics generally overlooked), a king threatens to kill his unborn child if it is female, and so his wife raises the daughter to whom she gives birth as a boy named Iphis. Iphis eventually becomes engaged to a duke's daughter and Cupid, in order to prevent their love from being unnatural, turns Iphis into a man. This tale directly follows the Tale of Pygmalion and the Statue; if that tale demonstrates that a statue can be a convincing woman, then the Tale of Iphis shows that a woman can be a convincing man. In both cases, Genius approves the manipulation of nature. Iphis shows no struggle between his/her identities or natures, and in fact does not even seem to be conscious that he/she is anything other than the gender he/she was raised to be. In Ovid, Iphis is disturbed by his/her love for Ianthe, but Gower eliminates any reference to that inner struggle. Throughout the tale, Genius refers to Iphis using masculine pronouns, showing no more consciousness of Iphis's conflicting natures or identities than Iphis himself/herself. In this tale, nurture successfully overcomes nature and finally Cupid refigures the latter.

As with Achilles, the education begins with the proper clothing. Iphis is "clothed and arraied so / Riht as a kinges Sone scholde" (IV, 472–73). Because he/she is betrothed at ten years old, there is no discussion of how Iphis functions socially as male. We do not see him/her undergo any experiences other than the betrothal and subsequent sexual experimentation. The tale quickly proceeds to the problem of desire, which is between two characters of the same sex but different gender identities. At the moment that Iphis desires a woman, however, Genius recalls Iphis's sex by applying the feminine pronoun to him/her for the first and only time. After the betrothal

> . . . ofte abedde
> These children leien, sche and sche,
> Whiche of on age bothe be.
> So that withinne time of yeeres,
> Togedre as thei ben pleiefieres,

Liggende abedde upon a nyht,
Nature, which doth every wiht
Upon hire lawe forto muse,
Constreigneth hem, so that thei use
Thing which to hem was al unknowe. (IV, 478–87)

The two are "constreign[ed]" by Nature here, but the phrase "sche and sche" evokes the more complex issue of Iphis's nature. In the midst of Genius's otherwise consistent use of masculine pronouns, this phrase is doubly disruptive. Here Gower reverses his strategy from the Tale of Florent, where he dispelled tension in the bedroom scene with an quick transformation; rather than allowing the reader to forget (as Iphis apparently has, if indeed he/she ever knew) that this character is a woman acting as a man, Gower reminds us at the moment where it might seem most problematic for medieval readers.[45]

Unlike Achilles, Iphis experiences the sexual desire of his/her adopted gender (within a heteronormative framework) and this more extreme situation apparently necessitates supernatural intervention. Despite the earlier portrayal of this same-sex desire as in accord with Nature, Genius now depicts the love of Iphis and Ianthe as unnatural:

For love hateth nothing more
Than thing which stant ayein the lore
Of that nature in kinde hath sett:
Forthi Cupide hath so besett
His grace upon this aventure,
That he acordant to nature,
Whan that he syh the time best,
That ech of hem hath other kest,
Transformeth Iphe into a man. (IV, 493–501)

The passage suggests that their love is unnatural because Iphis is biologically female, even though we have seen no evidence of womanly nature from her/him. However, as is typical of Gower's language when describing such issues, there is ambiguity: the love may be unnatural because it is queer desire or because Iphis's womanly nature has been so completely subsumed in his/her manhood.[46] In other words, it is not clear whether the sexual encounter itself is unnatural or whether it merely brings to the forefront the problem of Iphis's unusual nature.

The physical transformation that resolves the situation has no visible impact on Iphis. There is no relief, no puzzlement, and no acknowledgment. Still, the ending is happy: "thei ladde a merie lif, / Which was to kinde non offence" (IV, 504–5). Lochrie maintains that "gender itself proves to be merely a disguise in the story—it neither provokes the desire of the two girls for each other nor constrains them."[47] Gender does operate as a disguise, but desire is an important part of that disguise. Desire for women is part of manhood, and desire for men is part of womanhood. This tale suggests that desire is not necessarily more natural than clothing and actions.

Most women learn womanliness and most men learn manliness. As the exaggerated cases in these tales show, however, any person can demonstrate manhood, womanhood, beastliness, or some combination of these aspects; even sexual desire appears acquired rather than innate. It is not surprising that Gower presents both men and women as possessing the potential for beastliness. It is more interesting that he presents womanhood, manhood, and beastliness as overlapping identities defined primarily by what is displayed, not what is essential, and potentially present in women as well as men. This is not to say that the problem is identical for both sexes. Only women can be beastly because of their appearance (as in the Tale of Florent) and only women become beasts through the violation of their bodies (as in the tales of Tereus, Cornix, and Calistona).

"Mi ladi, which a womman is"[48]

Throughout the *Confessio Amantis,* Amans believes his problem to be unrequited love. In other words, his lady does not act within the romance conventions that the text supplies through its own tales. Gower implies, however, that the problem lies not in the fact that the lady does not comply with the courtly love role but in the very attempt to force reality to accord with romance, a misuse of social power.[49] "Chivalry," Winthrop Wetherbee writes, "is in effect the villain of the *Confessio.*"[50] Influenced by his own idea of chivalry, Amans allows his beastly and womanly aspects to be uppermost and needs to develop a manly heart, as Achilles did in his early education. Amans reveals his beastliness in his desire to violate the lady, like Tereus, and his womanliness in his inability to allow reason to overcome love, like Sardanapalus.

In the exempla, Genius tries to correct Amans's views of his lady and himself by portraying women sensitively and highlighting male responsibility. Rather than applying these stories to himself, however, Amans uses them to accuse his lady of improper behavior, comparing her to the Gorgons and Sirens—a misreading that confirms his love is overruling his reason. This tendency increases through Books I–VI; aspects of the narrative that invite misinterpretation further encourage Amans.[51] For instance, in the tales of Iphis and Araxarathen, Rosiphelee, and Jephthah's Daughter, Book IV seems to judge women for refusing to engage in love. Although Genius relates these tales to masculine sins, Amans draws on them to critique his lady. In Book V, the difficulty of adapting financial sins to love leaves room for Amans to argue that the lady owes him for the love he has given her. Genius combats this reading by refiguring the value of the exchange between Amans and the lady. In the end, Amans must recognize himself as primarily a man rather than a lover, minimizing his beastly and womanly aspects by reading female behavior sympathetically and his own less indulgently.

The romantic representations in the tales contrast with the relative reality of the frame narrative; this gap allows the lady to refuse Amans. In her reading of the *Franklin's Tale,* Crane has argued that romance rhetoric does not allow a woman to refuse a man who pursues her.[52] Because the lady in the *Confessio Amantis* is not completely contained by these rules of courtly love, she is able to reject Amans's suit. This interest in the malleability of desire marks another radical aspect of Gower's conception of gender; the lady can step outside courtly love conventions without morphing into an antifeminist stereotype. If she inhabited one of the tales, she might be constrained to reciprocate or suffer punishment; in the frame, she has the power to act on her own feelings and wishes. Nonetheless, all of the tales that involve womanhood reflect on the representation of the lady. These tales help to define womanhood and Amans, Genius, and even the reader measure the lady against this definition. However, the lady and her connection to the tales have not figured prominently in the critical tradition,[53] which has taken for granted that Amans's attitude toward his lady is relatively straightforward and of minor importance to the text.[54] In an influential reading, G. C. Macaulay argues that the lady is a paragon: "Gower, who was quite capable of appreciating the delicacy and refinement which ideal love requires, has here set before us a figure which is both attractive and human, a charming embodiment of womanly grace and refinement."[55] Although Amans does represent the lady as an ideal, he also bitterly tallies the ways in which she falls short of that ideal.

Amans's education on this point develops from the first book through the end of the text; his ambivalent attitude toward the lady is apparent from the outset but becomes increasingly acerbic through Book VI. His earliest critique compares her to the Gorgons and Sirens, figures who mix womanliness with beastliness. In the Tale of Medusa, the Gorgons are clearly unnatural; Genius calls them "Monstres" (I, 404 and 425) and "dredful Monstres" (I, 435). However, he also refers to them as daughters and sisters, portraying them as unfortunate rather than evil. This departs from Ovid's version, where the Gorgons' nature is a punishment. Genius explains that the Gorgons are the result of "the constellacion" at their births (I, 393) and places the responsibility for their effect on men who "Misloke, wher that thei ne scholde" (I, 418) and thereby turn themselves to stone. In this way, the Tale of Medusa draws on the first tale in the text, that of Acteon, which showed that men should not violate women by looking when (or where) they should not. The moral of these stories is not about the women but the men; Genius emphasizes to Amans

"That thou thi sihte noght misuse" (I, 437) because a man must "wel his yhe kepe / And take of fol delit no kepe" (I, 441–42). However, in absolving the Gorgons in this way, Gower also robs them of any true agency.

The treatment of the Sirens is similar. Genius also calls them monsters (I, 485, 514, and 526), but they are further over the border between woman and beast than the Gorgons. The mixture of woman and beast that the Sirens represent is literal: women "Up fro the Navele" and fish "doun benethe," singing with "wommanysshe vois" (I, 489, 490, and 495). They are "Lik unto wommen" (I, 488) and "wommanysshe"—womanlike rather than womanly. With their seductive singing, the Sirens display slightly more agency than the Gorgons. Nonetheless, Genius blames not the monsters but the men who ignore "reson" and "here Ere obeie, / And seilen til it so befalle / That thei into the peril falle" (I, 504 and 510–12).

Amans uses images of both the Gorgons and the Sirens to make sense of his lady's behavior. He admits that he is guilty of the sins of the eye and the ear:

> I have hem cast upon Meduse,
> Therof I may me noght excuse:
> Min herte is growen into Ston,
> So that my lady therupon
> Hath such a priente of love grave,
> That I can noght miselve save.
>
> . . .
>
> [And] whanne I may my lady hiere,
> Mi wit with that hath lost his Stiere:
> I do noght as Uluxes dede,
> Bot falle anon upon the stede,
> Wher as I se my lady stonde;
> And there, I do yow understonde,
> I am topulled in my thoght,
> So that of reson leveth noght,
> Wherof that I me mai defende. (I, 551–56 and 559–67)

Following the models of the Sirens and Gorgons, Amans absolves the lady of responsibility for her effect on him. She is the object of his gaze and her speech is more overheard than directed at him. At the same time, these comparisons to monster-women enable Amans's criticism of the lady's failure to reciprocate his love. His consequent divided feelings, which intensify as the poem progresses, are here already visible. Amans's recourse to courtly rhetoric only emphasizes the lady's resemblance to the womanish monsters. If anything, she is more active and hence more blameworthy, for she engraves "a priente of love" on Amans's heart. Although he admits to the initial acts of looking and hearing, the lady then takes over and produces effects that are beyond his control.

By Book III, Amans's romantic rhetoric begins to break down. Addressing the sin of hate, he qualifies his feelings for the lady after she rejects him: "Thogh I my ladi love algate, / Tho wordes moste I nedes hate; / . . . / The word I hate and hire I love" (III, 875–76 and 883). Amans's tone is not that of a wistful lover but of a sulky rejected suitor. He returns to the lady's lack of mercy later in the same book with a direct accusation. If he were to die, he claims, she would be guilty of homicide; she has "Withoute pite gentilesse, / Withoute mercy wommanhede" (III, 1606–7). This is the first overt criticism of the lady Amans has ventured and his first reference to womanhood. The accusation bears some relation to courtly rhetoric, where unrequited love may result in death (as it will in the Tale of Iphis and Araxarathen). Because Amans takes his idea of womanhood from romance, he sees mercy or pity as its fundamental characteristic—an idea that we have already seen in Chaucer's *Knight's Tale* and that Genius later seems to support.

In Books IV and V, Amans seizes upon several of Genius's remarks in order to mount a stronger critique of the lady. The tales of Rosiphelee and Jephthah's Daughter provide a basis for Amans to disparage the lady for not returning his love. Departing from Genius's practice of relying on male examples, both tales offer female examples of idleness in love.[56] Although they provoke little direct response from Amans, the tales provide rare instances of female sin against which he can measure the lady. Rosiphelee, the daughter of a king, has no desire to marry but receives a supernatural warning not to delay. Learning that she will be sacrificed, Jephthah's daughter laments that she has not married and had children. These tales present another way in which womanhood can be endangered or damaged, if not lost altogether: if she fails to marry and produce children, a maiden never achieves full womanhood. Jephthah's daughter bewails that "sche no children hath forthdrawe / In Mariage after the lawe, / So that the poeple is noght encressed" (IV, 1569–71). She goes to mourn with a group of maidens, each of whom "hire maidenhiede / Compleigneth upon thilke nede, / That sche no children hadde bore" (IV, 1585–87). Maidenhead is an important element of womanhood, but only within a limited time frame. Some of the urgency that Genius represents women as feeling (or needing to feel) may be the result of the prospect, which has been vividly represented, of losing womanhood in ways that are not under a woman's control.

Amans applauds the condemnation of women's behavior. He is pleased "That ye the wommen have noght spared" (IV, 1600). He easily sees how women sin, but does not follow Genius's application of Rosiphelee and Jephthah's daughter to masculine behavior (IV, 1602–7). As Rosiphelee "was chastised," Genius explains, "Riht so the knyht mai ben avised, / Which ydel is and wol noght serve / To love" (IV, 1455–58). It makes sense for Genius to adapt these two tales that focus on female behavior for his primary audience, Amans. But it is curious that Gower selects such stories, rather than ones that might be more obviously relevant, at this moment and nowhere else. If idleness in love is a problem particularly for women (a logical conclusion, since the time for marrying and child-rearing is most limited for

women), then why does Amans need to hear about it? If love idleness is not a specifically female issue, then why does Genius use not one but two female examples
to illustrate it, when female examples are absent elsewhere in the text? It may be
that the extreme nature of the example makes it more effective. In other words,
it seems more unusual for a woman not to want to marry and so the behavior is
that much more reprehensible. But these stories also introduce the possibility that
Amans most wants to deny: that women (and hence his lady) may not be interested
in love.

Genius does not stop his elucidation of the moral of the Tale of Rosiphelee with
the application to men. He continues, "Bot forto loke aboven alle, / These Maidens, hou so that it falle, / Thei scholden take ensample of this" (IV, 1463–65). He
then discusses at length how peculiar it is that a maiden would not want the kind of
love that leads to marriage:

> A gret mervaile it is forthi,
> How that a Maiden wolde lette,
> That sche hir time ne besette
> To haste unto that ilke feste,
> Wherof the love is al honeste. (IV, 1480–84)

Genius suggests both that marriage is an unalloyed good and that all women should
participate in it.[57] Further, the passage imagines wifehood followed by motherhood as the only conceivable outcome for women. Genius goes on to explain that
women should not wait to get married because they must have children for the
world to continue.

In the *Confessio,* the only sinful behavior discussed through female examples
is withdrawing from the system of marriage by refusing or failing to marry and
have children (a passive rather than an active sin).[58] The implication might be that
a woman's sole responsibility is to fulfill these two roles; other issues of behavior in
love can be taken up with men. Unlike Amans's ideas about the lady, which draw
on courtly representations of women, Genius's concerns about female behavior are
firmly grounded in social reality and concerned with social ramifications. There is
no discussion of how women ought to act as love objects or as wives and mothers,
only the assertion that they should take on both of the latter roles. Since courtly
love is not a necessary predicate for wifehood and motherhood, the lady is not
obligated to love Amans but only to marry and have children eventually. As the
conclusion will reveal, Amans's age makes him a weak candidate for love with these
practical purposes.

The Tale of Iphis and Araxarathen licenses Amans to attack his lady's behavior
from a new angle. Araxarathen resists Iphis's advances in an attempt "To save and
kepe hir wommanhiede" (IV, 3534). When Iphis hangs himself, the tale seems to

blame Araxarathen's lack of pity: she asks the gods to punish her and they turn her to stone. In the end, however, Genius interprets the tale as an example of why men should not despair. Iphis, rather than Araxarathen, is the negative example; her self-accusation and punishment make her the victim of his improper behavior rather than the other way around.[59] The twist in the middle of the tale toward blaming Araxarathen (which is more in keeping with Ovid's version) becomes a digression rather than the point. Still, it is easy to understand why Amans may have concluded that women who do not reciprocate love are culpable rather than that men should not despair. The accusations he will later make against his lady seem to draw in part on the depiction of Araxarathen's lack of mercy.

The issue of mercy returns us to the problem of matching romance with reality. In courtly rhetoric, women respond mercifully to their lovers. Those who do not, like Araxarathen, are blamed and punished. Amans wants and expects his lady to play this role; if she does not conform to romance models, he does not know how to behave. He struggles to reconcile or at least adapt literary representations to the social reality of women, and the reader experiences this struggle with him. He wonders how the lady can have womanhood if she is not behaving as she would in a romance, how she can be the reasonable and desirable object of his affections and yet reject him, and whether the lady's behavior or the literary role is unnatural. The romance version of womanhood would seem to dictate that she reward his loyal love and devotion, if only in some small way. What we have learned about Amans's behavior, however, makes her treatment of him understandable, even appropriate. As with Araxarathen, the lady's rejection of Amans may preserve her womanhood rather than undermining it.

Influenced by these tales, Amans becomes much freer and more overt in his critique of the lady and her behavior. Lack of mercy in the mode of Araxarathen becomes the basis for accusations of usury against the lady; idleness in love in the mode of Rosiphelee and Jephthah's daughter becomes the basis for accusations of parsimony. In this same book, Amans first expresses a troubling desire that critics have largely disregarded: to violate his lady.[60] After the Tale of Tereus, Amans said he would rather be drawn apart by wild horses than go against his lady's will (V, 6053–58). Here he anticipates that tale and his vow by describing how, at night, he will "thenke upon the nyhtingale" (IV, 2872). He then details how his heart virtually satisfies his contrary wish:

> Ther is no lock mai schette him oute,
> Him nedeth noght to gon aboute,
> That perce mai the harde wall;
> Thus is he with hire overall,
> That be hire lief, or be hire loth,
> Into hire bedd myn herte goth,

And softly takth hire in his arm
And fieleth hou that sche is warm,
And wissheth that his body were
To fiele that he fieleth there. (IV, 2879–88)

Although such thoughts go against Genius's teaching, they are in keeping with romantic discourse, as in the *Romance of the Rose*. Within that context, they are even relatively mild; the intent, however, remains disquieting. This passage is embedded in a much longer speech by Amans and Genius does not react to this point.

Amans's desire to possess his unwilling lady is a persistent theme; he refers to it again briefly near the opening of Book V. Although scholars generally consider the problem books to be VII and VIII, serious problems begin in the fifth book as Genius attempts to adapt the sins of avarice to love. The sexual economy is difficult to develop consistently and always skirts dangerous implications. As Nicola McDonald declares, "Book 5 simply does not work."[61] Here Amans makes his most serious condemnations of the lady, stimulated by the tales from Book IV and the problematic logic underlying Book V. To a certain extent, Genius does act to correct these misinterpretations, but Amans's behavior in making the accusations is remarkable. They undermine his sense of himself as an ideal lover and expose his attitude toward the lady as far from the easy admiration critics have assumed it to be.[62] He denies avarice, but only because he has never gotten what he wants. What he wants, in this context, seems to be sex, although he claims that kissing the lady would be enough. He says, "If I that swete lusti wif / Mihte ones welden at my wille, / For evere I wolde hire holde stille" (V, 76–78). This language uneasily recalls the violation fantasy of the previous book. Amans may be using "wif" in the general sense of "woman" or he may be imagining the lady as his wife, a woman subject to his will and required by law and custom to submit to his sexual overtures. If she were his wife, he could truly "welden [her] at my wille."

The troublingly inexact adaptation of avarice to love in Book V allows room for Amans to misapply the sins to the lady's behavior. First, he claims that he has given her much and she has granted him nothing in return. His tone becomes increasingly bitter. Amans begins by mourning his general misfortune in love and the speech quickly becomes a specific attack as much as a complaint:

And if sche of hire goode leve
Rewarde wol me noght again,
I wot the laste of my bargain
Schal stonde upon so gret a lost,
That I mai nevermor the cost
Recovere in this world til I die. (V, 4470–75)

At this point Amans's words are still primarily mournful and focused on himself. He then fully excuses himself and turns to the guilt that he perceives on the part of his lady: "So that the more me merveilleth, / What thing it is mi ladi eilleth, / That al myn herte and al my time / Sche hath, and doth no betre bime" (V, 4481–84). I argued earlier that the location of the frame outside the courtly love tradition created a space for the lady to refuse Amans's suit. Nevertheless, Amans continues to locate himself within that tradition and, as a result, he cannot comprehend the lady's behavior. He "merveilleth" at her actions and can only imagine that something "eilleth" her. He plays his role and she does not respond as he expects; the Tale of Iphis and Araxarathen reinforced his idea that the lady should have mercy on him and return his love, to avoid divine punishment if for no other reason. The disappointment of his expectations leads to his harsh accusations.

Amans appeals to Genius to support his judgment: "Touchende usure, as I suppose, / Which as ye telle in love is used, / Mi ladi mai noght ben excused" (V, 4490–92). Amans elaborates on the grounds for his accusation, casting the lady as responsible for his love and therefore bound to repay him, at least in some part:

> That for o lokinge of hire yë
> Min hole herte til I dye
> With al that evere I may and can
> Sche hath me wonne to hire man:
> Wherof, me thenkth, good reson wolde
> That sche somdel rewarde scholde,
> And yive a part, ther sche hath al. (V, 4493–99)

Amans plays the trump card: reason. Her act of "lokinge" takes his "hole herte," he argues, and she should repay him somehow. He cleverly reverses the idea of "mislooking" by aligning the lady with the men who looked where they should not in Book I but his logic here also exploits the difficult nature of Book V. Gower's reasoning throughout the text has removed the agency of love from women, placing the responsibility on the men who should be able to control their reactions when a woman's appearance affects them. Although Amans's application of usury to the lady's behavior violates this central tenet, it does seem reasonable when judged solely based on the problematic description Genius provided earlier in the fifth book.

Usurious lovers, Genius explained, "thogh thei love a lyte, / That scarsly wolde it weie a myte, / Yit wolde thei have a pound again" (V, 4411–13). Placing the lady within this economy of love, Amans sees her as giving the "myte" of a look and receiving the "pound" of his "hole herte," an obviously uneven exchange. He continues to build on this metaphor:

I not hou sche hire conscience
Excuse wole of this usure;
Be large weyhte and gret mesure
Sche hath mi love, and I have noght
Of that which I have diere boght,
And with myn herte I have it paid. (V, 4506–11)

Amans's tone becomes increasingly angry and self-pitying. His most condemna-
tory expression comes near the end: "Hire oghte stonde in ful gret doute, / Til sche
redresce such a sinne, / That sche wole al mi love winne / And yifth me noght to
live by" (V, 4514–17). Amans blames the lady completely, leaving himself as the
injured bystander. Not realizing that Iphis was at least as guilty as Araxarathen,
Amans declares his lady to be guilty of "sinne" and vaguely threatens punishment.
He retreats somewhat at the end of his speech, however, reiterating that he is inno-
cent of usury and stating that "if mi ladi be to wyte, / I preie to god such grace hir
sende / That sche be time it mot amende" (V, 4530–32). This wishful conclusion,
pious on the surface, is self-serving: if the lady "amende[s]" her usury by the system
that Amans has described, she must return his love. She cannot refund it as one
might money, so she must give him something else of value. Genius has elsewhere
presented maidenhead as a woman's treasure, but even Amans does not directly
demand this as payment.

Rather than acknowledging that love cannot be explained entirely in economic
terms, Genius extends his logic to correct Amans's view. Genius says sternly "that
thou tellest in thi tale / And thi ladi therof accusest, / Me thenkth tho wordes
thou misusest" (V, 4536–38). In characterizing Amans's speech as a "tale," Genius
implicitly compares it to his own exempla and finds its application of usury to the
lady flawed; he exposes Amans's narration of his love as a romance. The potential
of words for misuse is a theme in the *Confessio*, and something that the text itself
guards against. Genius's refutation of Amans's accusation turns on a revaluation of
the lady's behavior. He explains: "Sche mai be such, that hire o lok / Is worth thin
herte manyfold; / So hast thou wel thin herte sold, / Whan thou hast that is more
worth" (V, 4542–45). Genius counters Amans's depiction of the situation by revising the relative weight of the values rather than by replacing the system. He plays
with Amans's inflated rhetoric regarding the lady's value by suggesting that her
"lok" may be of more "worth" than his "herte." Genius also casts Amans himself
as the active agent in the exchange. In Amans's description, he was an unwitting
(if not unwilling) buyer; in Genius's description, Amans is the seller. He "sold" his
heart and so accepted whatever price he was paid.

We do not see any reaction from Amans, but he tries another accusation two
sins later. He charges the lady with parsimony because "sche wol noght take, /
And yive wol sche noght also, / Sche is eschu of bothe tuo" (V, 4746–48). She

does this, Amans acknowledges, to prevent him from having "eny cause of hope" (V, 4751). Whereas usury was a misuse of love's economy, parsimony is a refusal to participate in it. Here Amans sees in his lady the idleness in love against which (in his interpretation) the tales of Rosiphelee and Jephthah's Daughter warned. His real complaint, though, is that she participates in the exchange with others while excluding him:

> Bot toward othre, as I mai se,
> Sche takth and yifth in such degre,
> That as be weie of frendlihiede
> Sche can so kepe hir wommanhiede,
> That every man spekth of hir wel.
> Bot sche wole take of me no del. (V, 4753–58)

This passage indicates that the lady's womanhood is at stake in this system of exchange. In friendly exchanges with others, she is able "kepe hire wommanhiede." The implication is that an exchange with Amans would not allow her to do this, either because of his character (an interpretation supported by his repeated wish to violate her) or because he wants an exchange of love rather than of "frendli-hiede." At one level, "wommanhiede" suggests the lady's chastity or virginity, but it also includes her honor or reputation (two things which cannot be separated for women, as the Rape of Lucrece shows). Genius does not respond to this accusation of Amans's, but quickly moves into the next tale.

In the context of the sin of ingratitude, Amans renews his accusation of the lady's usury in a fresh guise: "I wol noght say that sche is kinde, / And forto sai sche is unkinde, / That dar I noght" (V, 5197–99). Although the expression is slippery, the basis of this complaint is similar to his earlier one:

> That sche for whom I soffre peine
> And love hire evere aliche hote,
> That nouther yive ne behote
> In rewardinge of mi servise
> It list hire in no maner wise. (V, 5192–96)

Amans appeals over Genius's authority to "god above" (V, 5199), emphasizing his own innocence and hinting at the lady's guilt (and perhaps wishing for an Arax-arathen-style punishment from the "god above," since Genius is not inclined to corroborate Amans's judgments). Here the complaint is not as explicitly situated in an economic context; Amans's desire to be "rewarded" for his "servise" draws more on the language of chivalry, recalling the romance ideals of womanhood dear to his heart.

Genius responds to Amans's accusation in the same terms, turning the tables by accusing him of unkind behavior:

> Mi Sone, of that unkindeschipe,
> The which toward thi ladischipe
> Thou pleignest, for sche wol thee noght,
> Thou art to blamen of that thoght.
> For it mai be that thi desir,
> Thogh it brenne evere as doth the fyr,
> Per cas to hire honour missit,
> Or elles time com noght yit,
> Which standt upon thi destine. (V, 5207–15)

When Amans's complaint was made within an economic system of love, Genius responded in kind. When Amans recasts it within a chivalric system (still with economic overtones), Genius again responds within the terms Amans himself set. Genius's references to "desir" that burns like fire and to concepts like "honour" and "destine" signal this context. Measured against his own romance ideal, Amans falls short.

Again, we do not witness any response from Amans. Whether Genius's speech convinces him or he sees that Genius will not sympathize with his self-pity, Amans does not attempt any further criticisms of his lady. This change in behavior does not correspond to any noticeable shift in attitude, however; he continues to voice his desire to violate the lady in the sections on the stealth and sacrilege of lovers. We might expect some eventual change in Amans's outlook or behavior, but the text makes this impossible. Genius's approach to educating Amans about the sins of love relies on the effectiveness of the illustrative tales. However, those tales depend on the listener's empathy for the women depicted, since Genius portrays male behavior primarily through its effects on women. Amans does not demonstrate an ability to empathize with the lady; his ignorance of the impact of his own behavior on her confirms that he is unable to interpret Genius's tales correctly.

The last significant references to the lady occur in Book VI; the trajectory ends here in part because the themes of the seventh and eighth books (the education of Alexander and incest, respectively) are less relevant to Amans's critique of the lady and in part because he appears to acknowledge the beastly nature of his desire for her. Having expressed that desire and perhaps beginning to recognize the impossibility of its fulfillment, he ceases to reaffirm it. When Amans admits to love delicacy in the sixth book, his imagery reveals the beastliness of his wish to violate the lady:

> For loke hou that a goshauk tireth,
> Riht so doth he [my eye], whan that he pireth

And toteth on hire wommanhiede;
For he mai nevere fulli fiede
His lust, bot evere aliche sore
Him hungreth, so that he the more
Desireth to be fed algate. (VI, 817–23)

In comparing himself to a "goshauk," Amans shows the beastly side of his nature: that side which, as we have seen throughout the text, wishes to possess the lady against her will. More specifically, this passage suggests a likeness between Amans and Tereus, who was also described as a "goshauk." This disturbing passage figures consummation as consumption. Genius is trying to reveal this aspect of Amans's nature to him and thereby eradicate it. The text is about the education of Amans in love, but more fundamentally about his education in manhood. He must learn where he is crossing the line from manly to beastly.

In the course of his confession, Amans reveals the multiplicity of his own nature: manhood, womanhood, and beastliness. He cannot separate the first from the other two and his ideas are too dependent on romantic conventions to be accurate. In being ruled by love, Amans is like the "evil example" of Sardanapalus, exhibiting womanhood.[63] In his wish to violate the lady, Amans shows his beastly side.[64] His reactions to the lady reveal his nature, but she acts as more than a foil; she also represents womanhood. Gower uses the representation of the lady to discredit the inaccessible ideals of romance and offer a more realistic example of womanly nature. Amans must allow reason to modify romance ideals. He has suggested that he is doing so by trying to figure his love for the lady as a reasonable reaction to her qualities, but true reason involves the recognition that Venus offers him: that he is too old and the lady does not love him.[65] He must use reason to distinguish between romance and reality, and his new idea of manhood must be based on a new understanding of womanhood. By the end of the text, Amans needs to be able to answer Venus's initial question "What are you?" correctly by saying, "A man," playing down his identity as a lover as well as his beastly and womanly aspects.[66]

Womanhood is a significant subtext in the *Confessio* because it plays a vital role in constructing and transmitting the ideas about manhood that Amans must recognize. The tale of King, Wine, Woman and Truth presents the argument that "Thurgh hem [women] men finden out the weie / To knihthode and to worldes fame; / Thei make a man to drede schame, / And honour forto be desired" (VII, 1904–7). Although the point that truth is the strongest force later supersedes the argument of which this expression is a part, its validity is evidenced throughout the tales and the frame. It is through women that the effects of sin are vividly demonstrated and through Amans's representation of the lady that we can measure his progress (or lack thereof) toward reason and reality. The point of the text was to reveal "thilke love which that is / Withinne a mannes herte affermed" (VIII, 3162–63) and, more importantly, to create the "mannes herte" in which that love could exist. The lessons contained in the text cannot be extended from male behavior to female. Creating the proper "woman's heart" would be a different project altogether.

Nevertheless, womanhood remains a critical issue in the *Confessio Amantis* and functions importantly in the ending. After Genius finishes, Amans is still unconvinced, explaining—in a shift into the first person—that "Tho was betwen mi Prest and me / Debat and gret perplexete" (VIII, 2189–90). He writes a plea to Venus and Cupid seeking the resolution he has wanted from the outset: "This wold I for my laste word beseche, / That thou mi love aquite as I deserve" (VIII, 2298–99). Rather than requiring the lady to return his love, however, Venus forces Amans to withdraw it and "tak hom thin herte ayein" (VIII, 2421). Speaking with "scorn" (VIII, 2397), she points out that he is old and likely impotent. This intervention finally shocks Amans and, swooning, he has a vision of the company of love. In narrating this vision, he is able to condemn negative male behavior, identifying Theseus as "untrewe" (VIII, 2511), for example. Amans then describes the complaints of various women, including Dido, Phyllis, Ariadne, Medea, Deidamia, Procne, and Philomena. Although he did not recognize their suffering in Genius's tales, he acknowledges it here. But "above alle" (VIII, 2605), he sees four exemplary women—Penelope, Lucrece, Alceste, and Alcione—and tells their stories. He specifically commends Penelope for keeping "hir wommanhiede" (VIII, 2629) but all four are models of womanhood.[67] In this vision, Amans proves his recovery: he is able to censure male misbehavior, sympathize with female victims, and recognize female virtue. The lady has disappeared from the narrative, but would no doubt appreciate this resolution.

Unlike Chaucer, Gower focuses on the performative nature of gender, the significance of its observable aspects such as clothing, behavior, and speech, and hence the possibility that it can be counterfeited. For Chaucer, womanhood includes certain specific virtues; for Gower, womanhood is a virtuous state, but the more interesting issues are how it can intersect with other identities, how it can be signaled to others, and how the ability to interpret such signals correctly can help to develop manhood. Gower's female characters embody the effects of male characters' actions, whether honorable or not, and the ability to recognize those effects and adjust one's behavior accordingly proves to be a key test for Amans. While both poets participate in the initial phase of the evolution of womanhood, then, Gower goes even further than Chaucer by illustrating not only that womanhood can span various possibilities for femininity but also that any figure can encompass womanliness, manliness, and beastliness to varying degrees (and that this composition may change radically through transformation or over time). We might see this approach as another way of drawing on the mediating possibilities of womanhood: Chaucer conceives womanhood as mediating between different female roles and traditions of feminine representation while Gower imagines it mixing with manhood and beastliness.

Gower's more radical take on identity also indicates a divergent approach to the relationship between gender and language. Whereas Chaucer was interested in the mediating function of language, Gower emphasizes its potential for ambiguity and multiplicity: words, like the observable signifiers of gender, are malleable. But, rather than leading to moral indeterminacy or relativism, the need for interpretation means that careful attention to such signals—whether embodied, spoken, or written—becomes a moral imperative. The connections between the exempla and the frame story underscore that necessity and allow the *Confessio* to provide a template for how literary representations can affect "real" experiences or mindsets; readers might learn the same lessons that Amans does from Genius's stories, or might learn other lessons from the careful interpretation of other texts. In the next chapter, I will explore how John Lydgate and Robert Henryson receive and revise these powerful and distinct fourteenth-century views of womanhood and of the possibilities for gendered language. If Chaucer and Gower are working to pin down some of the central aspects of femininity and how they operate, then the fifteenth-century poets are scrutinizing the limits of the categories that terms like *womanhood* and *femininity* might describe; in the process, Lydgate and, to an even greater degree, Henryson push these words in recognizably modern directions.

CHAPTER 3

LYDGATE'S LADY AND HENRYSON'S WHORE

Womanhood in the Temple of Glas *and the* Testament of Cresseid

B y the fifteenth century, *womanhood* has moved out of the earliest phase of its development but writers continue to use the term and concept in innovative and flexible ways. While John Lydgate, Thomas Hoccleve, Robert Henryson, and James I all employ the word in their texts,[1] the ways in which Lydgate's *Temple of Glas* and Henryson's *Testament of Cresseid* develop the idea are especially significant. In constructing their own versions of womanhood, these poets draw on both Chaucer and Gower—using their combined influence to reexamine romance ideals of femininity—but Lydgate and Henryson also establish new associations that move *womanhood* closer to its more general modern meaning. As the term comes to indicate a broader concept, my analysis becomes correspondingly more conceptual; I rely on gendered vocabulary as an index of not simply when writers are invoking the related ideas but, more precisely, when they do so with a heightened consciousness of fresh possibilities for gender representations, possibilities that take advantage of this new vocabulary and its still unstable definitions. In these fifteenth-century texts, womanhood becomes a larger gendered category rather than a condition featuring specific virtues, appearances, or actions, and its ties to moral concerns begin to loosen. Lydgate shows the idea in the midst of this transition but, in Henryson's later usage, womanhood evolves into a primarily physiological condition that includes all women.

Recently, scholars have brought new insights and approaches to Lydgate; monographs by Robert Meyer-Lee, Nigel Mortimer, and Maura Nolan and essay collections edited by Lisa Cooper and Andrea Denny-Brown and by James Simpson and Larry Scanlon have energized Lydgate studies.[2] This work has also contributed to the ongoing reevaluation of fifteenth-century texts; perhaps because of that context, critics have shown particular interest in Lydgate's innovations and relationship to literary traditions. However, the sheer size of his canon means that there are still many texts, such as the *Temple of Glas,* and issues, such as gender, that invite more detailed consideration.[3]

In the *Temple of Glas,* Lydgate examines the relationship between womanhood and power from a new angle, illustrating how womanhood itself can act as a social script that compels certain actions, some of which may be contrary to an individual woman's desires. The female role in courtly love is virtually predetermined, raising the possibilities that a lady might have to act in ways she does not wish to and become vulnerable to men who know this code of behavior and can exploit it (much as Walter did in the *Clerk's Tale* and Amans attempted to in the *Confessio Amantis*). Lydgate's representation erodes the tie between womanhood and morality, however, because the primary imperative behind the script is aesthetic and cultural rather than ethical—in other words, femininity in the *Temple of Glas* involves characteristics and behaviors determined by literary and social precedent rather than moral considerations. Venus, whose ambiguous morality contrasts with the Virgin Mary's perfection, takes a prominent role in defining and enforcing the script, thereby underscoring that shift.

The possibilities and constraints of the lady's womanhood—rather than, as most critics assume, an existing marriage—operate as the central problem in the poem. Lydgate represents womanhood as having a limited relationship to social power. The lady exercises some power in choosing the knight and attracting him but, having chosen, she has a prescribed role to play in responding to his approaches: she must demonstrate pity, the hallmark of Lydgatian womanhood. Because Venus drives the lady's choice, the reader cannot ascertain how much power to choose the lady might have on her own. Further, by employing the language of constraint in the lady's response to the knight, Lydgate gestures toward the prospect that womanhood might require women to be as receptive to male suitors whom they have not chosen; this presents an implicit critique of courtly womanhood. Nonetheless, while the lady may be required by womanhood to demonstrate pity, the ability to exercise pity is also a marker of authority for rulers (like Theseus in the *Knight's Tale*) and supernatural figures (like Venus in this text); from that perspective, womanhood may be enabling as well as limiting.

Although there has been less recent work on Henryson, his treatment of gender has received substantial attention from critics such as Felicity Riddy and Lesley Johnson; most studies interpret his representation of femininity as negative, if nuanced. Within the overarching narrative of the evolution of *womanhood,* however, Henryson occupies a crucial position: he imagines it in its most literal sense, as the condition of being a woman. He suggests that even non-virtuous behavior can exist within womanhood because women are vulnerable by nature. Henryson's existential conception of the term represents the more generalized usage that becomes common by the late fifteenth century, marking the endpoint of the development of *womanhood* from specific yet variable denotations to the broad definition it still carries today; however, the *Testament* explores that broader version in unusual detail. In short, Henryson offers the first sustained medieval representation of womanhood to approximate our modern understanding of it.

Henryson's expanded concept reduces any association with specific virtues such as submission and pity and links womanhood instead with a weakness common to all women. He extends Lydgate's idea that women might be vulnerable to the compulsions of womanly virtue in relation to men: women become weak and vulnerable to men simply by nature. Womanhood, while not necessarily a powerless state, is a condition subject to male authority. Henryson uses this notion in the *Testament of Cresseid* to critique Chaucer's portrayal of Criseyde in *Troilus and Criseyde*. Although scholars have traditionally interpreted Chaucer's narrator as sympathetic while often reading Henryson's as misogynistic, the *Testament* strives to represent Cresseid more positively and casts her terrible punishment as the unavoidable conclusion to Chaucer's judgmental narration of her story. Cresseid is considerably less powerful than Lydgate's lady—rather than choosing her lovers, Cresseid is dependent on their treatment of her and, rather than being aided by supernatural influences, she has them arrayed against her. This situation, however, is the basis of Henryson's defense: Cresseid is pitiable because she is a weak woman in unfortunate circumstances.

A "quene of womanhed" in Lydgate's *Temple of Glas*[4]

Before the recent reinvigoration of Lydgate studies, the seminal work was Derek Pearsall's 1970 *John Lydgate* and, while its aesthetic valuations have been challenged, many of its readings remain influential.[5] Pearsall notes that Lydgate uses, expands, and even undermines antifeminist images of women in many of his texts but concludes, "What Lydgate actually thought of women is irrelevant: I doubt whether he thought much about them at all."[6] What Lydgate "actually thought of women" may indeed be irrelevant, but he did think and write about them. The *Temple of Glas* demonstrates an interest in women and specifically in the idea of womanhood-what it means and how it operates.

Womanhood plays into the larger theme of the poem: constraint in love. The dreamer introduces the idea of "constreint" in the first line and continues to refer to it throughout, noting the opposition the lovers experience between "eleccioun" and "subieccioun" (569–70, 1075 and 1077) as they are "bound" together (e.g., 335, 568, 810, and 990). Critics have usually identified the overarching constraint on the lovers as the lady's marriage; nearly every scholar who has recently written about the *Temple of Glas* has assumed that the lovers' relationship is adulterous.[7] This assumption has a substantial critical history. C. S. Lewis states unequivocally, "The heroine of the poem is certainly married, and not married to her lover. . . . [H]er marriage is the heroine's chief grievance . . . and seems to be regarded as an insurmountable obstacle to her desires."[8] Similarly, Pearsall argues that

> [The poem treats] a literal human situation, in which the true love of the Knight and his Lady is temporarily frustrated by the fact that she is married. This at any rate is the purport of the lines quoted above [335–41], and of many other dark hints in the course of the poem, though Lydgate does not make the situation very explicit.[9]

Pearsall is more tentative than the critics who follow him; in spite of the caveat that Lydgate is not "very explicit," they have taken up Pearsall's conclusion virtually unexamined.[10] Even Bryan Crockett, who proposes a fundamental rereading of the poem as ironic, follows Pearsall on this point: "The lady explains the situation: she is married but is in love with another man, one with whom she sees no chance of consummating her love."[11]

In identifying the constraint as a husband or marriage, Pearsall is influenced by a variant of the poem that its primary editor, J. Schick, rejected as a corruption. This variant includes a group of stanzas at the conclusion of the lady's complaint to Venus in which the lady refers directly to jealousy and invokes the love triangle of Venus, Vulcan, and Mars. Pearsall interprets this as an earlier version of the poem and describes Lydgate's portrayal of the lady "as complaining, not of the frustration of her true love by a rather vaguely identified and unmalicious husband, but violently and bitterly against 'Jelusye.'"[12] Pearsall suggests that Lydgate removed this "complaint against an old, crabbed, and jealous husband" in the later version of the poem because "he saw how inappropriate in its violent tone and language it was to the Lady."[13] If, in fact, Lydgate wrote and then revised these stanzas, then his changes work to weaken the possibility that the lady is married; neither version, however, directly mentions marriage or a husband. While a plausible reading of the unspecified constraint, marriage is neither the only nor the most persuasive interpretation. The "dark hints" can be read differently, and they point to a previously overlooked aspect of the poem: womanhood.

The critical focus on marriage has obscured a larger meditation on the constraints and possibilities of the ideal of womanhood. The poem traces the dynamics of power between the two lovers as first one and then the other gains the upper hand in the relationship until they are fairly equally bound together in the closing ceremony. While Venus imposes the knight's constraints, however, the lady's are a result of her womanhood. Feminine virtues become a prescription for behavior and Lydgate raises the possibility that the prescribed actions may not accord with what women truly desire or how they wish to act. Such a reading of womanhood might be implied in Griselda, whose face Walter studies for signs that her emotions are at odds with her submissive behavior, or in Florent's loathly lady, whose appearance belies her true self, but Lydgate develops these implications and considers their impact on the female subject.

Lydgate uses *womanhood* frequently; the eleven occurrences of the word in the *Temple of Glas* suggest its importance as a concept.[14] The reader encounters it throughout the text, in the frame as well as the dream, and, within the dream, in the narrative as well as the characters' speeches. It first surfaces in the dreamer's description of the lady, but all three major characters—the knight, the lady, and Venus—use the term. Related words also appear, such as *womanli* (307, 731, and 1020), *femynyne* (526), and *femynynite* (1045). This pervasiveness contrasts with the single occurrence of *manhod* (1178). Every reference to womanhood applies to the lady, as a condition she either possesses or should and will exhibit. The importance of womanhood is tied to the importance of the lady; in this reading, the lady (rather than the knight) is the poem's focus. She is the dreamer's primary concern and she is the first figure to emerge from the crowd of lovers. Her complaint to Venus seems to summon the knight into being and his speeches center on the lady in a way that hers do not on him; even portrayals of the knight echo those of the lady.[15] The lady provides the impetus for the story and dominates it throughout.

Although Lydgate cultivates significant connections between the *Temple of Glas* and Chaucer's *House of Fame* and *Parliament of Fowls,* the central problem of the lady's womanhood is an original addition. Chaucer does not use the word in either of those poems, but it is critical for Lydgate; furthermore, his version departs substantially from Chaucer's usage in those texts where it does appear. Lydgate's concept differs primarily in its physicality and its exemplar, as I have suggested, and, whereas submission was vital to womanhood for Griselda and the Amazon sisters in the *Canterbury Tales,* Lydgate sees submission as a potentially undesirable restraint on the lady's will. In the first appearances of *womanhood,* it is one component of the lady's ideal character (and the basis for her attraction) as seen through the dreamer's and knight's eyes. As Venus and the lady herself apply the term, they uncover the limitations involved for women in embodying that ideal.

Rather than invoking the Virgin Mary as the model of womanhood, Lydgate presents Venus as its defining figure.[16] Her role here is parallel to Mary's elsewhere: the lovers complain to Venus, asking for her "grace" (333 and 710), and she intercedes for them. The imagery Lydgate uses to describe Venus recalls Mary; the lady addresses Venus as "O ladi Venus, modir of Cupide, / That al þis wor[l]d hast in gouernaunce" and "Causer of ioie, Relese of penaunce" (321–22 and 325).[17] Womanhood embodied by Venus must be substantially different from that exemplified by Mary, with a lesser emphasis on chastity, for instance. Nonetheless, one of the traditional qualities of womanhood—pity, sometimes called mercy or compassion—is a vital feature of this alternate version as well. Because Venus is the object of lovers' appeals and the lady is the object of the knight's plea, the issue of feminine pity is crucial. This conception of womanhood draws less on the spiritual authority of Mary than the secular authority of Venus, which centers on her ability to respond to lovers with or without mercy.

Lydgate's representation of Venus is tailored to this poem and its interest in womanhood and love constraints. Although Venus is often seen as a figure of changeability or symbol of courtly love, Theresa Tinkle has emphasized the range of meanings associated with her and available for manipulation by medieval poets: "Venus may be historically a prostitute; naturally, a planet; allegorically, feminine vanity; morally, libido or licit and illicit loves; philosophically, celestial or earthly love. Mythographers typically develop more than one of these models, and Venus may signify all of these meanings within a single text."[18] Depicting Venus in the *Temple of Glas,* Lydgate constructs an importantly female character (rather than a purer symbol or more distantly addressed goddess) and focuses on her role as an arbiter of love, the force responsible for binding lovers, individually and together. The poem first mentions Venus as the one who can redress or reject lovers' complaints; immediately, the question is whether or not she will have "pite" on them (54). By using Venus rather than the Virgin Mary as the primary figure of womanhood, Lydgate changes its principal qualities but also conceives it as something more than virtue. Womanhood requires virtuous behavior but that requirement creates further—and quite significant—effects in the realms of love and life.

Womanhood is important in the *Temple of Glas* at multiple levels: as a theme, as the source of the lady's complaint, and as a constraint that develops and operates throughout the lovers' interactions. Lydgate introduces it through the painted group of lovers the dreamer sees when he first enters the temple of glass. He describes the famous and virtuous women depicted, including two women from the *Canterbury Tales* for whom womanhood was vitally important, Griselda and Emelye (75 and 106), and figures associated with womanhood in the *Confessio Amantis,* including Medea, Penelope, Achilles, Philomena, Procne, and Lucretia. As the first characteristic of the temple's interior, the paintings establish that the text is concerned with women and their natures. Although the paintings represent the women as lovers, they do not portray the women with their partners. The text mentions men—some appear in the painting, while others are alluded to as the betrayers of or sources of pain for the women—but couples are rarely represented together and the majority of the lovers are female. Lydgate describes these women as being "deceyued" (58) and "falsed" (63); one "lost hir life" (72) and another suffered "turment" and "cruel wo" (78). The attention to the unhappiness they suffered indicates a Gower-like interest in how men behave toward women and what effects that behavior might have on the women.

Introduced with the portrayal of the legendary women, the issue of woman-hood comes into focus with the appearance of the lady herself. Three questions preoccupy the characters as well as the poet: what virtues womanhood includes, what actions it involves, and how it affects those who exhibit it. The paintings set up these issues—introducing the ideas that women suffer in love and are vul-nerable to men—but the poem explores them in relation to the lady. When she first speaks, she complains of a restraint that prevents her from having what or whom she desires. Critics have cited the lovers from the crowd in the temple that complain of being bound in marriage to someone they do not love (for example, 209–14) as additional evidence for reading the lady's constraint as marriage. How-ever, this complaint is one among many; Lydgate represents almost every imagin-able love complaint in the poem. The lady can more profitably be read in relation to the notable women in the paintings than the anonymous masses. Lydgate links these famous women to the lady by their shared exemplary status and some details of representation: Dido and Alcestis are called "quene" (56 and 70), as is the lady, and Penelope's coloring is "pale and grene" (69), the same colors worn by the lady (299). In her exemplarity, individual depiction, and formally voiced and detailed plea, the lady is distinguished from the crowd of complaining lovers and connected to the famous women in the paintings. Womanhood—not adultery—is the central matter and the constraint of which the lady speaks.

Soon after the narrator describes the paintings, the lady first mentions her con-dition of constraint:

> For I am bounde to þing þat I nold;
> Freli to chese þere lak I liberte;
> And so I want of þat myn hert[e] would;
> The bodi [is] knyt, al þouȝe my þouȝt be fre,
> So þat I most, of necessite,
> Myn hertis lust out[e]ward contrarie;
> Thogh we be on, þe dede most[e] varie.
>
> . . .
>
> To my desire contrarie is my mede;
> And þus I stond, departid euen on tweyn,
> Of wille and dede Ilaced in a chaine. (335–41 and 353–55)

The lady makes two significant points here: she is somehow bound and cannot freely choose to do what she would like, and this restriction imposes a division between her heart/desires/will and her body/deeds/actions. She does not refer either to marriage or to a husband.[19] Although this speech could allude to an undesired marriage, the context of the poem as a whole argues for a broader constraint, that of womanhood. It may be, as Alain Renoir suggests, that the lady is complaining of being unable to address her lover and being forced to wait for him to address her.[20] Rather than reading the lady's desires as transgressive but reined in by her virtuous womanhood, we can read her desire as appropriate but frustrating; courtly codes of behavior cast women as the respondents in love and not the initiators. Though her desire itself may be proper, there is no way of acting on that desire while maintaining the ideal of womanhood.[21] While not the only situations in which womanhood might restrict the lady, marriage and courtly love are the most salient.

After hearing the lady's complaint, Venus responds by comparing her situation to that of some virtuous and famous women: Griselda, Penelope, and Dorigen. What these figures show, however, is that women are rarely able to act freely in love. In reminding the lady of these stories, Venus is highlighting the restrictions as well as the potential rewards of womanhood—if women behave according to its ideals, they are largely dependent on men to take action. When this formula works, it can be to a woman's benefit and may end happily. But womanhood will not only prevent the lady from acting in certain ways, it will also compel her to take other actions. Her womanhood constrains her at each phase of the love affair: before it begins, when the knight approaches her, and when they are joined at the end of the poem.

In the first half of the poem, however, the two men concerned with the lady's womanhood—the dreamer and the knight—are the only characters to use the term and they see it only as ideal. When the dreamer first sees the lady, he describes her "semelines, / Hir womanhed, hir port, & hir fairnes" (265–66) and then discusses her "condicioun" (284). He treats "womanhed" as one element in the catalog of the lady's perfections (285–97), associating it with seemliness and status, beauty and behavior, and physicality and virtue but preserving it as a discrete quality. He does not develop an exact definition of womanhood, but connects it to the lady's identity as a true womanly ideal, emphasizing her superlative nature.

The knight shares the dreamer's view of the lady as ideal, but his primary concern is whether this ideal woman will react favorably to his suit. Answering the lady's initial complaint, Venus has bound the knight to the lady (440–46) and he is feeling the fire of love. His complaint echoes the language of the lady's but with an opposing dynamic: she was bound but has apparently gained some measure of power with Venus's help, while he was free and is now bound.[22] The lady intimated that she could not approach or obtain her love; the knight knows that he could speak to the lady, but is not sure that she will react favorably (669–75). He worries that the lady's womanhood is without pity:

For in myn hert enprentid is so sore
Hir shap, hir fourme, and al hir semelines,
Hir port, hir chere, hir goodnes more & more,
Hir womanhede, & eke hir gentilnes,

Hir trouth, hir faiþ & hir kynd[e]nes,
With al vertues, Iche set in his degre;
There is no lak, saue onli of pite. (743–49)

The knight's description is an abbreviated echo of the dreamer's but the final line bemoaning the lady's lack of "pite" is distinctive. The dreamer does not claim this virtue for her, though neither does he note its absence; demonstrated through actions, pity may not be discernible at sight. Indeed, the question is not so much whether the lady possesses pity as whether she will act as if she does. From the knight's perspective, pity is the crucial virtue because it would ensure a sympathetic hearing for his suit. The lady's apparent ability to dispense or refuse pity—a reversal of Chaucer's *Knight's Tale* and *Clerk's Tale,* where monarchs hold that authority—empowers her at this point in the exchange.

Beyond the question of whether it includes pity, womanhood does not have a specific meaning for the knight any more than for the dreamer; however, both closely associate it with the lady's ideal nature. A few stanzas after the passage above, the knight revisits the lady's lack of pity in spite of her womanhood:

What wonder þan þouȝ I be wiþ drede
Inli supprised forto axen grace
Of hir þat is a quene of womanhed?
For wele I wot, in so heigh a place
It wil not ben; þerfor I ouerpace,
And take louli what wo þat I endure,
Til she of pite me take vnto hir cure. (764–70)

In this passage, womanhood does seem to be the culmination of virtue and beauty, a term that stands in for excellence in many qualities, rather than being one among many. The lady's exemplary status is that of a "quene of womanhed"; in other words, she is not only a model for her sex but also, more specifically, an ideal of womanhood. The knight draws an analogy between nobility and virtue: as a queen is superior to other women, the lady's womanhood is superior to other women's. The word "quene" may imply that womanhood is a quality of noble women and not of women in general; it certainly conveys that the knight views the lady as unattainable and unapproachable. He portrays her as virtuous and beautiful but without feeling, rather like Venus. The knight pleads for Venus to "restreyne" the lady's heart since he cannot "restreyne" himself from serving her (726 and 735). Although she is the object of many petitions, there is no indication that Venus will have pity on the lovers in her temple, and those figures painted on the wall (such as Dido) remind us that she does not always show mercy even to the most exemplary lovers. The knight views the lady as possessing womanhood in Venus's image, and

with the former as the object of his desires and the latter as the object of his sup-
plication, he has little hope of obtaining relief.

The two male characters, who at this point have had no interactions with the
lady beyond gazing at her, speak the first four appearances of *womanhood*. This
usage suggests that the idea is constructed from the male point of view, based on
qualities that men might value in a woman—most notably, beauty. The context
also indicates that womanhood can be identified visually: it is apparent at a glance
whether a woman can lay claim to it (or whether a man can claim it for her)
or not. The version of womanhood that the knight sees in the lady, however, is
incomplete.

In her response to the knight's complaint, Venus corrects the knight's idea of
womanhood by revealing that pity is an indispensable, if not immediately visible,
component:

> But vndirstondeþ þat al hir cherisshing
> Shal ben grovndid opon honeste,
> That no wiȝt shal, þurugh euil compassing,
> Demen amys of hir in no degre:
> For neiþer merci, rouþe, ne pite
> She shal not haue, ne take of þe non hede
> Ferþer þen longiþ vnto hir womanhede. (869–75)

Now "womanhede" begins to seem a limitation as well as a condition of excellence.
Venus reveals the constraints that exist for the lady, decreeing that she can act no
"ferþer þen longiþ vnto hir womanhede." The lady is still a paragon of virtue and
beauty, but Venus uncovers the corollary of this situation, showing that the lady
must conform to the model that she epitomizes. Because she is an exemplar of
womanhood, her behavior and options are circumscribed and she is exposed to the
machinations of Venus and the approaches of the knight. Although the lady apparently wants to respond favorably to the knight, Venus's language suggests that the
lady would have to respond equally favorably to any male suitor regardless of her
desires; she is bound to have "merci, rouþe," and "pite," and to behave within the
restrictions of "hir womanhede."

Concluding her response, Venus gives the knight explicit instructions and outlines the reception he can expect from the lady:

> Therfore at ones go in humble wise
> Tofore þi ladi & louli knele adoun,
> And in al trouth þi woordis so deuyse,
> That she on þe haue compassioun:
> For she þat is of so heigh renoun

In al vertues as quene & souerain,
Of womanhed shal rwe opon þi pein. (925–31)

Here again womanhood is associated with class in an analogical relationship; the
lady is a "quene" and a "souerain" because of her "vertues," a description that
equates her ideal nature with a kind of nobility. As before, however, this exemplary status has a corollary in specific reactions. The previous passage revealed the
lady's womanhood as a curb on her behavior; here it also compels her to behave
in particular ways. However she feels about the knight's suit, she must "rwe opon
[his] pein." Venus corrects the knight's view of womanhood by informing him that
"compassioun" or pity is an element on which he can depend and of which he can
take advantage (in the case of lady, if not Venus herself).

Accordingly, the knight's address to the lady begins by lauding her model womanhood:

Princes of iouþe, & flour of gentilesse,
Ensaumple of vertue, ground of curtesie,
Of beaute rote, quene & eke maistres
To al women hou þei shul hem gie,
And soþefast myrrour to exemplifie
The ri3t[e] wei of port & womanhed:
What I shal sai of merci takeþ hede. (970–76)

This opening gambit stresses the lady's exemplarity and nobility, two crucial aspects
of her womanhood. The final line of the passage hints that the knight, as Venus said,
is able to direct the lady's response. The knight is no longer being compelled (as he
complained of to himself and to Venus) so much as compelling the lady, based on
Venus's instructions. This scene marks a shift in power from lady to knight.[23] She
began by claiming to be bound and not free but seemed to be gaining power as
Venus assured her that she would get her love and he would be faithful forever. The
knight did seem to be in thrall, complaining about being struck by love and not
receiving pity. Now, however, having chosen to enter the pattern of courtly love
conventions, the lady is bound in a new way: she cannot choose how to respond to
the knight's plea. Even if she desires the knight, the language of compulsion that
surrounds her response to and union with him suggests that she lacks the liberty
"Freli to chese" (336) now as much as in the beginning.

In the process of gaining the knight as a suitor, the lady has lost any power over
her own response or ability to change her mind. Moreover, her response seems to
substantiate Venus's interpretation of womanhood, which implied that the lady
would have to act similarly regardless of the man making the petition. Lydgate
draws out that underlying problem: while the lady has engineered herself into this

exchange with the knight, she might find the same constraints less amenable with another suitor and pity might easily become something she is bound to against her will. Womanhood suggests compulsion even as it enables choice.

When the lady finally uses *womanhood,* in her response to the knight's plea, she directly portrays it as a restraint upon her actions:

> But as for me, I mai of womanhede
> No ferþir graunt to ȝov in myn entent
> Thanne as my ladi Venus wil assent.
>
> For she wele knowiþ I am not at my laarge
> To done riȝt nouȝt but bi hir ordinaunce;
> So am I bound vndir hir dredful charge,
> Hir lust to obey withoute variaunce. (1065–71)

This does not seem like the welcoming response that the lady's original complaint might have led readers to expect. Her phrasing here ("so am I bound") recalls her earlier complaint ("For I am bound"), relating the two restrictions. Her description of womanhood as a constraint upon her behavior is consistent with Venus's speech to the knight and the expectations that he then expressed in his petition.[24] Still, whether the lady is demurring or whether she is truly not empowered to respond to his suit is in doubt. The last two lines of the passage suggest that womanhood and obedience to Venus are unpleasant restraints: Venus's charge is "dredful" and the lady must obey her "lust," a word that connotes unreasonable desires (as it did in describing Walter's motivations in the *Clerk's Tale*). Because the lady has expressed her desire for the knight, it is odd that the language of compulsion would reappear at the moment when her desire is fulfilled, but that language reminds us that she now plays a conventional role.

The lady does continue, "But for my part, so it be plesaunce / Vnto þe goddes, for trouþe in ȝour emprise, / I ȝow accepte fulli to my seruyse" (1072–74). Since this follows her avowal of constraint, this may be part of the lady's prescribed social performance rather than an accurate representation of her desires.[25] In other words, here we see the lady acting as she must according to womanhood: responding with compassion to the knight's address by accepting him to her "seruyse." This may also be an attempt to reassert some power over the situation by emphasizing that the knight, by the conventions of courtly love, must serve her. Lydgate gives us no insight into how the lady feels at this moment, and perhaps this is the point; we see the lady acting as a model of femininity, more icon than character (a perception increased by her namelessness). Her own declaration that Venus "myn hert haþ in subieccioun, / Which holi is ȝoures and neuer shal repent, / In þouȝt nor dede, in myn eleccioun" supports the reading that she suffers under a constraint (1075–77).

Both Venus and the knight bind the lady and her choice of words suggests that she performs as womanhood demands rather than freely expressing her desires. "Subieccioun" overrules "eleccioun."

After the exchange between the knight and the lady concludes, the couple approaches Venus and the goddess gives a speech in which she outlines how womanhood also guarantees the lady's future behavior, like an invisible chastity belt: "Your honour saue, and eke ȝour womanhed, / . . . / Siþ he is bound, vnder hope & drede, / Amyd my cheyne þat maked is of stele" (1117 and 1119–20). In this sense, womanhood serves a practical function by ensuring the lady's faithfulness and hence the legitimacy of any offspring. It is analogous to the steel chain that binds the knight; in exchange for this binding, Venus tells the lady, "Ȝe must of merci shape þat he fele / In ȝov som grace for his long seruise" (1121–22).[26] A mutual state of constraint was created only by Venus's intervention, however; the lady is restricted—however naturally or gently—by the ideal of womanhood, while the knight is not equally bound by manhood but must have a physical chain. In order to make the constraints equivalent, the knight's has to be forged supernaturally whereas the lady is bound by an ideal condition she cannot discard or disavow without serious social consequences.

Venus mentions womanhood once more in her response to the couple (1207), but the last occurrence of the word is in the dreamer's speech after waking. He announces his intent to write

> A litil tretise, and a processe make
> In pris of women, oonli for hir sake,
> Hem to comende, as it is skil & riȝt,
> For here goodnes, with al my ful[le] myȝt—
> Prayeng to hir þat is so bounteuo[u]s,
> So ful of vertue and so gracious,
> Of womanhed & merciful pite
> This simpil tretis forto take in gre,
> Til I haue leiser, vnto hir heiȝ renoun
> Forto expoune my forseid visioun,
> And tel in plein þe significaunce,
> So as it comeþ to my remembraunce,
> So þat her-after my ladi may it loke. (1380–92)

This closing note reaffirms the connection between "womanhed & merciful pite." We have seen, however, that pity can mean not only sympathy for those in trouble or need but, more specifically, receptivity to the advances of men. The knight sought a positive reception for his suit; the dreamer seeks a positive reception for his poem. By saying that he is "Prayeng to hir þat is so bounteuo[u]s, / So ful of vertue and so gracious," the dreamer commingles the lady, Venus, and the Virgin Mary. The language is typical of that used about Mary but the context of the poem confirms the other two female figures as referents. This elevates the status of the lady and Venus while also connecting them firmly to womanhood by likening them to its most famous exemplar.

If womanhood is the restraint the lady laments, this reinterpretation must affect our reading of the rest of the poem. It is no longer about suffering, as Pearsall contended, but the possibilities and limitations of womanhood. And while external factors restrict all of the characters in some way, only the lady is restricted by her own nature and excellence. There are two larger conclusions that we might draw from this. Lydgate might be commenting on courtly love as a convention that binds all lovers to predetermined roles that may not accord with their desires. In light of Lydgate's oft-remarked orthodoxy, he might be contrasting the constraint of pagan religion, in which even the gods are bound by human desires, with the freedom from the material world promised by Christianity. While these broader conclusions are plausible, the text consistently emphasizes womanhood as a determining factor in the lady's behavior, particularly her demonstrations of pity.

To say that Lydgate is interested in how womanhood binds women is not to say that he is a protofeminist, a label scholars sometimes apply to Chaucer. It is not clear that Lydgate is advocating reform or even attempting to raise awareness about the situation he describes; nonetheless, the text provides an illuminating insight into the nature of womanhood. The *Temple of Glas* takes up the concept as a code of behavior that may enforce a division between women's thoughts and actions by compelling them to respond in certain ways to specific situations, particularly situations in which women interact with men. Although the poem treats the relationship between lovers, the dynamics of the situation might be generalized to any relationship between a woman and a male authority figure—lover, husband, father, lord, king, or even God.[27] In any such relationship, womanhood—if a woman posses it or if others recognize her as possessing it—both licenses and circumscribes her actions and reactions.

Critics have begun to explore Lydgate's areas of innovation, and this is a crucial one: he imagines womanhood in an original way in his most original text. While some scholars have viewed the *Temple of Glas* as a rewriting of Chaucer's *House of Fame*, the two poems are quite different and any resemblances exist primarily between Lydgate's poem and the first book of Chaucer's. Still, the *Temple of Glas* is clearly shaped by Chaucer, and not only by the *House of Fame* or the *Parliament of Fowls*; the *Book of the Duchess* and the *Legend of Good Women* are other potential influences, if not direct sources. Although A. C. Spearing called the *Temple of Glas* an "unintelligent imitation of Chaucer," it is, as Pearsall points out, "the longest sustained composition in which Lydgate does not work from a direct source."[28] The *Temple of Glas* is Lydgate's invention in a way that most of his other texts are not and in this independent creation he develops his own idea of womanhood, one influenced by earlier usages and by the historical circumstances in which he was writing, but still an idea that represented a new stage of development in the term *womanhood* and the concept it denoted.

The "flour of womanheid" in Henryson's *Testament of Cresseid*[29]

The leap from Lydgate to Henryson is a large one, spanning decades and crossing geographical boundaries. While Lydgate is at the beginning of the Chaucerian tradition, producing as well as participating in it, Henryson is near the end of the medieval phase of it; he is also part of the developing literary tradition in Scotland.[30] The critical difference between the two for this study involves their uses of *womanhood,* which react to diverse strands of existing usage and reflect each poet's individual notions of gender. The *Temple of Glas* is not the only text of Lydgate's in which the term appears; he uses it dozens of times in the *Troy Book,* for example, and six times specifically in reference to Criseyde.[31] This statistic is not surprising since Chaucer also employed *womanhood* in his version of the story, *Troilus and Criseyde;* his usage there is his most negative.[32] When Henryson draws on that text for the *Testament of Cresseid,* he places the word at the center of two of the most significant moments in the relatively brief poem: when the narrator first professes his sympathy for Cresseid and assigns the blame for her situation and in the three-line epitaph engraved on her tomb. Both the opening and closing notes of this version of Cresseid's story invoke her womanhood.

In these critical moments, Henryson uses the word in the broadest sense that we have yet seen, as a term that describes the general condition of being a woman and so approaches the modern usage. This definition testifies to an important shift that occurred during the fifteenth century—as the conclusion to this book will explore in greater detail—from seeing *womanhood* primarily as a condition with moral associations to seeing it more broadly as an existential condition. In most fifteenth-century uses, the term is still associated with virtue and with positive models like the Virgin Mary, but Henryson pushes existential *womanhood* to an extreme: it no longer appears within catalogues of virtue and beauty, has no apparent exemplar, and can express a sullied state. Lydgate implied that the virtues of womanhood enforced specific behavioral constraints; conversely, Henryson will suggest that even unpleasant appearances or improper actions can be combined with womanhood. For Henryson, however, the word still has some moral overtones; he implies that weakness is the identifying characteristic common to women and hence to possess womanhood means to be vulnerable.

While that construction of female nature as weak opens Henryson to charges of misogyny, his divergent usage of *womanhood* in the *Testament of Cresseid* reveals his particular compassion for Cresseid and his strategy to expose Chaucer's portrayal of Criseyde as unsympathetic.[33] Ironically, this strategy echoes Chaucer's own positioning of his text as rejecting the more antifeminist elements and attitudes in his sources; Henryson reconfigures Chaucer as the primary source. Henryson develops his critique through a series of narrative choices: picking up the narrative at the moment where the *Troilus* narrator's sympathy fails most noticeably; shaping the *Testament* as a continuation dependent on Chaucer's version of events and hence figuring Cresseid's excessive punishment as the inevitable outcome of that earlier text; using the epithet "fair Cresseid" consistently to remind the reader of her positive qualities; and alluding to Anelida from *Anelida and Arcite,* whose womanhood Chaucer depicts more compassionately, in order to suggest that alternative portrayals of Criseyde were possible. The basis of the critique, however, is Henryson's deployment of the narrator. His narrator provides sympathetic interjections that surpass the half-hearted performances in *Troilus* and reveal that womanhood is a potential excuse for questionable actions rather than—as Chaucer's narrator represents it—a kind of beauty that conceals motivations and manipulations.[34]

The relationship between Chaucer's and Henryson's texts has been a primary feature of the critical history of the *Testament.*[35] However, most scholars have seen Chaucer's narrator as genuinely sympathetic while they have evaluated Henryson's variously as charitable or antifeminist.[36] Jennifer Summit summarizes the critical consensus on Chaucer's portrayal of Criseyde: "[I]n representing Criseyde anew, Chaucer not only humanizes her by making her a complex individual who faces difficult choices, he also examines the very conditions of medieval misogyny that shaped her literary history, asking why and how women become the objects of so many narratives and legends that debase them."[37] If there is no similar accord regarding the nature of Henryson's depiction, many scholars do agree in reading the *Testament* as a record of the growth of Cresseid's self-awareness and, by extension, her recognition of her sin and repentance.[38] Such interpretations often reflect a view of Henryson as more rigidly moral than Chaucer; in her study of exemplarity, Elizabeth Allen contrasts Chaucer's "interrogations of exemplary morality" via Criseyde with Henryson's "explicit effort to make Cresseid a clear and stable exemplary figure." Allen sees Cresseid's exemplarity as definitively negative and suggests that the narration of her story "look[s] like an act of antifeminist violence."[39] But Henryson's narrator stresses Cresseid's vulnerability rather than her culpability throughout the poem: whereas Chaucer's Criseyde is a fickle beauty, Henryson's Cresseid is a weak woman. The line of influence cannot be drawn straight from Chaucer to Henryson, however; Lydgate writes a version of the story that also influences the Scottish poet.[40] Before discussing Henryson's treatment of Cresseid in detail, this section will establish its context by briefly considering Chaucer's and Lydgate's portrayals.

The *Troilus* narrator's lack of sympathy for Criseyde centers importantly on his descriptions of her womanhood, although the term appears mostly in connection with Troilus's perceptions. Chaucer uses it slightly differently here than in the later *Canterbury Tales*; from the moment that he introduces *womanhood* in relation to Criseyde, it signifies the single virtue of her beauty. When Troilus first sees her, her appearance stuns him; he observes that "alle hire lymes so wel answerynge / Weren to wommanhod, that creature / Was nevere lasse mannyssh in semynge" (I, 282–84). This beauty inspires his love, but does not seem to be attached to other virtues as it is for Griselda and Hippolyta. Instead, Criseyde's beauty masks what the poem eventually uncovers as her shallow and changeable character. Even at this early stage, Chaucer ties Criseyde's womanhood to deception; her appearance "Shewed wel that men myght in hire gesse / Honour, estat, and wommanly noblesse" (I, 286–87). The narrator has already told us, however, that Criseyde will forsake Troilus (I, 56) and so we know that such a "gesse" based on her beauty and womanhood would prove incorrect.

Chaucer continues to develop the idea that Criseyde's womanly beauty is deceptive because it conceals her thoughts and motivations. Trapped in "Criseydes net" (III, 1733), Troilus speaks to Pandarus "of hire wommanhede, / And of hire beaute" (III, 1740–41). His overriding impression continues to be of her beauty; it has captured him and keeps him from foreseeing her betrayal. Before Criseyde leaves for the Greek camp, Troilus does worry that her father will convince her to marry a Greek: "His olde sleighte is yet so with hym laft / Ye shal nat blende hym for youre wommanhede, / Ne feyne aright; and that is al my drede" (IV, 1461–63). Troilus fears that Criseyde's womanhood will render her vulnerable to the machinations of others by preventing her from "feyn[ing]" convincingly. The irony, of course, is that her womanhood "blende[s]" Troilus himself. It also blinds the reader because Chaucer's narrator does not allow us to see beyond it. When Criseyde betrays Troilus for Diomede, the only explanation seems to be that her womanhood did indeed "feyne" effectively when she made promises to Troilus. After Criseyde has gone, Troilus reads her letters, "Refiguryng hire shap, hire wommanhede, / Withinne his herte" (V, 473–74), but this gives him no insight into her character or behavior.[41]

Nor does the reader get this kind of insight from the narrator, in spite of his ostensible sympathy for Criseyde. Significantly, most of his expressions of sympathy are generalized and appear in the prologues to the books rather than alongside the actual events. There are several points at which the reader might be predisposed to sympathize with Criseyde, such as when Pandarus lies to her and tries to coerce her into loving Troilus by threatening her with their deaths, or when she faces being traded to the Greeks like a prisoner, but the narrator does not provide any material to develop the reader's sympathy.

We do not get the same insight into Criseyde's character that we do into Troilus's or even Pandarus's. She changes her mind about serious issues—loving Troilus, not loving him—without the narrator offering any reason, however speculative. This absence of explanation is most frustrating with her betrayal of Troilus (if it is indeed a betrayal), which is only minimally narrated. We do not hear the speech of Diomede's that sways Criseyde (V, 1030–36) or witness any scene that portrays her change of heart. The narrator observes that "bothe Troilus and Troie town / Shal knotteles thoroughout hire herte slide" (V, 768–69). The moment of betrayal slides away from the reader, as well; the narrator takes refuge in his sources, saying "And after this the storie telleth us" and "I fynde ek in stories elleswhere" and "But trewely, the storie telleth us" (V, 1037, 1044, and 1051). He ascribes his inability to describe her change of heart to gaps in these other texts (V, 1086–99). He then returns to the story and its focus on Troilus, not only leaving the reader with the final picture of Criseyde as shallow and changeable but also going on to emphasize the effects of her inexplicable betrayal on noble Troilus.

When Lydgate takes up this tale in his *Troy Book,* his depiction of Criseyde largely follows Chaucer's but also foreshadows Henryson's. Lydgate's narrator explains

> How Cryseyde for-soke hir owne kny3t,
> And 3af hir herte vn-to Dyomede
> Of tendirnes and of wommanhede,
>
> . . .
>
> I can noon oþer excusacioun,
> But only kyndes transmutacioun,
> Þat is appropred vn-to hir nature.[42]

Like the *Troilus* narrator, this narrator is unable to sympathize with Criseyde or to make the reader do so. He hides behind Criseyde's womanhood, which, he says, led her to betray Troilus for Diomede; it was in her nature and hence no excuse is possible. Lydgate uses Criseyde's womanhood more explicitly than Chaucer to explain her bad behavior (she "3af hir herte vn-to Dyomede . . . of wommanhede") and, in doing so, suggests that her womanhood is the source of her weakness, as Henryson will do in the *Testament* to different effect. Henryson's narrator wants to excuse Cresseid on the basis of her womanhood; Lydgate's can give "noon oþer excusacioun" except for her womanhood, which he connects to her changeable nature. In each case, womanhood is the excuse, but Henryson's use of the concept is more sympathetic. Although both Chaucer and Lydgate influence Henryson's *Testament of Cresseid,* he focuses on revealing Chaucer's representation as unfair. The rest of this section will explore how Henryson develops this critique—of which *womanhood* becomes an important emblem—through his method of narration and in particular passages, including the narrator's interjections and Cresseid's blasphemy, complaint, and epitaph.

In the opening of the *Testament,* Henryson lays the foundation for his critique by expressing a dubious attitude toward Chaucer's version of events, especially those involving Criseyde. The narrator describes Chaucer's text as primarily concerned with Troilus's "cairis" and contrasts that with his own interest in Cresseid (60). When he wonders whether "all that Chauceir wrait was trew," Criseyde's experience is directly in question (64).[43] In spite of these doubts about Chaucer's veracity, the narrator casts himself as a helpless observer of events set in motion by Chaucer's poem (glossing over the fact that Chaucer also inherited the story from other sources), preparing us to see Cresseid's coming punishment as the result of that unsympathetic portrayal rather than of any antifeminist sentiment on Henryson's part. If Chaucer's depiction of Criseyde's betrayal of the noble Troilus is correct, any continuation of the story demands that she suffer horribly to compensate for the suffering she caused him. The *Testament* will comply by chronicling "the fatall destenie / Of fair Cresseid, that endit wretchitlie" (62–63). As the epithet "fair Cresseid"—and its persistence after her apparent act of betrayal—suggests, however, the *Testament* narrator will focus on Cresseid's positive aspects.

The narrator immediately begins his reinterpretation of the central incident from Chaucer. The *Testament* picks up the narrative after Cresseid has gone to Diomede, the betrayal that apparently puts her beyond redemption in *Troilus and Criseyde.* This new account focuses on Diomede's actions rather than Cresseid's and thereby implies that he bears much of the fault: he had "his appetyte / . . . fulfillit" and then "hir excludit fra his companie" (71–72 and 75). The episode is not about Cresseid's betrayal of Troilus, but about Diomede's inconstancy to her. Even after he mistreats her, she remains a "fair ladie" (72); when the narrator mentions Cresseid's promiscuity, he characterizes it as hearsay, something "sum men sayis" (77). Henryson recasts the interpretation of this watershed event and, by taking it as the origin of his narrative, sets the tone for the rest of the *Testament:* we should be thinking about Cresseid as a "fair" but vulnerable woman in a tricky situation.

Criseyde's apparent betrayal was the crucial moment where Chaucer's narrator failed to provide any explanation or express any pity. Henryson's narrator establishes his sympathy by stepping in at this point with a lengthy interjection:

> O fair Creisseid, the flour and A per se
> Of Troy and Grece, how was thow fortunait
> To change in filth all thy feminitie,
> And be with fleschelie lust sa maculait,
> And go amang the Greikis air and lait,
> Sa giglotlike takand thy foull plesance!
> I haue pietie thow suld fall sic mischance!
>
> 3it neuertheles, quhat euer men deme or say
> In scornefull langage of thy brukkilnes,

I sall excuse als far furth as I may
Thy womanheid, thy wisdome and fairnes,
The quhilk fortoun hes put to sic distres
As hir pleisit, and nathing throw the gilt
Of the—throw wickit langage to be spilt! (78–91)[44]

The narrator suggests that Cresseid is worthy of pity because she was the victim of "fortoun"; she was "fortunait / to change in filth all thy feminitie." In other words, she may have acted wrongly but those actions were determined by fate. He also maintains that Cresseid's situation came about "nathing throw the gilt / Of the." This passage clearly professes sympathy and argues that Cresseid is not blameworthy by displacing the guilt onto her unfortunate circumstances.

The narrator's sympathetic attitude is also apparent in his descriptions of Cresseid as "fair" and a "flour." Douglas Gray contends that "the adjective 'fair' becomes almost the inevitable epithet of Cresseid in the *Testament*" but this epithet always invokes a past Cresseid, the beautiful and loved noblewoman from the beginning of Chaucer's poem.[45] "Fair Cresseid" is a role that Cresseid never occupies within Henryson's narrative; he shows us a later version of her. His consistent use of the epithet, however, reminds us that she was once a positive figure even in Chaucer's version; under more favorable conditions, she might have preserved that identity. Cresseid's status as the "flour" of Troy and Greece is also always in the past in the *Testament.* Henryson returns to the flower imagery throughout the poem until it finally reaches full bloom in Cresseid's epitaph, where she is described as the "flour of womanheid," a traditional courtly phrase (608).[46] We already know that "fair" Cresseid will become "lustie Creisseid" (69) and meet a wretched and woeful end (63 and 69). Even while describing that end, however, the rest of the text will continue to remind us of her previous status as a fair flower.

The poem complements such direct rehabilitation of Cresseid with disparaging remarks about her critics. Other men (such as Chaucer) may speak of Cresseid with "scornefull langage," but Henryson's narrator resolves to "excuse . . . thy womanheid." This is exactly what Chaucer did not do: explain what happened underneath Criseyde's womanhood. As the rest of the *Testament* will reveal, the narrator regards Cresseid as weak and weakness as characteristic of womanhood. From this perspective, womanhood lands Cresseid in her lamentable situation; it is the basis of her downfall. This concept is an important variation on Chaucer: womanhood obscured Criseyde's weaknesses in *Troilus* but becomes her weakness in the *Testament.* For Henryson, womanhood is not a state of virtue, as it was in the *Canterbury Tales* and, to a certain degree, the *Temple of Glas,* but the state of being a woman.

Three characteristics of Henryson's usage reveal that he is defining the concept of womanhood in a new way. First, the term does not appear in the context of a list of superior qualities (like those describing Griselda in the *Clerk's Tale* or the lady in the *Temple of Glas*). This demonstrates that womanhood is no longer firmly connected to feminine virtues and allows Henryson to attach it to a woman who has betrayed her lover. The dispensability of virtue to womanhood responds to Gower; Henryson extends the idea that womanhood is based on observable signs by defining it by sex (and the fundamental nature he associates with that sex) rather than a set of behaviors. Second, there is no exemplar of womanhood such as the Virgin Mary or Venus. Cresseid herself is representative rather than superior; in the *Testament,* women are weak by nature and she typifies this. If, as Henryson implies, womanhood is a condition common to every woman, then there is no possibility of a true paragon. There may, however, be sullied as well as unsullied womanhood; this is the third and most interesting aspect of Henryson's usage. Cresseid's weakness and lustful actions do not cause her to forfeit her womanhood; she still possesses femininity, albeit a "maculait" version (81). Felicity Riddy argues that Henryson's line "To change in filth all thy feminitie" (80) implies "that femininity is purity, and so an unclean femininity is a contradiction whose unthinkableness produces the outrage of this line, and eventually requires the dissolution of Cresseid."[47] Certainly there is something pure about femininity here. What is remarkable, however, is that Cresseid's femininity continues to exist even in an impure state. "Unclean" womanhood is exactly what Henryson does think about, and this makes him unusual in the tradition of usage that we have seen up to this point.

The idea that there can be a sullied version of womanhood is a critical sign of the term's changing meaning. In Chaucer, this could not have existed; Griselda and Hippolyta had to demonstrate their virtue in order to prove their womanhood. Although the womanhood Chaucer associates with Criseyde is shallower, it relies on the virtue of her extraordinary beauty. Because Gower conceived of womanhood as dependent on actions and appearances, he considered figures who counterfeited womanhood (like Achilles) or displayed its lack (like the lady of Florent), but these were incomplete or contradictory manifestations rather than damaged or dirty forms. In other words, if a Gowerian character performed some actions or displayed some characteristics of womanhood but not others, his or her womanhood would be unfinished and confusing but not "maculait." Lydgate hinted that conforming to a feminine ideal might require a woman to exhibit certain behaviors, but Henryson's definition eliminates this possibility. Not only does womanhood not require Cresseid to behave according to a standard, it allows her to misbehave to any degree. Regardless of how ugly or sinful Cresseid becomes, she can only pollute—not destroy or forfeit—her womanhood. By broadening the term, Henryson flattens out more specific denotations but extends its applicability.

Cresseid addresses her polluted womanhood in her first speech, suggesting that it has been sullied not by her actions but through a "translation" beyond her control. She blames Venus and Cupid:

> ȝe gaue me anis ane deuine responsaill
> That I suld be the flour of luif in Troy;

Now am I maid ane vnworthie outwaill,
And all in cair translatit is my ioy.
Quha sall me gyde? Quha sall me now conuoy,
Sen I fra Diomeid and nobill Troylus
Am clene excludit, as abiect odious? (127–33)

Like the narrator's interjection, Cresseid's speech focuses on how outside forces have influenced her situation and employs the "flour" image to suggest what might have been. She figures herself as a victim, suggesting that neither her exemplary status nor her dejected condition were of her own making. Instead, she has been "maid" an outcast; others have "translatit" her identity without her knowledge or understanding.[48] This translation has thrust upon her a new version of womanhood. The principal trait of this version, as of the one she formerly possessed, is weakness: she implies that she was subject to the actions of "Diomeid and nobill Troylus" and now that she lacks any "gyde," she is at a loss. In the *Temple of Glas,* the lady's womanhood dictated her behavior; here, the very fact that Cresseid is a woman and hence dependent on male guidance circumscribes her options. Submission, a characteristic of Chaucerian womanhood, has become exaggerated and involuntary in Cresseid's case.

Cresseid believes that her life could—and should—have been different. Whereas the narrator described her as the "flour . . . of Troy and Grece," she claims the gods promised that she would be the "flour of luif." Cupid did plant the "seid," which "grew grene" until it was "with froist . . . slane" (137–39). Before this seed could fully bloom, she became "ane vnworthie outwaill." While some critics have interpreted "flour of luif" to mean that Cresseid would be attractive to many lovers, the "flower of womanhood" tradition suggests instead that the phrase indicates that she would be known as an exemplary lover in the courtly love tradition, like the women painted on the walls of Lydgate's glass temple. While Lydgate's lady attained similar status with Venus's aid, Cresseid received no such aid and has lost that status, if she ever had it. As a result, she blasphemes against the goddess instead of appealing to her.

This blasphemy is the proximate cause of Cresseid's punishment, but to understand why her speech against Venus and Cupid is blasphemous, we have to go back to Chaucer's version of events (which, of course, draws on other versions in turn). The opening of the *Testament* established that text as dependent on *Troilus* and now, as Cresseid's punishment nears, the narrator permits a more specific reference to the betrayal he has set outside the text. In Cupid's refutation of Cresseid, the god hints at that event by adopting her flower image. He had made her "sum tyme flour of lufe," he says, but she is blaming him and Venus for her downfall when the true cause is "hir leuing vnclene and lecherous" (279 and 285). Henryson has not shown any unclean living or lechery by Cresseid, so Cupid's phrase must allude to the infidelity in Chaucer. Criseyde betrayed Troilus and therefore Cresseid must suffer. While not denying that Cresseid is at fault, the narrator directs the reader back to Chaucer for evidence of that fault.[49] Thus Cresseid's leprosy and death—which scholars generally cite as evidence for interpreting the *Testament* as excessively harsh—result from what Henryson constructs as Chaucer's attitude toward her rather than his own.

After Cresseid has become a leper, she gives a lengthy complaint mourning her misfortune and underscoring that weakness is common to her sex. She interrupts a litany of what she has lost to address other women:

> O ladyis fair of Troy and Grece, attend
> My miserie, quhilk nane may comprehend,
> My friuoll fortoun, my infelicitie,
> My greit mischeif, quhilk na man can amend.
> Be war in tyme, approchis neir the end,
> And in ʒour mynd ane mirrour mak of me:
> As I am now, peraduenture that ʒe
> For all ʒour micht may cum to that same end,
> Or ellis war, gif ony war may be. (452–60)

Cresseid identifies the ladies in her audience with her earlier self. By addressing them as "ladyis fair," she echoes her own original epithet ("fair Cresseid") and underscores the commonality between her previous state and their current one.[50] She cautions them, "Nocht is ʒour fairnes bot ane faiding flour" (461). As a lover and a beauty, Cresseid was a flower but has lost that bloom. This change has divided her former and current selves, and she describes a parallel distance between herself and her audience: her "miserie" is one that "nane may comprehend." By encouraging the women to make a "mirrour" of her, Cresseid highlights both her separation from and her similarity to the ladies: she is on the other side of the mirror, but she is their reflection.

Henryson also exposes Cresseid's weakness not as an individual quality but as characteristic of women in general; "for all [her] micht," any woman might "cum to that same end." Later passages will continue to characterize Cresseid as a warning of what might happen to any unfortunate woman. She is trapped between fortune and nature: she is responsible for her fate, but only to the extent that she is a woman and therefore weak. Although critics have seen this speech as representing an incomplete stage in her development—one in which she has not fully realized her own guilt—I would disagree.[51] The message of this passage, and most of the poem, is that Cresseid is a typical woman in an atypical situation, one into which the weakness of her womanhood led her and hence one into which any woman could fall, given the wrong circumstances. Women are vulnerable because, the *Testament* suggests, womanhood is a condition of weakness and dependence. While this view allows women little agency or authority, it does enable a more sympathetic representation of Cresseid by suggesting that the line between a "fair" lady and a "faiding" one is easily crossed and the lady herself may have little control over the shift.

The form of Cresseid's complaint, which is distinct from the rest of the *Testament,* is another subtle critique of Chaucer. Henryson borrows the AABAABBAB stanza form from Anelida's complaint in Chaucer's unfinished *Anelida and Arcite.*[52] Chaucer apparently invented this form but does not employ it in any other text; by using it, Henryson draws from two opposing depictions of women and versions of womanhood in Chaucer's canon. This juxtaposition highlights a way in which Chaucer could have portrayed Criseyde—speaking for herself and revealing a fully formed character in the process—but chose not to. The distance between Anelida and Criseyde is not only a function of their characters but also of the definitions of womanhood Chaucer associates with each. Whereas *Troilus* links Criseyde's womanhood with her beauty and double self, Anelida represents her own womanhood as a courageous and honorable state.

Anelida is almost the antithesis of Criseyde. Anelida has been betrayed by Arcite, who was "double in love" (87) while she was "So pleyn . . . and dide her fulle myght / That she nyl hiden nothing from her knyght" (116–17). He leaves her for another woman and accuses Anelida of doubleness in order to excuse himself. In response, she constructs a complaint that is technically complex and dramatically moving. Even as the victim of a false lover, Anelida is assertive and articulate. Although Criseyde has assertive moments, they are largely near the beginning of the text, as when she declares, "I am myn owene womman" (II, 750)—a sentiment later events belie. The difference is not merely in the nature of her character but also in the complexity and completeness of its development. Within the brief space of her complaint, Anelida becomes a fully fleshed out character. Chaucer represents her compassionately, showing the reader her strength as well as her sorrow. On the other hand, while the *Troilus* narrator leads us to believe that we will come to know Criseyde in depth, she instead slips from the reader's grasp as the poem progresses.

Chaucer shapes correspondingly different versions of womanhood for each character; while it is about beauty for Criseyde, it is a source of power and honor for Anelida. The word appears in the antistrophe of her complaint:

And shal I preye, and weyve womanhede?—
Nay! Rather deth then do so foul a dede!—
And axe merci, gilteles—what nede?
And yf I pleyne what lyf that I lede,
Yow rekketh not; that knowe I, out of drede;
And if that I to yow myne othes bede
For myn excuse, a skorn shal be my mede.

Your chere floureth, but it wol not sede;
Ful longe agoon I oghte have taken hede. (299–307)

In this stanza, Anelida rejects the possibility of abasing herself by praying to her lover or complaining in front of others. She demonstrates a strength of heart and character missing in Chaucer's portrayal of Criseyde. Rather like Arcite's "chere" here, the *Troilus* narrator's sympathy "floureth" but does not "sede" for Criseyde. Anelida admits her error—"I oghte have taken hede"—but maintains her sense of self, a self closely identified with her womanhood. It is what sustains her and what she refuses to yield.[53]

Among Chaucer's longer works in which *womanhood* appears, *Troilus and Criseyde* contains his most negative use of the term; the *Canterbury Tales, Anelida and Arcite,* and the *Legend of Good Women* contain different ideas about womanhood, but all are more firmly associated with various virtues. His treatment of Criseyde and the way in which he imagines her womanhood are choices that Chaucer makes while rejecting more positive or sympathetic options that he develops elsewhere. Through the juxtaposition of Anelida and Criseyde/Cresseid, Henryson reveals not only the *Troilus* narrator's lack of sympathy but also the deployment of Criseyde's womanhood as a shield for her incomprehensible behavior. Womanhood is not a resource for Criseyde as it is for Anelida; it is a cover the narrator draws over her.

Far from concealing Cresseid's thoughts or motivations, Henryson's narrator provides her with a voice in the climactic moment of his narrative. Troilus has encountered the lepers and, although he did not recognize Cresseid, she reminded him of his former love and so he gave her gifts for "memoriall / Of fair Cresseid" (519–20). When she finds out that the man was Troilus, she finally breaks down and blames herself for her misfortunes. Abandoning the "fair" epithet, she repeatedly calls herself "fals Cresseid" (546, 553, and 560). She claims that she was wanton and fickle (549 and 552) and concludes, "Nane but my self as now I will accuse" (574). The narrator does not offer any sympathetic interjection, but Cresseid is sympathetic enough on her own at this point. He has encouraged readers to see her as the victim of fortune, Diomede's inconstancy, the gods' cruel judgment, a fatal disease, and her own womanhood. This context mitigates Cresseid's guilt and her confession becomes a poignant expression of remorse—something markedly absent from Chaucer's portrayal. Having fulfilled this last purpose, Cresseid writes her testament and dies.

After Cresseid's death, Troilus composes her epitaph, which offers an interpretation of her life commensurate with the narrator's:

Sum said he maid ane tomb of merbell gray,
And wrait hir name and superscriptioun,
And laid it on hir graue quhair that scho lay,

In goldin letteris, conteining this ressoun:
'Lo, fair ladyis, Cresseid of Troy the toun,
Sumtyme countit the flour of womanheid,
Vnder this stane, lait lipper, lyis deid.' (603–9)

The narrator couches this penultimate stanza of the poem in terms of possibility rather than actuality, connecting it to the hearsay about Cresseid's promiscuity and to his questioning of the reliability of Chaucer's text. This attitude stresses the nature of Cresseid's life as fiction, something that has been constructed by a series of male writers (including Chaucer, Lydgate, Henryson, and now Troilus) and hence something that can be represented (or misrepresented) in different ways. By avoiding epithets, the epitaph further suggests that Cresseid cannot ultimately be described so simply. In death, she is not fair or lusty or false; she is only Cresseid. Instead of being firmly established, her identity is eternally elusive; Cresseid's body has been laid to rest but her life continues to be open to interpretation.[54]

Critics have read the epitaph primarily as an end to Cresseid's story that offers nothing new.[55] However, the epitaph instructs us to read her story as about not leprosy—the overwhelming image from the *Testament* for many readers—but "womanheid." The "flour" imagery finally reaches completion as Troilus joins it to this idea. As other speakers have, he uses the flower to symbolize Cresseid's former life but he specifies that she was the flower not only of her region or of love but, more widely, of "womanheid" itself. Her womanhood is less firmly in the past than her "lait" leprosy and will continue to be linked to her story in the future; she may still be remembered and "sumtyme countit the flour of womanheid." Furthermore, the rhyme scheme of the epitaph links her death not with her disease but with her womanhood. There is no direct indication that Cresseid dies of leprosy; because she dies immediately after finishing her testament, her death seems to have some larger cause—perhaps the final recognition of her stained womanhood.

The narrator's closing stanza again extends the issue of womanhood beyond Cresseid to all "worthie women":

Now, worthie wemen, in this ballet schort,
Maid for ȝour worschip and instructioun,
Of cheritie, I monische and exhort,
Ming not ȝour lufe with fals deceptioun:
Beir in ȝour mynd this sore conclusioun
Of fair Cresseid, as I haue said befoir.
Sen scho is deid I speik of hir no moir. (610–16)

Henryson's use of the word "wemen" in the first line is unusual. "Wemen," like the linguistically related "womanheid," occurs relatively rarely in the poem; although the narrator demonstrates apparent concern for and interest in women, he usually refers to them as "ladies" (as the epitaph in the previous stanza does). The only other appearance of "wemen" is in Cresseid's confession, when she praises Troilus as being, for her sake, "Of all wemen protectour and defence" (556); this usage highlights the inclusiveness of the term. In the concluding stanza, addressing the poem to "wemen" reminds us of every woman's connection to womanhood as Henryson has imagined it. Rather than excluding some "unworthy" women, the adjective "worthie" reminds us that even the most virtuous woman might be vulnerable in Cresseid's circumstances and so the lesson of her life is valuable even for "worthie wemen."

As his final message, the narrator instructs these "worthie wemen" that they must "Ming not [their] lufe with fals deceptioun." This directive implies that Cresseid's actions led to her "conclusioun." It is not clear, however, how the moral relates to the story of her life as the *Testament* has recounted it. Are we to understand that she deceived Troilus? That she was deceived by Diomede, or Cupid and Venus, or love itself? All of these seem defensible and, given the weakness of womanhood, it is unclear how Cresseid might have changed her fate (or how other women—similarly weak by nature—might avoid it). The moral again reaches back beyond the bounds of this text to its source and makes sense only because Henryson's Cresseid has a past as Chaucer's Criseyde. If Criseyde was as fickle as the *Troilus* narrator tacitly encourages us to believe (in Henryson's interpretation), she deserves an ugly fate. Still, in a last show of sympathy, the *Testament* narrator's final mention is of "fair Cresseid."

With her death, says the narrator, he can "speik of hir no moir." This closing echoes the words spoken by Troilus when he learns of Cresseid's death—"I can no moir" (601)—but the two men use this tactic to opposing ends. Troilus follows his pronouncement with a reminder of Cresseid's sin and refocuses attention on himself ("Scho was vntrew and wo is me thairfoir" [602])—a fairly unsympathetic reaction to her death. The narrator marks the end of his text with the declaration that he cannot say more. Since words spoken by and about Cresseid have caused her considerable suffering, like the "scornefull" and "wickit langage" he referred to in his first interjection (86 and 91), ceasing to speak of her may be a merciful move. The narrator leaves us with the image of fair Cresseid, whose punishment has finally ended.

Henryson's usage of *womanhood* reveals how much it has evolved since the earliest appearances in Chaucer and Gower. In the *Testament of Cresseid,* womanhood becomes not only an abstract noun but also a conceptual category defined solely by gender. In some ways, this is a return to the antifeminist discourse from which Chaucer broke away—in the process of excusing Cresseid's behavior, Henryson suggests that women are weak by nature. Still, this move does not necessarily mark Henryson himself as antifeminist. He exploits that discourse to critique Chaucer's treatment of Criseyde, a move that argues for a certain amount of sympathy toward women. In addition, Henryson relies on a strand of usage that exists in Chaucer; antifeminist overtones that manifest themselves in Henryson were latent in *Troilus and Criseyde.* The line of influence does not end with Henryson, of course; although it is impossible to trace precisely, his usage certainly affected other writers, perhaps most deeply in relation to the story of Cresseid.[56] This completion of the story became widely known and was frequently attributed to Chaucer and printed with his works. As a result, when Shakespeare has Troilus exclaim "Let it not be believ'd for womanhood!" in response to news of Cressida's betrayal, he may be drawing from Henryson as well as Chaucer and from the ideas of womanhood expressed in both texts.[57]

In the *Testament of Cresseid* and the *Temple of Glas,* Henryson and Lydgate shape their own ideas of womanhood and significantly advance the development of its meanings. These fifteenth-century poets consider the larger ramifications of the concept and both poems display surprisingly sympathetic attitudes toward women (if in convoluted ways). This new stage in the evolution of collective gendered terms involves two shifts: from denoting specific characteristics to denoting a category or condition and from identifying primarily positive attributes of womanhood to identifying potential problems with that mode of thinking or negative ways in which such a classification might operate. In other words, both the concepts and the terms move closer to their modern incarnations as Middle English poets move from establishing the meaning of such terms to testing their limits; the word *womanhood,* for instance, becomes increasingly abstract and gathers additional layers of connotation in the process. From a broad perspective, these poems illustrate how linguistic innovation continues, albeit in different forms, after the preliminary phase of invention. Up to this point, I have concentrated on a small group of related courtly poems by male authors; hereafter, I will widen the focus by considering first, how the two contemporary women writers in Middle English responded differently to the same conceptual and linguistic gaps and, finally, how both strategies fared when a variety of fifteenth-century discourses took up and popularized new and newly redefined gendered vocabulary.

CHAPTER 4

VERNACULARITY, FEMININITY, AND AUTHORITY

Reinventing Motherhood in The Shewings of Julian of Norwich *and* The Book of Margery Kempe

argery Kempe's and Julian of Norwich's lives suggest some of the ways in which women's experiences in the late fourteenth and early fifteenth centuries exceeded the extant gender stereotypes and vocabulary—in other words, the very issue that *womanhood* and related coinages began to address. But these women writers are not merely examples of a problem that concerned male poets; Julian and Margery are also grappling, perhaps even more urgently, with gender representations and terminology in their texts. These women are critical to a study of gender and language in the later Middle English textual tradition, then, not because they are female writers within that tradition (they are far from the only women in this category; as recent work by Mary C. Erler, Rebecca Krug, Catherine Sanok, and Claire Waters has underscored, women were involved in the production, circulation, and reception of religious and literary texts in multiple and complex ways)[1] or because they significantly deal with gender in their texts. Julian and Margery are critical to this study because they consciously manipulate gendered vocabulary in order to address the shortcomings inherent in existing ways of imagining and labeling women and explore fraught questions about female power and authority. In other words, they participate in the processes that comprise the central focus of this book: developing terms for and representations of new concepts of femininity.

Margery and Julian not only share the general cultural and aesthetic context of the male writers in the previous chapters but also work with many of the same materials, including portrayals of the Virgin Mary and notions of feminine virtue. However, they employ a different strategy as they edge up to the same linguistic gap: rather than using the new word *womanhood,* they refashion *motherhood.*

It is impossible to know whether Julian and Margery never encountered the former term or knew and avoided it. However, the fact that Julian employs related words—*manhood, childhood, fatherhood,* and *motherhood*—while she does not use *womanhood* or a word often substituted for it, *femininity,* lends some credence to the latter scenario. If that hypothesis is correct, then there are many possible reasons for it. Perhaps these women writers did not wish to adopt a term that was being developed and employed primarily by men; perhaps it was already becoming—or had the potential to become—more limited in its denotation; or perhaps, conversely, they did not want to distract from the other purposes of their texts by putting forward their own construction of a word that was still unsettled enough to require a fresh definition with each usage.

We might also interpret Margery and Julian's avoidance of *womanhood* as characteristic of medieval women writers who, Nicholas Watson posits, tended to reshape established categories of femininity rather than proposing alternatives. They respond to gender stereotypes "neither by accepting nor by rejecting them, but rather by thinking through them in as active and positive a way as possible, identifying with them and even intensifying them to the point where their 'authorized' meaning (as understood, for example, by institutionally powerful men) undergoes basic shifts." Watson continues, "For these women, it was less the stereotypes themselves that were seen as being the problem than a given interpretation of the stereotypes, which constantly threatened to devalue what women were concerned to think of as their 'proper,' positive meaning."[2] Perhaps this explains why Julian and Margery refashion the existing stereotype of motherhood rather than participating in the evolution of a wholly new term.

In this particular case, I would argue that there is a further positive justification for the choice: motherhood offers a clearer (and possibly less threatening) model for women's access to power. That model derives from various secular and spiritual sources, including depictions of the Virgin Mary as an authoritative figure, the traditional role of wives and mothers as mediators, and the acceptance of maternal nurturing as a power dynamic not only within earthly families but also between spiritual "parents" and "children." Rather than trying to define a new model of feminine power, in other words, Julian and Margery can tweak established female roles to provide one that is consonant with their projects. Theresa Coletti's and Nancy Bradley Warren's recent studies demonstrate that female spirituality offered a complicated but rich ground for creating an associated authority and these women writers took advantage of that as part of their literary strategies.[3]

Even as they reform rather than refuse the stereotype, Julian and Margery create new possibilities for representing femininity in the vernacular. In other words, they contribute to the same project that the male poets undertook through coinages like *womanhood* and *femininity,* but from a different perspective. Paradoxically, on this issue Julian and Margery are not writing from outside the literary tradition—a position that Jennifer Summit has shown as conventionally constructed for women writers even in the Middle Ages[4]—but instead from more fully within it than the male poets examined in the previous chapters. The women adapt motherhood, a much older concept than womanhood that is also denoted by a more established term, and make use of the long literary history of Mary as mother. In this instance, the male poets whom we retrospectively perceive as foundational to the canon are, in fact, writing from a less central position. However, this does not make Julian and Margery's approach any less novel or significant, nor does it sever their use of gendered vocabulary from male writers'; because motherhood is a component of womanhood, a reimagining of the former concept necessarily affects the latter, as well. Medieval authors had previously used *motherhood* to define a religious relationship and applied it almost exclusively to Mary herself, but Julian reshapes it as a category that applies to human women, as well, and both she and Margery use that altered concept to authorize themselves and their texts.

In making this move, both women redefine the idea of motherhood from human as well as spiritual perspectives. Caroline Walker Bynum identifies three primary maternal characteristics in spiritual writers: "the female is generative (the foetus is made of her very matter) and sacrificial in her generation (birth pangs); the female is loving and tender (a mother cannot help loving her own child); the female is nurturing (she feeds the child with her own bodily fluid)."[5] Julian moves beyond a vision of motherhood as dependent upon specific events ("birth pangs" and "feed[ing]) to encompass the emotional experiences of mothering for biological and spiritual mothers. Margery acknowledges the negative and painful aspects of human motherhood, but uses that suffering to compare herself to Mary and then claim a parallel intercessory power and intimacy with Christ that eventually exceeds Mary's.

These redefinitions of motherhood participate in the larger project of inventing womanhood. By increasing the value of motherhood, these writers are also revaluing womanhood; the former is an essential subcategory of the latter. By becoming authors and spiritual figures themselves, these women are also expanding potential female roles in society. As we have seen in previous chapters, male authors sometimes portrayed womanhood as a limiting rather than contributing factor in feminine power. Motherhood was an alternative available for reinvention in terms favorable to these women's spiritual and authorial enterprises and accordingly becomes an important source of authority for them.

I. Redefining Motherhood: Maternal Images and Words in the *Shewings*

The Shewings of Julian of Norwich is a novel undertaking: the first known book by an English woman and the first known attempt to describe the experience of a female visionary from a first person perspective in vernacular English. In this project, Julian's contemporaries are not only other English mystics such as Richard Rolle and Walter Hilton but also Chaucer and Gower.[6] Later Middle English poets share with devotional authors—particularly Julian—concerns about language and representing women. Nicholas Watson and Jacqueline Jenkins's excellent recent edition of the *Shewings* identifies language as Julian's primary focus, arguing that her text "is less concerned with ideas than it is intent to give birth to words that will be 'gretly stirrande to alle thaye that desires to be Cristes loverse.'"[7] One mark of the critical divide between poetry and devotional texts, however, is that scholars tend to perceive Middle English as an up-and-coming literary language in poetry while seeing it as a common language—more accessible but also less authoritative than Latin—in religious texts of the same period. In Julian's case, new attention to the poetic qualities of her text is beginning to reverse this perception,[8] but I want to stress here that all literary and devotional writers are making Middle English: they are developing more precise vocabulary to suit religious as well as aesthetic needs. Like the poets from the Chaucerian tradition, Julian is engaged in the process of creating language to meet her rhetorical requirements: she experiments in order to adapt or coin the words that will express her original ideas.[9] Describing a vision from God demands, for her, a new vocabulary. And, also like the poets, Julian brings her interest in language to bear on the issue of how to think and write about women, which was at least as pressing in religious texts as courtly ones. The crucial term *motherhood* illustrates Julian's linguistic project and signifies her corresponding redefinition of women's spiritual and worldly roles.

Critical attention has generally focused on Julian's theology or on the differences between her short and long text in structure and content, but there is now also a renewed attention to her language and aesthetics.[10] Denise Baker declared some time ago that Julian's *Shewings* "deserves to be acknowledged as the prose masterpiece of Ricardian literature," and this chapter contributes to the critical work that has taken up this perspective.[11] While scholars have examined Julian's rhetoric, however, none has yet explored in detail her inventiveness with language—a sign that she participates in the evolution of Middle English as much as the courtly poets did—and how carefully she manipulates it as an aesthetic tool.[12] This section considers her uses of language and feminine imagery to describe the motherhood of Jesus and examines how these narrative strategies address her two great challenges: writing about holy things and writing as a woman. I argue that Julian manipulates language to mark her descriptions and concepts as novel and sacred. Her representation of Christ as mother is the most significant example of that tactic; most critical attention has focused on how that representation affects medieval understandings of Christ, but I suggest that it also affects understandings of motherhood. Julian redefines *motherhood* to include not only spiritual nurturing but also the continuing emotional and physical experience of human mothering. This redesigned motherhood creates space for Julian's identity as a female spiritual authority and author and allows a different interpretation of the famous excision of the "I am woman" passage from the long text.

Julian's redefinition of feminine roles overlaps with another of her primary aims: developing the language to express her holy visions and the theology they inspire. She resorts to the inexpressibility *topos* at several points, saying "I can not ne may not shew it as openly ne as fully as I would" (157), alluding to things that are "so mervelous that I can it not discrive" (287), and explaining that "for the gostely sighte, I have saide somedele, but I may never fulle telle it" (351).[13] Julian never explicitly mentions English as a constraint, suggesting instead that the problem is rendering the holy in human language.[14] Liz Herbert McAvoy identifies the phallogocentric nature of language as an additional barrier for Julian, one that she overcomes by paradoxically emphasizing the body and "collapsing . . . gender binaries."[15] It is not that the English vernacular fails where literary French or religious Latin might succeed; language itself falls short in multiple ways. Nonetheless, God supplies Julian with words as well as images and she must undertake the intellectual task of explicating both.

Julian deploys the inexpressibility *topos* in a literal fashion by combining it with word coinage. In part because she is engaged in a highly individual undertaking, it is impossible to ascertain what, if any, influences she had—textual or oral, literary or religious, direct or indirect.[16] As a result, we cannot determine which words she might have encountered (including *womanhood*) and which she was creating for her own purposes. There are several words that she seems to be using in a special sense, including *onnyng, homlyhede, fulhede, blindhede,* and *rightfullehede. Fulhede,* for example, does appear in other texts but Julian uses it to convey something specific to her theology.[17] The term often appears in the phrase "fulhede of joy," designating the divine sense of completion and rightness that Christians should experience at the knowledge that Christ wishes to be "homely" with them and that, as Julian famously explains, "all shall be well." For the words she creates and for the more generally known terms she modifies, Julian is precise in her usage. Describing the "rightfullehede of Gods working" at the first occurrence of the word, she explains that it "hath two fair properties: it is right and it is fulle. And so be all the workes of our lorde" (165). Because *rightfullehede* also appeared in works contemporaneous with Julian's text, we cannot say with certainty that she originated the term. It is clear, however, that she is very conscious of the words she employs; here she breaks the word into its component parts to emphasize the exact meaning that she wishes it to convey to her audience.

As the examples above suggest, Julian makes particular and copious use of words with the *-hed* or *-hede* suffix throughout the *Shewings*.[18] The preference for *-hed(e)* over *-ness* marks her dialect,[19] but some of the words appear to be her inventions while others were commonly used. Some also appear in the works of other English mystics, including *blindhede* and *fulhede.* The Sloane manuscript, which critics generally accept as the closest to Julian's own language, contains more than fifty *-hed(e)* terms, most of them with multiple occurrences.[20] This feature of Julian's vocabulary takes on a significant pattern as the text uses the *-hed(e)* suffix with selective consistency. The same root may appear with that suffix in some instances and with a *-ness* suffix (or in another form with essentially the same meaning) elsewhere.[21] The *-hed(e)* words frequently appear in clusters and in passages with extraordinary visions or original theological concepts; they often mark a particular struggle to capture those ideas and images in language. I am not arguing that every time Julian uses a *-hed(e)* term she is actively struggling to find a language for her visions, nor that the use of *-hed(e)* words is the sole marker of those struggles in which she does engage. Relatively unusual words with the *-hed(e)* ending, however, do appear most often at these moments in the text and, in my view, she employs them to mark the distinctively divine nature of what she has seen.[22] She defamiliarizes the vernacular to fit it to spiritual discussion and the *-hed(e)* suffix aids in this project by drawing attention to otherwise everyday diction.

Julian tends to use these *-hed(e)* words for two purposes: to distinguish descriptions as spiritual and to explicate the concepts that develop from her visions. In descriptive passages, *-hed(e)* terms mark the qualities being described as godly rather than ordinary. In the seventh chapter of the long text, Julian explains that all of her visions took place within the showing of Christ's bleeding head:

> The gret droppes of blode felle downe fro under the garlonde like pelottes, seming as it had comen oute of the veines. And in the coming oute they were browne rede, for the blode was full thicke. And in the spreding abrode they were bright rede. And whan it came at the browes, ther they vanished. And notwithstonding the bleding continued tille many thinges were sene and understonded, nevertheles the *fairhede* and the *livelyhede* continued in the same bewty and livelines.
>
> The *plentuoushede* is like to the droppes of water that falle of the evesing of an house after a grete shower of raine, that falle so thicke that no man may nomber them with no bodely wit. And for the *roundhede,* they were like to the scale of hering, in the spreding of the forhede. Thes thre thinges cam to my minde in the time: pelettes, for the *roundhede* in the coming oute of the blode; the scale of herring, for the *roundhede* in the spreding; the droppes of the evesing of a house, for the *plentuoushede* unnumerable. This shewing was quick and lively, and hidous and dredfulle, and swete and lovely. (147; my emphasis)

Concluding the chapter, Julian refers to the "homelyhede" of this vision four times and describes the "fulhede of joy" it promises Christians (147–48). While "homely-

hede" and "fulhede" denote concepts specific to her developing theology, the other
-hed(e) terms do not. They are part of Julian's struggle to articulate a spiritual sight
in words that will illustrate for her reader how the showing appeared and how it signified to her. She needs words that are vivid and suggestive, that can be commonly
understood but are not merely ordinary descriptors. The "roundhede" of the drops
of Christ's blood, for instance, seems qualitatively different from the roundness of
a wheel. When the process of description or explication becomes particularly complex or troubling, she often makes use of these -hed(e) words. That is not her only
technique; in this passage, she also relies on figurative language, such as the images
of eves and scales, and the paradoxical adjectives at the close to communicate the
nature of the vision to the reader. Again, she is using the quotidian to express the
divine and render it comprehensible, but even while using these everyday images
and adjectives, Julian is working to signal the unique spiritual nature of her visions.

In the above example, the problem is one of description. In the forty-ninth
chapter, a similar cluster of -hed(e) words appears around a problem of explication.
Julian seeks to explain her ideas about the nature of God, including her view that
God cannot be angry with us: "For thowe we fele in us wrath, debate, and strife,
yet we be all mercifully beclosed in the *mildehed* of God and in his *mekehed,* in his
beningnite, and in his *buxomhede*" (269; my emphasis). Another cluster occurs as
Julian attempts to disentangle the multivalent symbolism of the servant's clothing in the lord and servant parable: "The whit kirtel is his fleshe. The *singlehede* is
that ther was right noght betwen the *godhede* and the *manhede.* The *straighthede* is
poverte. The elde is of Adams wering. The defauting is the swete of Adams traveyle.
The *shorthede* sheweth the servant laborar" (285; my emphasis). As in the descriptive passage, here the -hed(e) ending indicates the qualitatively different nature of
spiritual qualities even when the word she uses to describe them might, in its root,
be used to describe anything. Both of these examples involve the explication of
ideas that are new: *mildehed, mekehed,* and *buxomhede* express the nature of God
as incapable of real anger toward humanity while *singlehede, straighthede,* and *shorthede* illustrate human nature as not inherently evil or irredeemably sinful. Julian
seeks a new vocabulary to accommodate such new theological concepts. The -hed(e)
suffix may allude to established spiritual concepts that employ it, such as godhead
and spiritual fatherhood, or it may invoke the idea that "Crist is oure hede" (219;
see also 285 and 295). In addition, the suffix connotes a more substantial or enduring state of being than alternatives such as -ness and Julian may want to couch her
theology in these more concrete terms. While both -hed(e) and -ness indicate a
condition or quality, -ness was generally attached to adjectives and -hed(e), although
originally used with adjectives, was also extended to nouns.[23] *Fulhede,* as a result,
seems more robust than *fullness:* it suggests a condition of being rather than a quality subject to change.

The central -hed(e) term in the *Shewings* is, of course, *motherhood.* While Julian
does not coin this word, she does craft a new and individual definition of it as a

theological concept original to her visions: a condition of being that is spiritual as well as womanly. Critics have concentrated on her treatment of Christ's motherhood, but Julian uses the idea much more broadly; she bases it on the Virgin Mary and includes the human experiences of child rearing as well as childbearing. She increases the value of motherhood by presenting it from a child's point of view, as the child/Christian seeing mother/Jesus; recuperating its physical aspects; and imagining it as the common ground between the human and the divine—replacing manhood, which had previously been seen as the element that Christ shared with humanity—and ultimately revising ideas about womanhood.

Julian is not the first to apply maternal imagery to Christ. As Bynum discusses in *Jesus as Mother*, twelfth-century Cistercian monks famously used mothering as well as fathering imagery to describe their relationship to those in their care.[24] Julian was also not the first to use the term *motherhood*; however, it was traditionally associated with the Virgin Mary and Julian was among the first writers to apply *motherhood* to human women.[25] Like the new word *womanhood*, then, Julian's new definition of *motherhood* was significantly vernacular and secular. The word *motherhood* represents Julian's linguistic techniques in response to the first major problem she faces—expressing the divine—but her elaboration of the concept of motherhood also helps her to address the second problem, writing as a woman. Julian uses her idea of motherhood to reassess the physical and womanly and then to authorize herself and her text.

Julian explains *motherhood* as follows:

> This fair, lovely worde, "moder," it is so swete and so kinde in itselfe that it may not verely be saide of none, ne to none, but of him and to him that is very mother of life and of alle. To the properte of moderhede longeth kind love, wisdom, and knowing; and it is God. For though it be so that oure bodely forthbringing be but litle, lowe, and simple in regard of oure gostely forthbringing, yet it is he that doth it in the creatures by whom that is done. (313–15)

As she defines "moderhede," Julian reminds us of the connection between human and spiritual mothering: if "bodely" motherhood is "litle, lowe, and simple" (adjectives similar to those that Julian will later apply to Mary herself), it is still the foundation for the figure of "gostely" motherhood. The very word "moder" is an honorific, applicable to Christ and, in the Sloane manuscript, Mary,[26] but commonly used to describe many women (or, in Julian's language here, "creatures"), whose roles as mothers were important aspects of their social and marital value. Julian presents *motherhood* as estimable, a condition that encompasses important virtues and bridges the fleshly and the heavenly.

Julian's emphasis on the word *motherhood* indicates a shift from the Cistercians' focus; she imagines it as an emotional as well as physical experience and connects the concept to women rather than, as the Cistercians do, to men and their relationships. I would argue that *motherhood* is significantly different from *mother:* while the verb *to mother,* particularly as the Cistercians use it, encompasses the physical acts of conceiving, giving birth, and breastfeeding, *motherhood,* particularly as Julian uses it, goes beyond such acts to the continuing experience of mothering. One is a biological condition (albeit applied metaphorically); the other is a largely emotional state of being and interacting. The Cistercians employ mother imagery in order to mediate relationships between men—a possibly problematic venture that this imagery facilitates by minimizing homoerotic overtones. Bynum suggests, "The Cistercian conception of Jesus as mother and abbot as mother reveals not an attitude towards women but a sense (not without ambivalence) of a need and obligation to nurture other men, a need and obligation to achieve intimate dependence on God."[27] For the Cistercians, maternal imagery is about men; Julian's motherhood imagery and theology applies more universally to humankind, but has a firm basis in womanhood.

Grace Jantzen has shown how Julian's idea of motherhood is indebted to the notion of Holy Church as mother, but it also grows out of the popular conception of Mary's motherhood.[28] As a result, the basis of Julian's concept of motherhood is both spiritual and womanly. Before moving into a detailed explication of the theology of Christ's motherhood, Julian is careful to distinguish Mary's motherhood from Christ's: "Thus oure lady is oure moder, in whome we be all beclosed and of her borne in Crist. For she that is moder of oure savioure is mother of all that ben saved in our saviour. And oure savioure is oure very moder, in whome we be endlesly borne and never shall come out of him" (305). Mary's motherhood—both literal and metaphorical—is the antecedent of and precedent for Christ's motherhood. By grounding her concept in the motherhood of the Virgin Mary, Julian firmly claims the human as well as spiritual origins of the term. She draws an analogy between Christ's enclosure in Mary and our enclosure in Christ, making Mary—the paragon of motherhood and womanhood—the basis for the concept of Christ's spiritual motherhood. Julian often associates motherhood with Christ, or the "second person" of the Trinity, but also with God and the Trinity as a whole. These links strengthen the spiritual connotations of motherhood. She defines it as having sensual and substantial natures as well as mercy, pity, grace, and deep wisdom (307–11). Some of these—most notably mercy and pity—are conventional qualities of womanhood, as we have seen in the previous chapters. These associations recall that motherhood is a condition specific to women. In the *Shewings,* Julian founds motherhood on the exemplar of womanhood and female spirituality and, from this basis, extends it to Christ.

Most medieval theologians perceived and depicted Mary's motherhood in terms of its main events: the Immaculate Conception and the birth and nursing of the holy infant. The scriptures describe few "mothering" experiences and indeed it is hard to imagine that God-made-flesh would require much human mothering.

Those moments that are described, such as Jesus's visit with the scholars in the temple, indicate his independence and Mary's limited role as a human mother. Although Julian founds her consideration of motherhood in Mary's maternity, she expands it to include the larger experience of human motherhood, a lifetime of caring and service. As a byproduct of changing ideas about women, Julian alters conceptions of Mary. By pointing to Mary as a foundation, Julian's theological concept of motherhood includes human women; by invoking the larger motherhood of Christ, Julian revalues women's experiences more generally.

Julian maintains this focus on motherhood as an ongoing experience when she describes the motherhood of Christ, in spite of his presumed nature as a male figure. She explains that he "is oure very moder: we have oure being of him, where the ground of moderhed beginneth, with alle the swete keping of love that endlesly foloweth" (309). Motherhood, in other words, involves not only its beginnings—those images commonly utilized by the Cistercians and, more conventionally, by writers describing the maternity of Mary—but all "that endlesly foloweth." Once the experience of motherhood begins, it never ends, whether for a human mother, Mary, or Christ. "Moder" is a persistent and enduring identity. In this concept, Julian relies not only on Mary's holy motherhood but also on the human experience of motherhood, a vital aspect of womanhood; the love that "foloweth" the beginning of motherhood exists for human mothers, as well.

This wider vision of Christ's motherhood requires a child's perspective, drawing on scriptural injunctions to come to him as a child. All of Julian's "evencristen" (235) are children in this metaphor and, speaking to and on behalf of them, she repeatedly identifies Christ as "our" mother: "oure very moder" (309, 311, 313), "oure precious moder Jhesu," and "oure tender mother Jhesu" (313). Correspondingly, we should "use the condition of a childe," "done as the meke childe," and "use the properte of a childe" (317). Jennifer Bryan demonstrates that Julian portrays this mother-child connection as more positive and more enduring than was common in devotional texts.[29] Furthermore, she builds on this metaphorical relationship with specific references to acts of mothering and what they signify in spiritual terms: "The moder may geve her childe sucke her milke. But oure precious moder Jhesu, he may fede us with himselfe, and doth full curtesly and full tenderly with the blessed sacrament that is precious fode of very life" (313). And in a longer passage:

> The kinde, loving moder that woot and knoweth the neede of her childe, she kepeth it full tenderly, as the kinde and condition of moderhed will. And ever as it waxeth in age and in stature, she changeth her werking, but not her love. . . .
>
> Thus he is our moder in kinde by the werking of grace in the lower perty, for love of the hyer. And he wille that we knowe it, for he wille have alle oure love fastened to him. (315)

Here Julian shows the "condition of moderhed" for human women in very positive terms, as analogous to Christ's caring for us. Both passages above depict motherhood as experienced by the child; we are on the receiving end of these motherly emotions and actions rather than exhibiting them ourselves. Julian's approach establishes the value of motherhood in its own right as a virtuous and holy condition that is feminine in its origins. Placing adult Christians in the position of children encourages an appreciation for what is being signified—Christ's humanity and love—but it also implies an appreciation for the signifier—motherhood and mothers.

Julian's broader treatment of motherhood also stresses its human physicality. She describes Christ's motherhood as a condition of his Incarnation: "he arayed him and dight him all redy in oure poure flesh, himselfe to do the service and the office of moderhode in alle thing. The moders service is nerest, rediest, and sekerest: nerest, for it is most of kind; rediest, for it is most of love; and sekerest, for it is most of trewth" (313). Here again, all aspects of a "moders service" are highly valued. Motherhood is not any one event but an "office" and a "service"; indeed, the closest and best "service." While traditional interpretations of Christ's humanity described him as taking on *manhood,* opposing that term to *godhead,* Julian makes *motherhood* the mediating category—a category that opens the connection to women rather than focusing on men's relation to Christ. Such motherhood is necessarily physical; in order to perform this "office," Christ had to take on human flesh.

The Incarnation connects Christ to mankind (and, in the *Shewings,* womankind), but the dynamic also works in the opposite direction by connecting us to him. Julian emphasizes the value of our physical natures throughout the *Shewings;* in the sixth chapter, for example, she uses flesh as a metaphor for the relationship between humans and God: "For as the body is clad in the cloth, and the flesh in the skinne, and the bones in the flesh, and the harte in the bowke, so ar we, soule and body, cladde and enclosedde in the goodnes of God" (145). Flesh is not merely the metaphor here, however; it is also part of what gets recuperated—the "body" as well as the "soule" is "enclosedde" in God. This greater value for human physicality becomes the foundation of Julian's theology of motherhood: "God knit him [Christ] to oure body in the maidens wombe" and Mary's motherhood prefigures Christ's role as "oure very moder" (305), which leads to the reassessment of human motherhood. Christ's connection to humanity through his physical nature is a necessary predicate for his motherhood, as Mary's status as mother of Christ was a necessary predicate for her status as a spiritual mother to humanity. Rather than being diminished by its associations with the flesh, motherhood is elevated by those associations even as Julian expands its definition beyond them.

By founding her conception of motherhood on Mary, extending it to include the more complete experience of mothering, and asserting the worth of its physical as well as spiritual aspects, Julian honors motherhood and, by extension, women and womanhood. In her *Shewings,* motherhood is an experience and an identity that is and should be valued. The fleshly aspect of motherhood does not detract from it but rather strengthens the connection between biological and spiritual motherhood: mothers are Christ-like. Julian does not praise women above men because of this—she consistently mentions *motherhood* with its counterparts in the Trinity, *fatherhood* and *lordhood*—but she creates for women a privileged position that potentially places them on equal standing with men. And by redefining motherhood, she revalues womanhood.

One of the other benefits Julian derives from her redefinition of motherhood is an implicit licensing of her own position as a woman writer. Significantly, the visions do not present this concept of motherhood directly; Julian develops it as she creates imagery to expound their teachings. If many medieval religious texts imagined fatherhood as a property of God and a quality of male religious authority, then motherhood might provide a model for a parallel form of female authority. Critics have suggested that, when she moves from the short text to the long, Julian excises references to herself as a woman in order to move toward a more universal view. However, I interpret this omission as a result of her theology of motherhood, which Julian develops only in the long text. This theology obviates any defense of her identity as a woman because her ideas about motherhood authorize her as a female writer; by creating a position analogous to Mary's as mother, Julian shapes her text as a maternal gesture. She both gives birth to the text and, through it, serves as a spiritual mother and instructor to others.[30]

Julian's identity as a woman licenses her text in one way, then, but it also creates some obstacles. The problem of language is exacerbated for a female mystic, as Sarah Beckwith notes: "the mystic must be a transmitter, and not a representer of that word [of God]. Her voice must not mix with, fuse with, talk with his."[31] Julian wrestles with this problem in a well-known passage from the short text of the *Shewings:*

> Botte God forbede that ye shulde saye or take it so that I am a techere. For I meene nought so, no I mente nevere so. For I am a woman, lewed, febille and freylle. . . . Botte for I am a woman shulde I therfore leve that I shulde nought telle yowe the goodenes of God, sine that I sawe in that same time that it is his wille that it be knawen? And that shalle ye welle see in the same matere that folowes after, if itte be welle and trewlye taken.
>
> Thane shalle ye sone forgette me that am a wreche, and dose so that I lette yowe nought, and behalde Jhesu that is techare of alle. (75)

This is the only moment in the short or long texts (aside from titles or chapter headings, which are likely scribal) that identifies Julian as a woman. Scholars have traditionally read this passage as a defense against charges of Lollardy, addressing Paul's injunction against women teaching or preaching. Julian does directly reject the identity of "techere" and position herself as merely the conduit for the message of "Jhesu that is techare of alle." In other words, she crafts herself as vessel rather than voice. She omits this move in the later long text, however.[32]

Even without the "I am a woman" passage, the long text preserves a clear sense of its author as female. Scribal headings identify the speaker as a "woman" and her status as an anchorite, the only religious way of life more popular with women than men, appears to have been relatively well known to her audience.[33] Julian's visions are necessarily filtered through her prior experiences as a woman in medieval society and possibly as a female religious figure in the Church; some scholars have argued that Julian was not only a laywoman before becoming an anchoress but also possibly a widow and even a mother.[34] As Felicity Riddy observes, "Clearly *A Book of Showings to a Young Widow* would have a very different set of resonances."[35] Although Riddy is pointing up the differences between this title and *A Book of Showings to the Anchoress Julian of Norwich,* it is also crucial to note the similarity between these two possible titles: in both cases (as, I would argue, in the various versions of the text itself), the showings are marked as those of a woman. This feature is integral to Julian's authorial identity within the text.

Whether or not Julian was herself a biological mother, she conceives motherhood broadly enough to authorize her writing, as a condition with implications for women as a whole. By insisting on the relevance of human motherhood to the spiritual motherhood of Mary and Christ and by expanding motherhood to include emotional as well as physical experiences, Julian finds ways for human women to claim spiritual motherhood more fully. This metaphor, which was an important figure for spiritual authority among the Cistercians, now works powerfully for women, as well. In accessing the metaphor of spiritual motherhood herself, Julian concentrates on her likeness to Mary, its feminine exemplar.[36] Julian's revelation is highly personal; in spite of its minimal biographical details, the text is narrated from the first person and concerns her private visions and interpretations. She constructs the speaker within the text, however, as a self who speaks for and to humanity—hence, "I" often becomes "we" and, as Julian states, "by me alone is understonde alle" (235). Because she is writing as a woman, it seems a bold move to present herself as characteristic of mankind. Julian's position is special (as the recipient of the visions) but representative (because her role is to share the visions widely). This makes her position as visionary author analogous to Mary's position as holy mother: Mary is also special (as the mother of Christ) but representative (because she is a human woman). When Julian has a vision of Mary, she is conscious of "the littlehead of herselfe" but she is also "more then all that God made beneth her in worthines and in fullhead" (137–39). Similarly, Julian figures herself as a "simple creature" (125) but her complex and vivid visions mark her as divinely favored. In both cases, the women themselves are modest while others are left to read the evidence of their special spiritual status.

Julian traces her connection to Mary even more directly through the eleventh revelation. In this showing, Julian first describes God's love for Mary as symbolic of his love for "all mankind that shall be saved": it is "as if he saide: 'Wilt thou se in her how thou art loved?'" (203–5). But Julian receives a more personal lesson: "hereof am I not lerned to long to see her bodely presens while I am here, but the vertuse of her blissed soule—her truth, her wisdom, her cherite—wherby I may leern to know myself" (205). This connection between Julian and Mary is not based on Mary's role as a human woman but on her role as a spiritual and virtuous model. By considering Mary in this light, Julian learns "to know myself." If Mary can be both "litille and simple" and "high and noble and glorious" (205) through her status as "blessed mother" (203), then Julian can aspire to a similar if not equal spiritual status because of their acknowledged likenesses and parallel spiritual motherhoods.

Mary gains reverence and authority due to her roles not only as the mother of Christ but also as the spiritual mother to humanity. The qualities of such motherhood include "mercy" and "tender love" (267), the very qualities that Julian thematizes in her text as she assures readers that "all shall be well." In the context she has created, her identity as a woman makes her claim to spiritual motherhood stronger and more natural. In other words, because Julian has connected spiritual motherhood to human women, the authority inherent in that concept is more available to her because she is a woman. The *Shewings,* then, might be read as an act of spiritual motherhood—a tender attempt to teach Christ's message of mercy and love to all Christians. The text seems designed to instruct its readers and inspire them to act accordingly, as a mother might instruct a child. Thus, "This boke is begonne by Goddes gifte and his grace, but it is not yet performed, as to my sight" (379): acting as a spiritual mother, Julian has presented her text but its effect on the children of humanity remains to be seen.

It is possible that Julian, in her guise as spiritual mother, influenced Margery on these same ideas during their meeting, which Margery's *Book* describes.[37] Motherhood is absolutely central to both texts and their claims to authority; still, there are many and various differences between the two texts and their conceptions of motherhood and womanhood. This relationship is similar to that between Chaucer and Gower, where the former was the originator of the term *womanhood* but the latter was in some ways more radical in expanding and using the concept; Julian creates a new set of meanings for *motherhood* but Margery utilizes these meanings in dramatic new ways. While motherhood is at least as important in Margery's text as in Julian's, however, scholars have rarely remarked on Margery's use of it. In the next section, I will argue that she is fully conversant with existing Maryology and other devotional models of motherhood but that she employs these models mainly to revise them in a more assertive, protofeminist direction. It may have been Julian's ideas about motherhood that inspired Margery's use of the concept to appropriate authority for herself as a spiritual speaker and writer. While Julian connects spiritual motherhood to physical motherhood and implicitly licenses herself as a woman and a spiritual mother, however, Margery explicitly exploits her physical motherhood to gain the authority of spiritual motherhood and combines maternal with sexual imagery to express her extreme intimacy with Christ.

II. Reimagining Motherhood: Maternity, Sexuality, and Spiritual Authority in the *Book*

Sex is never far from Margery Kempe's mind. In 1436 she creates *The Book of Margery Kempe,* one of the first English texts by a woman and perhaps the first autobiography in English, in order to chronicle her transformation from middle-class married businesswoman to traveling spiritual figure.[38] However, sex remains a persistent feature of her thoughts and experiences throughout this transition, which paradoxically seeks both to leave behind and to build on her identity as wife and mother. One of the first things Margery tells us in her *Book* is that she wants to stop having sex with her husband. In fact, she says, "the dette of matrimony was so abhominabyl to hir that sche had levar, hir thowt, etyn or drynkyn the wose, the mukke in the chanel."[39] Her revulsion is the result of a spiritual awakening, but Margery soon reveals that she has not lost her sexual passion: sex becomes more significant in her spiritual life than it was in her earthly one. In most medieval devotional texts, sexual imagery expresses spiritual longing, and scholars have generally agreed that Margery's use of sex is inappropriately literal (or insufficiently figurative). However, they have dismissed this as a minor element in the *Book* and a somewhat clumsy maneuver by a woman whose desire for sainthood outstrips her qualifications.[40] This section will argue that Margery's sexual imagery is not a misstep but instead a conscious authorial strategy, the capstone of her effort to fashion a distinctive form of spiritual authority that is modeled on the Virgin Mary but incorporates the material of Margery's worldly life in order to surpass even Mary's level of intimacy with Christ. Margery does not misuse or misunderstand devotional traditions; she modifies them to suit her purposes.

There is a long-standing debate over the degree to which Margery controls the text and whether she can be considered the author of her *Book*. Early critics saw her as simply dictating her memories to scribes (in between bouts of her famous weeping) and credited those men for any narrative structure or devices. Lynn Staley challenged this assumption in *Margery Kempe's Dissenting Fictions,* distinguishing the narrative persona Margery from the authorial presence Kempe and viewing the text as a largely fictional construct.[41] A. C. Spearing also sees the text as a construct but stresses the scribe's role in shaping the representation of Margery, calling the book, "The Diary of a Nobody."[42] As a recent pair of essays by Nicholas Watson and Felicity Riddy illustrates, the fundamental issue of authorial responsibility remains unresolved.[43] Watson carefully separates out which features of the text are attributable to Margery and which to the second scribe, finally concluding that Margery is primarily responsible for the shape of the narrative. Riddy, on the other hand, argues that the text must be read as the result of a collaborative effort and that it is neither possible nor desirable to assign responsibility for its effects.

While Riddy's reading is persuasive, and we must not discount the mediating function of the scribe, I see the connection between the sexual and the devotional as a principal element of Margery's innovative vision for her spiritual life, and a testimony to her control as author. Her literal deployment of sex in a spiritual context is not wholly unprecedented, as scholars have demonstrated; Virginia Burrus has shown in her study of ancient hagiography, *The Sex Lives of Saints,* that an "exuberant eroticism" was an important part of saintly discourse, often imagined in definite and material ways.[44] It is unclear whether Margery would have known those ancient texts, but Burrus demonstrates that embodied eroticism is an inherent quality of hagiography. And, although most medieval devotional texts use sexual imagery metaphorically, some female mystics do engage in more literal descriptions of an erotic connection with Christ.[45] While the image of Christ as lover is conventional in mystical texts, then, Margery's use of maternal imagery in combination with concrete sexual imagery complicates what might otherwise be traditional metaphors.[46] She uses her mixed imagery to a specific end: to enhance her authority as a religious figure in the image of the Virgin Mary.

Margery's spiritual life begins too late for her to be a holy virgin and too early for her to be a chaste widow, but she builds on her earthly roles as a wife and mother to create unusually firm connections to her model, the mother of Christ.[47] Although a few female saints had also been wives and mothers (most notably St. Bridget, an early fourteenth-century saint who was a favorite of Margery's), they defined their devotional lives as a departure from those roles rather than—as Margery does—an extension of them.[48] While scholars have frequently connected Margery's text to *imitatio Christi,* I want to suggest that the more significant devotional model in the *Book* is the lesser-known *imitatio Mariae.* This *imitatio* might focus on various iconic traditions—the immaculate virgin, the nursing madonna, the suffering mother, or the sympathetic intercessor—but Margery chooses to concentrate on the primary ground of her identification with Mary: motherhood. Margery's transition from physical to spiritual motherhood mirrors Mary's transition from biological mother of Christ to spiritual mother of humanity. Margery carefully shapes her *imitatio* to take advantage of Mary's authority to instruct and intercede for others while negotiating the divergent challenges posed by her own lack of both virginity and humility.

So where does sex fit into *imitatio Mariae?* For Margery Kempe, everywhere. She continually insists on the connection between motherhood—whether physical or spiritual—and sexuality. While the experience of childbirth recalled Eve's original sin and resulted in the sexual impurity of the mother, and Mary's motherhood remained pure because of her virginity, *sponsa Christi* tradition did attach sexual imagery to her.[49] Like Mary Magdalene and other female saints, the Virgin Mary was sometimes imagined as the bride of Christ; Song-of-Songs-type language might be used to portray this relationship, but it was preserved as only a figure for spiritual desire and intimacy. Other religious women made use of similarly figurative language, but sometimes fell into a more literal eroticism as well. Margery, however, concretizes the image of the divine bride of Christ, and then appends that earthly eroticism to her *imitatio,* creating an intimate role for herself that combines the sexual and the maternal and draws on her secular roles. She also has parallel familial-yet-erotic relationships with the rest of the holy family. This conflation increases both the authority of her religious teachings and their potential for heterodoxy. In her intimacy and authority, Margery eventually seeks to exceed the Virgin Mary.

This section traces how Margery deploys that strategy, linking the sexual, maternal, and devotional to create authority for herself and her text. It begins by discussing the significance of motherhood in the *Book* and how Margery ties it to sex and uses her physical motherhood to justify a form of spiritual motherhood that permits her far-reaching authority. I then examine how Margery aligns herself with the Virgin Mary, focusing on their parallel transitions from physical to spiritual motherhood and emphasizing two related aspects of *imitatio Mariae:* Mary as *Mater Dolorosa* and intercessor. Finally, I explore how Margery combines maternal imagery with other kinds of familial and—more interestingly—sexual imagery to create a multiple and intense intimacy with Christ, again mingling the physical and the spiritual to achieve religious authority.

From Physical to Spiritual Motherhood

Carolyn Dinshaw observes that Margery Kempe is "a creature that itself is not clearly categorizable in her community's bourgeois heteronormative terms . . . a creature whose body does not fit her desires."[50] Yet as Dinshaw's shift in pronouns from "itself" to "her" might signal, Margery manipulates those terms—and that body—to fulfill her singular desires. In the Middle Ages, mothers were expected to be loving and nurturing figures who provided early religious and moral instruction for their children within the home.[51] Margery reshapes this concept of motherhood by drawing on a wide variety of maternal experiences and images while exploiting the relationship between physical and spiritual motherhood. Scholars have overlooked the abundance and importance of maternal imagery in this text, focusing instead on issues of authorial versus scribal control, and on the questionable orthodoxy of Margery's devotional practices.[52] Clarissa Atkinson, whose 1983 *Mystic and Pilgrim* marked the beginning of a resurgence of interest in Margery, downplays the significance of motherhood in the *Book:* "Kempe used few maternal images and metaphors, and she rarely mentioned her children or her experience of motherhood."[53] Anthony Goodman's recent observation is a typical extension of this view: "*The Book* does not dwell on her role as mother, or on her children, because these subjects were largely irrelevant to its purposes."[54] On the contrary, motherhood and maternal imagery are prevalent and pervasive in Margery's text.

The *Book* begins by drawing attention to her status as a physical mother. Margery's claim to this form of motherhood is indisputable: she has fourteen children. Although we hear little about those children, she frames the *Book* with depictions of herself as a mother; the story of her life begins with the birth of her first child—the impetus for all that follows—and ends with her interactions with her adult son. Opening not with Margery's birth but with a sentence briefly describing her marriage and first pregnancy, the *Book* then describes how, "aftyr that sche had conceyved, sche was labowrd wyth grett accessys tyl the chyld was born, and than, what for labowr sche had in chyldyng and for sekenesse goyng beforn, sche dyspered of hyr lyfe, wenyng sche mygth not levyn" (21). The experience of labor leads to sickness and later madness—a progression that highlights the connections between motherhood, fleshliness, and sinfulness by focusing attention on the weaknesses of Margery's body[55]—and brings on the divine intervention that changes the course of her life. Margery becomes a mother and spiritual figure almost simultaneously. The language of the description closely associates the two events of becoming a mother and of going mad (as the result of an unconfessed but probably sexual sin).[56] She returns to the term "labowryd" to describe the struggle she has with the spirits (22). Margery's experience as a mother is the foundation for all of the experiences with which the rest of the text is concerned; her first difficult childbirth leads to her first vision of Christ and ultimately to her life as a spiritual figure and author.

The associations between maternity and spiritual uncleanness could be remedied through the ritual known as churching, which followed the precedent Mary set after Christ's birth.[57] The *Book* later describes another mother's churching, but Margery's extreme case, with the additional peril of madness, demands a more individual solution. In the midst of her postpartum struggles, Christ appears, sitting on her bed. Her insanity is so enduring and disturbing that she requires this divine intervention to recover—and she is apparently so special that she deserves it. This episode signifies a privileged relationship with Christ and emphasizes the connection between Margery's sexual body and her spiritual experience, even suggesting that the first is somehow integral to or carried over into the second. Christ appears to her as an attractive young man, saying: "Dowtyr, why hast thow forsakyn me, and I forsoke nevyr the?" (23). He invokes his role as her father and crucified savior, but appears in the guise of a lover.

The erotic presence of Christ in the bedroom was not anomalous. In his Letter to Eustochium, St. Jerome exhorted the virgin to "Let the seclusion of your own chamber ever guard you; ever let the Bridegroom sport with you within."[58] Here, as elsewhere in the *Book,* however, it is the context of Margery's earthly life and her conflation of the maternal and the sexual that make the difference. She is not in virtuous "seclusion" but has recently become a mother and still bears the sexual stigma, even though she is now figured as Christ's "Dowtyr" in this bedroom tryst. Her sinful physicality is prominent in this moment and the appearance of Christ like a lover in her bedroom underscores this in the act of resolving it. Despite her condition, Margery is in a position of power: Christ seeks her out, states his devotion to her, and addresses her in the same words he spoke to God the Father from the cross. By invoking the Passion, Christ suggests that her suffering, like his own, may have spiritual significance. This suggestion conforms to a common trope in hagiography. Other female spiritual figures, including Julian of Norwich, also suffer in the modes of Christ or Mary; however, while Julian's pain, for instance, is deeply physical, it leads to disembodied spiritual experiences and lacks the worldly sexual and maternal undertones that make Margery's postpartum suffering distinctive.[59]

Proving more effective than churching, Christ's words immediately return Margery to her sanity. She resumes her normal life and daily activities, asking her husband "that sche mygth have the keys of the botery to takyn hir mete and drynke as sche had don beforn" (23). Her keys are a symbol of her return to the very domestic world that caused her trouble, but they are also, as Staley points out, signs of female power.[60] However, the keys signify that Margery's power is still limited to and by her earthly roles as wife and mother; she will later adopt symbols of spiritual power, including her white clothing and engraved ring. Margery remains a mother and wife, but she will redirect her domesticity and sexuality into an intimate relationship with Christ. The text sets him up as a figure for whom both sexual and familial imagery is appropriate but, at this point, Margery is beginning that spiritual relationship while maintaining its earthly equivalents with her human family. The visions of the two religious figures closest to her, Bridget of Sweden and Julian, began in childhood and near-fatal illness respectively, but Margery's spiritual career originates from this first encounter with Christ and childbirth.

In the only other example in the *Book* of a woman's experience immediately after childbirth, the text makes it clear that the suffering of childbirth and motherhood is not an avenue that all mothers can follow to a religious life. Here madness again follows childbirth; the woman's husband explains that "sche knowyth not me ne non of hir neyborwys. Sche roryth and cryith so that sche makith folk evyl afeerd. Sche wyl bothe smytyn and bityn, and therfor is sche manykyld on hir wristys" (170). In this case, Margery, rather than Christ, heals the mother, emphasizing Margery's spiritual power—she can perform the same act for another that Christ performed for her—and her unique status—she merited direct divine intervention. After Margery intervenes, the new mother stops raving and is "browt to chirche and purifiid as other women be" (171). If Margery's ability to circumvent churching reveals her special status, then this episode shows that her spiritual power works within the established religious structure: her intervention facilitates the mother's churching rather than replacing it. In other words, although Margery's spiritual experiences may have been outside of the Church, she used her authority for orthodox objectives.

Before Margery could claim such authority, she had to perform a careful balancing act, overcoming the obstacles of physical motherhood in order to transform it into spiritual motherhood while still preserving the physical as a precondition for the spiritual. Her experiences of motherhood are not confined to her children, however; they begin again when she becomes a mother to her husband, John, after he suffers a head injury. She notes the commingling of her familial roles during this period, explaining that she "had ful mech labowr wyth hym, for in hys last days he turnyd childisch agen." The word "labowr" connects this episode with her experiences of motherhood and madness at the beginning of the text. Her husband's childishness is not solely a mental condition but also a physical one: he "cowd not don hys owyn esement to gon to a sege . . . but as a childe voydyd his natural digestyon in hys lynyn clothys." Margery's experience with his newly childlike body reminds her of the sexual pleasure they shared before Christ first appeared to her, when she had "ful many delectabyl thowtys, fleschly lustys, and inordinat lovys to hys [John's] persone" (173). Here again motherhood mingles with sexuality, which is in turn complicated by the familial relationships involved. Margery's husband is a passionate lover and a helpless son to her, while she is his wife and mother. It is her responsibility as his wife to become his mother in this situation; the people of Lynn believe that "yyf he deyd, hys wyfe was worthy to ben hangyn for hys deth, forasmeche as sche myth a kept hym and dede not" (172). Christ reinforces Margery's wifely responsibility, instructing her to "take hym hom and kepe hym for my lofe" (173). Both her community and Christ pressure her to care for her husband in this peculiarly dual role. Christ argues his point by asking Margery to do so for the "lofe" of her spiritual lover, a further mingling of spiritual, familial, and erotic elements.

By the time of his sickness, however, Margery's sexual relationship with her husband is in the past. Immediately after setting forth her credentials as a mother (and proving that motherhood can coexist with a sexualized spirituality), she distances herself from physical motherhood by portraying her withdrawal from earthly sex. Physical motherhood remains important; Margery sets it up as a prerequisite for spiritual motherhood, establishing it as the indispensable ground for the spiritual metaphor. In doing so, she—like Julian—follows the model of the Virgin Mary, whose status as the human mother of Christ led to her role as spiritual mother for humanity. However, physical motherhood is also a potential impediment to its spiritual counterpart. From a philosophical standpoint, physical motherhood is an incontrovertible sign that a woman is not a virgin (with Mary as the sole exception); from a practical standpoint, the responsibilities of wifehood and motherhood deplete the time, energy, and resources that a woman might otherwise devote to pursuing a spiritual life. Because Margery is crafting an authority based on her human roles as wife and mother, she cannot simply leave the physical behind; the physical—and the sexual—remain as the foundation of her relationship with Christ.

Once again, Christ directly intervenes. He helps Margery overcome the philosophical and practical obstacles and, once again, she mixes maternal and sexual imagery to create spiritual intimacy and authority. She cannot recapture her virginity, but she distances herself from the fleshly and sinful connotations of motherhood by establishing a chaste marriage. Her husband is initially reluctant to agree to an arrangement that would turn sex into a deadly sin. With Christ's mediation, the spouses strike a deal: Margery will pay her husband's debts and eat with him on Fridays and he will assent to a chaste marriage. She figures her request for chastity not as an end to sexual intimacy, however, but as a redirection of it, saying that her husband, by agreeing to the new terms, would "makyth my body fre to God." He consents and says, "As fre mot yowr body ben to God as it hath ben to me," a reference to their previously active sex life (38). This language suggests that Margery's body is being exchanged between her husband and God; she renounces "fleschly comownyng" (26) in favor of a more spiritual but scarcely less sexual communion. Having achieved her "desyr" (38), she goes on to visit "many other of owyr Lordys loverys" (39), confirming that she has moved from being John's lover to being the "Lordys." The confluence of Margery's spiritual and sexual experiences is unusual; the closest case is that of Bridget of Sweden, whose marital sexuality was much more controlled (she and her husband observed periods of chastity in their marriage) and was safely in the past by the time her spiritual life began in earnest during her widowhood. In her *Revelations,* Christ stresses this divide to Bridget: "And when at your husband's death your soul was gravely shaken with disturbance, then the spark of my love—which lay, as it were, hidden and enclosed—began to go forth . . . [and] you abandoned your whole will to me and desired me above all things."[61]

For Margery, a chaste marriage is not only about keeping her body pure but also about ceasing to bear children.[62] The text explains that this resolution conforms to a direct command from Christ. Although Christ consistently downplays to Margery the value of virginity, assuring her that he does not love her any less because she has an earthly husband, Christ makes a specific declaration against her continuing role as mother: "whyl thys creatur was beryng chylder and sche was newly delyveryd of a chyld, owyr Lord Cryst Jhesu seyd to hir sche schuld no mor chyldren beryn, and therfor he bad hyr gon to Norwych" (50). This is not only an exhortation to chastity but also a specific imperative against further reproduction. It comes after she already has many children; Christ does not want her to be childless but to prevent her from having "mor chyldren." The command is notable because it responds to Margery's experience as a mother, an experience that most female religious figures lacked. It also distinguishes her from male religious authorities; priestly celibacy required a renunciation of biological in favor of spiritual fatherhood, but Margery is able to experience and utilize both forms of motherhood while exploiting the figurative relationship between them. As she embraces chastity, Margery replaces—or, more accurately, supplements—her marriage to John with a relationship with Christ that proves to be more intimate, more exclusive, and more productive.

Christ follows his instruction to stop having children with a significant rationale: since Margery had complained that she could not travel because giving birth had left her too weak, she must renounce motherhood in order to continue her teaching. Christ presents her trip to Norwich as an alternative to or replacement for motherhood, but this new task also conflates the spiritual and the sexual. Christ tells Margery to meet with a vicar and "schew hym thy prevytés and myn cownselys swech as I schewe the" (50). "Prevytés" is a suggestive term that could denote "genitals" as well as "divine secrets";[63] while the latter meaning is clearly primary here, the former still hovers behind it. Margery's "prevytés" and Christ's "cownselys" are structurally equivalent in this passage, binding the two together and raising the value of the first. Christ has replaced the traditional vocation of women, motherhood, with teaching, a spiritual vocation. The circumstances surrounding this shift also endow Margery with spiritual authority; her activities may appear to violate scriptural and societal strictures against women as preachers, but a higher power has licensed her.

Christ makes teaching more suitable for her than bearing children, but Margery makes motherhood the basis for her authority, using her identity as a mother to warrant her actions and speech as a teacher. She advances this claim when a clerk questions her about God's imperative to be fruitful and multiply, a command that seems to conflict with Christ's injunction to her to stop having children. Margery glosses the phrase in a way that eliminates the apparent contradiction: "thes wordys ben not undirstondyn only of begetyng of chyldren bodily, but also be purchasyng of vertu, whech is frute gostly, as be heryng of the wordys of God, [and] be good exampyl gevyng" (121–22). Figurative interpretation of this passage is hardly an original move,[64] but Margery's adaptation is. She emphasizes the connection between physical and spiritual motherhood; the scriptural words are not simply figurative, as in most other interpretations, but refer to both forms of fruitfulness (one should "not . . . only" have biological children "but also" become a virtuous example for others, thereby producing spiritual children).[65] The command is twofold: a directive toward both physical and spiritual productivity.[66] Having satisfied the "bodily" component of the command, Margery has moved on to producing "frute gostly." Whereas Julian connected spiritual motherhood to its human equivalent, Margery reverses the trajectory by leveraging her indisputable claim to the latter (the ground for the metaphor) into a claim for the former.

Margery again draws on her status as a mother when she is examined by the Archbishop of York and has to defend her right to speak publicly. He finds her orthodox, but asks her not to "techyn ne chalengyn" his people. She refuses his request and quotes the words spoken to Christ by a woman who heard him preach: "Blyssed be the wombe that the bar and the tetys that gaf the sowkyn" (Luke 11:27). This scriptural passage is the basis of Margery's defense; it leads her to conclude that "me thynkyth that the gospel gevyth me leve to spekyn of God" (126). The passage offers dual grounds for Margery's right to speak. First, Christ affirms the unnamed woman's speech. Second, more subtly but more interestingly, the passage connects female speech with Mary's role as physical mother. As Mary, the "wombe" that bore Christ, is blessed, so is Margery, whose womb has borne many children. Her role as mother, not only possessing but also using her "wombe" and "tetys" to birth and nurture children, makes her "blyssed." And because she is blessed, she has the right to speak. Motherhood provides a foundation for some authority as a religious teacher; relying on examples of spiritual mothers who were "voices of holy wisdom," David Herlihy suggests that medieval mothers assumed a critical if not very visible role in their children's religious education.[67] Margery's conclusion certainly (and perhaps purposefully) misreads the passage, which concerns Christ's speech and makes no mention of Mary's right to speak or of the unnamed woman's right to speak more than the single sentence in praise of Mary. Furthermore, it offers only slim grounds for the deduction that other mothers are "blyssed" because Mary herself is. Whether Margery misrepresented the passage, however, is less important than the fact that she chose to stake her claim on this basis, the authority of motherhood. In doing so, she collapses the categories of physical and spiritual. She emphasizes that she is physically a mother, referring to specific body parts and to the acts of birthing and nursing, but she uses these references to justify herself as a spiritual mother in the mode of Mary who is permitted to teach her "children"—a category that seems to include everyone Margery encounters.

Throughout the *Book,* Margery talks about her physical motherhood strategically, using it primarily at the beginning to establish her claim to motherhood and to set up the connection between her sexuality and spirituality. She is trying to do a tricky thing: to insist that her physical motherhood is valuable and, in fact, the basis of her unusual claim to spiritual authority, but then to leave it behind quickly so that she can assume the spiritual motherhood that is thus enabled. She wants to make clear that her claim to physical motherhood is indisputable and represents an important connection to Mary, but its true value comes only when she makes the transition to spiritual motherhood. Once she has made that transition, she wants to inhabit the spiritual aspect fully. While Margery's representation is always mediated at some level by her scribe, the use of her own motherhood is so unorthodox and so dependent on her individual identity that it seems more likely to have its origin in Margery's view of her life than in the scribe's. Taking on the role of spiritual mother helps Margery to appear experienced and authoritative because it necessarily positions other people as children. But she is focused on the Virgin Mary and, for Margery, Mary's key characteristic is her maternity; even her virginity is a facet of her identity as Christ's mother. Margery makes use of her own unusual purchase on that imagery; throughout the *Book,* she stresses her superlative spiritual status—as the closest intimate of Christ, the most persecuted and therefore most worthy figure, the loudest weeper—and her motherhood is another distinguishing feature of which she can take advantage. As a result, Margery's motherhood, which might have been a major obstacle to her spiritual life, becomes the improbable foundation for it.

Imitating the Virgin Mary

The Virgin Mary was the most powerful and honored female figure of the Middle Ages, so it is hardly surprising that Margery, who is always concerned with spiritual status, would seek to imitate her.[68] Mary was the paragon of motherhood in all its forms. What may be more surprising, however, is that Margery's focus on Mary is unusual among women; Caroline Walker Bynum notes that "the humanity of Christ was a more prominent emphasis in women's piety than was devotion to the Virgin."[69] This may explain why so few critics have noticed the elements of *imitatio Mariae* in Margery's text, and why none has recognized the ways in which she strategically modifies that tradition in order to support her claim to spiritual authority through motherhood.[70]

Near the beginning of the *Book,* Margery has a trio of visions that emphasize how closely she identifies with Mary, and how tightly that identification is tied to maternal images. These visions are an early and important sign that Margery's ultimate model is Mary rather than the various other female saints who have similar characteristics. The visions begin with Christ's instruction to Margery to "thynke on my modyr, for sche is cause of alle the grace that thow hast" (32). Margery then sees herself as a kind of midwife at the births of Mary, John the Baptist, and Jesus (32–33); in all three births, Margery is most closely associated with Mary, regardless of Mary's changing role throughout. Margery is an active participant in these scenes, contrasting with the rather passive actual mothers, and she demonstrates a

fair amount of maternal authority, taking charge of the young Mary and announc-
ing that she will be the mother of Christ. Here, Margery becomes a spiritual mother
to the ultimate spiritual mother.

Through most of the *Book,* Margery focuses on Mary as the divine example of
physical motherhood transformed into spiritual motherhood, seizing on the two
devotional models clustered around that transformation: Mary as *Mater Dolorosa,*
or grieving mother, and as *Mediatrix* or intercessor. These models are connected
because Mary's suffering at Christ's crucifixion established her as the emotional link
between the human and the divine, and therefore as a mother to and intercessor
for humanity. These roles for Mary are developments particular to the later Middle
Ages and were popular in various medieval texts, including lyrics, Dante's *Paradiso,*
and Chaucer's "An ABC" and *Canterbury Tales.*[71] Most medieval literary representations of Mary, however, mention these roles in the context of other characteristics,
and emphasize the paradox of her power and humility.[72] Dante typifies this view
when he addresses Mary as "Virgin Mother, daughter of thy Son, humble and
exalted more than any creature."[73] Similarly, the prologues of both the Prioress and
the Second Nun in Chaucer's *Canterbury Tales* at once appeal to Mary as a powerful
intercessor and stress her humility. The Prioress prays for "help" in telling her tale,
addressing the Virgin as "O blisful Queene" and mentioning her "magnificence"
alongside her "humblesse" and "grete humylitee" (473, 481, 474, 470, and 475). The
Second Nun portrays Mary as one who helps not only those who request it but also
"er that men thyn help biseche, / Thou goost biforn and art hir lyves leche" (55–56);
she is "Mayde and Mooder," which makes her "humble, and heigh over every creature" (36 and 39).

By downplaying certain aspects of Mary's physical maternity—as well as her
own—and highlighting instead the suffering that marked the end of Mary's physical motherhood and the beginning of her spiritual motherhood and intercessory
power, Margery takes advantage of the power while virtually ignoring its counterpart: humility. This is a distinct departure from other mystical texts (including the *Shewings*), which habitually embraced humility and revered Mary for her
exemplary demonstration of that quality. There are some elements of humility and
subordination in Margery's text: she portrays herself as obedient to Christ and to
the Church (all the while remarking on her many encounters with clerical figures
who are less obedient than she). But her *imitatio Mariae* is a strategy for spiritual
authority, and so she focuses on those elements of the Marian model that provided
a link between Mary's earthly maternal experience and her authority as supreme
spiritual mother. Margery wants to duplicate that link. Her characteristic weeping
thus emulates Mary's suffering and facilitates her access to the associated intercessory power.

Some of Mary's experiences with earthly maternity are more useful for Margery's
project than others. She ignores perhaps the most popular element of Mariolatry:

Mary as the nursing mother of the holy infant.[74] Unlike many female saints—and some monks[75]—Margery does not have visions of herself nursing the Christ child. Mary most fully participated in physical motherhood through nursing; her conception was immaculate and it was believed that she did not experience labor pains. As a result, images of Mary as a nursing mother, *Maria Lactans,* became particularly important and symbolically charged. In the fourteenth century, such images had become symbols for female humility, a virtue that is not dear to Margery's heart. In her popular study of the Virgin Mary, Marina Warner describes the contemporary attitude: "if woman was considered inferior because of her greater subjection to biology, then the Virgin, by accepting that female destiny, by bearing and suckling a child, revealed her model humility."[76] The image was more complex than Warner allows; Bynum contends that Mary's breast was an empowering symbol and provided the basis for perceiving the female body "as powerful in its holy or miraculous exuding, whether of breast milk or of blood or of oil," but such "extraordinary flowing" in female saints, Bynum acknowledges, "was predicated on extraordinary closure."[77] Margery's lay existence deprives her of the ability to claim any "miraculous exuding," and the image remains problematically physical, even—or perhaps especially—for the Virgin Mary.

Margery does embrace the physicality of Mary's experience as Christ's mother, but primarily through her suffering. The most physical and perhaps best-known element of Margery's *imitatio Mariae* is her copious weeping, although the connection to Mary has gone largely unrecognized—perhaps because the weeping is so extreme that any precedent seems inadequate. Sarah Beckwith notes that "tears of compassion had long been considered a special sign of grace,"[78] but they were a sign specifically associated with Mary. Tears were a prominent feature in the cult of *Mater Dolorosa,* which reached its height in the fourteenth century, and Eamon Duffy identifies the devotion to the sorrows of Mary as "the most distinctive manifestation of Marian piety in late medieval England."[79] Many Marian lyrics described her sorrows; one late fourteenth-century poem speaks in Mary's voice, bewailing "Wel may I mone and murning maken, / And wepen til myn eyne aken. / For wane of wele my wo is waken, / Was nevere wif so wo."[80] We might guess that Margery's eyes ached from her repeated bouts of weeping, as well; in their very excessiveness, her tears are a testament to her Marian spirituality.[81]

The embodiedness of Margery's suffering, which scholars commonly claim as a facet of her *imitatio Christi,* strengthens her *imitatio Mariae.* Beckwith points out that Margery concentrates "on those parts of [Christ's] life which emphasize embodiedness most completely," his birth and death.[82] Margery focuses most frequently and most intensely on Mary's experience at these moments; her identification with Mary gives her access to these scenes. Karma Lochrie, in her influential reading of Margery's associations with the flesh, points to the originary moment of Margery's weeping as evidence that it is part of *imitatio Christi:* while visiting

Mount Calvary, she weeps uncontrollably as her body seems to mimic Christ's crucified body.[83] But Margery clearly associates these experiences with Mary rather than Christ. In spite of the physical mimesis, Margery never fully identifies with Christ on Mount Calvary but instead likens her suffering to that of people who "for inordinat lofe and fleschly affeccyon yyf her frendys er partyn fro hem, thei wyl cryen and roryn and wryngyn her handys as yyf thei had no wytte ne non mende" (77). This view aligns her with the audience at the crucifixion rather than with Christ himself. Soon after, Margery names the actual figure with whom she identifies in these moments of suffering, explaining that "sche thowt sche saw owyr Lady in hir sowle, how sche mornyd and how sche wept hir sonys deth, and than was owyr Ladiis sorwe hir sorwe" (78). Thus Margery's suffering is initiated by Christ's Passion, but it is the suffering of "owyr Lady," for which Margery has special empathy and that she takes as the object of her *imitatio Mariae*.

Mary was recognized as having had various sorrows, but the greatest was her pain at the Passion. This emphasis was the creation of later religious authors; it does not feature prominently in the biblical accounts. Margery's Christ intends her tears as a manifestation of Mary's grief, a visible human representation to inspire others. Late in the *Book,* he reveals this to Margery: "I geve the gret cryis and roryngys for to makyn the pepil aferd wyth the grace that I putte in the into a tokyn that I wil that my modrys sorwe be knowyn by the that men and women myth have the mor compassyon of hir sorwe that sche suffyrd for me" (175). Those who observed Margery's crying did not always comprehend this aim. Some who did recognize the connection rejected it, suggesting that Margery's suffering was excessive and admonishing her that "owr Lady, Cristys owyn modyr, cryed not as sche dede." In other words, Margery's Marian suffering surpasses even Mary's. Margery herself begins to feel that her suffering is too great and cries out, "Lord, I am not thi modir. Take awey this peyn fro me, for I may not beryn it" (159). Although Margery momentarily rejects the role of Christ's mother, her rejection makes it clear that her suffering—and her *imitatio*—is of Mary.

Mary's suffering for her crucified son links her physical motherhood with the much broader spiritual motherhood she achieves; with the death and resurrection of Christ, Mary assumes the position of mother to humanity. She becomes the "Almighty and al merciable queene, / To whom that al this world fleeth for socour," as Chaucer addresses her in the opening lines of "An ABC" (1–2). Mary's status as intercessor was tied to the actual roles of mothers as intercessors in medieval households. Because wives were often significantly younger than their husbands, women could bridge the generations within their families and mediate between fathers and children. Herlihy explains that, "used to seeking the help and intercession of their natural mothers, medieval people seem to have sought comparable services from their spiritual mother in heaven."[84] The crucial depiction of Margery's role as a "natural mother" is brief, but she often acts as an intercessor for her spiritual children, pleading with Christ for their salvation or healing. She has one such encounter with a priest: "be inqwyryng he cam into the place wher that sche was, and ful humbely and mekely he clepyd hir modyr, preying hir for charité to receyven hym as hir sone. Sche seyd that he was wolcom to God and to hir as to hys owyn modyr" (100). As his spiritual mother, Margery is able to assure the priest that he is "wolcom to God." Like Mary, she can act as an intercessor to God and guarantee a man's salvation.

In the only extended episode concerning one of Margery's biological children, she acts as a spiritual mother toward her son. She intercedes with him on God's behalf so that her son "schulde be the mor diligent and the mor besy to folwyn owr Lordys drawyng" (209). He becomes seriously ill, but her concern is for his salvation, even at the expense of his health. Others accuse her of actually causing her son's bodily sickness to prompt him to repent, saying that "thorw hir prayer God had takyn venjawns on hir owyn childe" (208). She shows no greater or lesser concern for her biological son than for her many spiritual children, for whom she also weeps and intercedes.[85] This episode, near the end of the book, demonstrates that Margery has moved beyond physical motherhood and sees herself primarily as a spiritual mother.

But Margery does not only intercede between men and God; she also intercedes within the holy family—this is where she begins to exceed Mary as a spiritual mother and intercessor, and where her idiosyncratic path to spiritual authority takes an unusual turn. Christ recognizes the expansive nature of Margery's spiritual motherhood and suggests that it benefits him, saying, "thu art to me a very modir and to al the world for that gret charité that is in the" (95). Christ also credits Margery with interceding for him with his mother, a peculiar permutation of the usual practice of intercession. He explains: "And also, dowtyr, thu clepist my modyr for to comyn into thi sowle and takyn me in hir armys and leyn me to hir brestys and gevyn me sokyn" (198). Here we do see Mary nursing her son, but this nurturing takes place at Margery's instigation and within her very "sowle." Here Mary remains a physical mother while Margery's mothering is spiritual. This substantiates Margery's spiritual authority: if she can intercede between Christ and Mary, then her messages from Christ to other people are surely credible.

A Maternal and Sexual Creature

While Margery's intercessions are unusual, her combination of sexual and maternal imagery becomes patently unorthodox. She finally shifts from a selective *imitatio Mariae* to exceeding any available precedent. It is not enough, in other words, for Margery to do *imitatio* differently than other female mystics; she must take it up another level to confirm her specialness. She goes beyond identification with Mary, and uses her *imitatio* as a springboard to her own inimitable intimacy with Christ. Margery returns to the physical and sexual aspects of her earthly life in order to transform her Marian spiritual motherhood into this insuperable spousal intimacy. Mary can be somewhat sexualized in this role through Song-of-Songs-type imagery, but her dominant sexual characteristic is her virginity, her experience of becoming a mother without engaging in sexual intercourse. In this final phase, Margery does not abandon her Marian model but instead radically alters it by suturing a new kind of intimacy onto it. She combines maternal and erotic elements, constructing a relationship with Christ that exceeds what anyone else—even Mary herself—could claim.[86]

The family roles played out in the spiritual relationships Margery has with God, Christ, and Mary are far from traditional. This, says Dinshaw, is "one big queer family"; it "shows up the earthly family for its limitations, especially for its lack of intimacy."[87] Yet Margery does experience a fairly deep intimacy with her husband and, at times, with her son, and that human intimacy becomes a critical factor in her unorthodoxy. Motherhood and sexual passion, which were (and still are) popular religious metaphors, have a physical basis in Margery's earthly life: just as she founded her spiritual motherhood on her physical motherhood, she founds her spiritual sexuality on its earthly equivalent.[88] Most female mystics renounced the earthly roles of wife and mother; rather than simply ignoring or denouncing those parts of her identity, however, Margery uses them to make her relationship with Christ distinctively intimate. She experiences spiritual sexuality through physical interactions and combines it with maternal imagery, producing unique and unsettling configurations of imagery and characters.

Critics have consistently seen Margery's sexual imagery as an unsuccessful attempt at affective piety,[89] which frequently utilized metaphors of marriage, love, or desire. In some texts—including the *Book*—this metaphorical language becomes surprisingly literal. Margery's use of the imagery of desire reworks those traditions in several important ways: by reforming its nature, by depicting its real-life context, and by combining it with other elements. This pattern is so pervasive in the text that it cannot be accidental or imposed. I see it as evidence of Margery's role in shaping her own story; even if the scribe is selecting, rephrasing, or restructuring her dictation, this combination of the maternal and sexual must come from the material of her life as she presented it to him. Certainly the representation of Margery is constructed, but this aspect of the constructed representation, I would argue, bears the stamp of Margery herself.[90]

Numerous female religious figures, including Angela of Foligno, Adelheid Langmann, and Catherine of Siena, envisioned themselves marrying Christ or God. Others used images of nursing the Christ child, or of Christ as lover. Such imagery was most often demonstrably metaphorical, as examples from Angela of

Foligno and Hadewijch will demonstrate. Margery may not have known these thirteenth-century female mystics, but they are typical examples of affective piety and contribute to the context in which scholars have read Margery's *Book*.[91] Hadewijch, for instance, says that Christ "came in the form and clothing of a Man, . . . took me entirely in his arms, and pressed me to him" but also interpolates the point that "he gave himself to me in the shape of the Sacrament, in its outward form," thus reminding us that this is a vision expressed in figurative terms.[92] Angela of Foligno also combines the imagery of Christ as lover with an explicitly metaphorical context: she "kissed Christ's breast . . . [and] then she kissed his mouth. . . . Afterward, she placed her cheek on Christ's own and he, in turn, placed his hand on her other cheek, pressing her closely to him." This intimate interaction, however, occurs while Angela is having a vision of herself with Christ in a sepulcher, and throughout he "lay[s] dead, with his eyes closed."[93]

The language describing such encounters sometimes borders on the orgasmic. Angela depicted another encounter in which she was "filled with love and inexpressible contentment which, satisfactory as it was, nonetheless generated in her a hunger so unspeakably great that all her members dislocated" (183). However, the metaphorical status of the description is again carefully preserved. Angela prefaces her description by specifying twice that she saw "with the eyes of her soul," and explains that these feelings were inspired by a vision of love as a sickle; she reiterates that "this should not be understood to mean that it could be compared to anything spatial or measurable" and the sickle "was not something that could be compared to anything spatial or material because it was a reality perceptible only to her mind through the ineffable workings of divine grace" (182–83). While Margery does sometimes make use of metaphors, as when she sees Mary nursing Christ in her "sowle," the metaphorical context for the sexual imagery often falls away and the context of her earthly life as a wife and mother replaces it. Margery's sexual imagery is not simply an attempt at affective piety that veers into the literal; she is deploying sexual imagery in a different context and to a different end. For Angela, Hadewijch, and other female mystics, desire is figurative and Christ is a divine lover; for Margery Kempe, desire is homely and familiar, and Christ is a daily partner with whom she shares an exclusive intimacy.

It is also worth noting that those female religious figures who were closest to Margery's experience and of whom she certainly knew—Bridget of Sweden and Julian—were muted in their descriptions of spiritual intimacy. Most studies that compare Margery and Bridget focus on their similarities as female spiritual figures who had experienced wifehood and motherhood rather than on the very different ways in which they use and depict those experiences.[94] Although Bridget is consistently described as the "bride" of Christ in her *Revelations,* this functions as an honorific more than as a metaphor. Rather than engaging in intimate conversations with Christ, Bridget records Christ's and Mary's virtual monologues or responses to organized "interrogations" from her visions. While Margery gains special authority from her homely intimacy with Christ, Bridget relies on the more established—and more masculine—model of prophetic authority.[95] As we have seen, Julian avoids sexualized imagery, focusing on herself as one of many "evenchristen," all of whom can be as close to Christ as a child to a parent, and authorizing herself primarily as a representative who received visions intended for that wider audience.

Within this context, Margery's sexual imagery is unusually concrete and familiar: less divine ravishing than daily affection. Other female mystics tended to use orgasmic language and rapturous imagery; Margery was not attempting to render the nature of an ineffable and transcendent experience but rather to certify her intimacy with Christ. He invites her to "kyssen my mowth, myn hed, and my fete as swetly as thow wylt" (95); in addition, he must "nedys be homly wyth the and lyn in thi bed wyth the" (94). This is not sexualized holy rapture; it is a domestic and "homly" sexual and spousal relationship.[96] For Margery, erotic descriptions are not as much about her soul being ravished or lifted up as about her closeness to Christ, and the ways in which that intimacy is beyond what others can approach; she is as close to him as if she were his real and only wife or lover—even closer because she is also his daughter and mother. Margery equates her experiences with those described in other devotional texts: "sche herd nevyr boke, neythyr Hyltons boke, ne Bridis boke, ne *Stimulus Amorys,* ne *Incendium Amoris,* ne non other that evyr sche herd redyn that spak so hyly of lofe of God but that sche felt as hyly in werkyng in hir sowle" (51). But she also goes further. Christ assures Margery that she is "a synguler lover, and therfor thu schalt have a synguler love in hevyn" (62).

Margery also depicts herself in bed with Christ and his mother. This is not a configuration that is conventional or, indeed, anything less than startling. Christ reflects, "And also, dowtyr, I thank the for alle the tymys that thu hast herberwyd me and my blissyd modyr in thi bed." For this act "and for alle other good thowtys and good dedys that thu hast thowt in my name and wrowt for my lofe thu schalt have wyth me and wyth my modyr . . . al maner joye and blysse lestyng wythowtyn ende" (201). Not only has this strange bedroom scene occurred, it has occurred many times and forms part of the basis for Margery's heavenly reward. This sexually suggestive scene cements her salvation, but noticeably lacks the explicit metaphoricity insisted on by other female visionaries. The bed, as far as we can tell, is indeed a bed. Even if we accept the premise that this spiritual family is not constrained by the incest taboos that regulate behavior in human families, this new trinity of bedroom partners is unusual. It creates an intimacy with Christ and the holy family that is hard to top, and an authority for Margery as a spiritual speaker that is hard to ignore.

Margery's religious sexual imagery is also bound up with her active earthly sex life (or, later, her recollections of it—even after her marriage becomes chaste, her sexual past provides the context for her relationship with Christ). While other female mystics may concretize their experiences with Christ, those can never be as literal as Margery's because she has the physical experience that they mostly lack. She is not imagining a physical and erotic relationship with Christ based on what she has heard or read; she is imagining it on the basis of the actual relationship she had with her husband. So when she kisses Christ's feet, head, or mouth, it is not as part of an idealized if literal spousal relationship that she has never had—it is a kind of replication, albeit a heightened and improved one, of a relationship she has already experienced. Most other female mystics envision Christ as their lover or husband; Margery envisions him as her alternative or replacement lover or husband.[97] Parallel to the ways in which her physical motherhood made her claim to spiritual motherhood more credible (because she indisputably had the ground of the metaphor), her experience with earthly sexuality makes her claim to spiritual eroticism stronger and more meaningful. And it adds to the authority that Margery can claim.

Whereas Julian's parent/child imagery downplays her individual presence and significance within the text, Margery's maternal imagery allows her some measure of power over the most impressive male figures of all time: God and Christ. As David Aers points out, only as a mother could a woman exercise power over a man at any age.[98] Throughout the *Book,* however, Margery has reminded us that sexuality and motherhood are linked. Not only does she, as the visionary, use sexual metaphors to talk about God but—in a departure from devotional tradition—the holy family also uses sexual metaphors to talk about her. Margery's treatment of the holy family has attracted attention, but has not been connected to her use of sexual imagery. Ralph Hanna sees Margery as seeking "a denatured family, one thoroughly spiritualized, in keeping with her efforts to enact a holy life" and as participating in a "textually based surrogate household, the Holy Family," derived from the *Meditationes vitae Christi.*[99] Beckwith contends that, rather than simply replacing the biological family, spiritual relationships that were figured as familial transformed and transcended their earthly models.[100] Aers argues specifically that Margery is struggling against traditional family roles.[101] But, as we have seen, something larger is at work in her mingling of the sexual with the familial and spiritual: a strategy for authority.

Margery derives authority from her over-the-top intimacy with the holy family. In her relationship with God, she occupies many roles simultaneously. This becomes apparent in a surprising context: when she is marrying him. Although she is reluctant to accept this sign of divine favor, Christ convinces her to go through with it, and excuses her cold feet to God. God speaks his vows, including the familiar "for richar, for powerar," but goes on to promise, "For, dowtyr, ther was nevyr childe so buxom to the modyr as I schal be to the bothe in wel and in wo, to help the and comfort the." The vows describe God as her "childe" immediately after he takes her as "my weddyd wyfe" (92). The marriage ceremony traditionally reinforces a wife's duty to obey and submit to her husband, but this one attributes some power to Margery as a mother to God.[102]

Margery is also figured as Christ's mother, a label that follows logically from her extended *imitatio Mariae* but that quickly leads into other roles. Christ identifies himself as "thy swete sone, for I wyl be lovyd as a sone schuld be lovyd wyth the modyr and wil that thu love me, dowtyr, as a good wife owyth to love hir husbonde" (94–95). Elsewhere he elaborates: "thow art a very dowtyr to me and a modyr also, a syster, a wyfe, and a spowse." The combination of these roles would be shocking and impossible in a biological family but, according to Christ, it simply agrees with scripture: "wytnessyng the gospel wher owyr Lord seyth to hys dyscyples, 'He that doth the wyl of my Fadyr in hevyn he is bothyn modyr, brothyr, and syster unto me'" (44). Although one hesitates to accuse Christ of misinterpreting scripture, and although incestuous representations of the Holy Family were not uncommon, the offered precedent is an inadequate basis for his words to Margery. The key role of "wyfe" and "spowse" is absent from the gospel version. As a result, it lacks the sexuality that makes the other so unusual; the scriptural version combines different family roles, but does not combine the familial with the erotic. Moreover, the role of brother, which draws on fluid ideas about gender roles that were more common, is eliminated in Christ's words to Margery.[103] Her human roles as mother and wife—the same roles the Virgin Mary had—distinguish Margery from most female religious figures and provide a natural foundation for her claims to the identities of spiritual mother and lover, also like Mary. While other women seeking spiritual lives renounced such earthly roles, Margery leverages them to construct a closer parallel between herself and Mary, and then stretches—even violates—that parallel to create a still closer intimacy with Christ as her son and lover.

The argument I have outlined might appear to be undermined by one word that Margery habitually uses: *creatur*. The use of this term, which emphasizes that human beings were created by God, might be interpreted as a strategy of modesty that also de-emphasizes gender. Such a reading would place Margery in a less feminine and thus less sexually charged position. But her use of *creatur* actually has the opposite effect, since every direct address to Margery identifies her as a woman. Christ, for instance, starts most of his speeches with "Dowtyr," reminding the reader repeatedly of her womanhood (especially in Christ's eyes). Margery is frequently asked about her marital status, her absent husband, and the identity of her father. The mayor of Leicester asks her "of what cuntré sche was and whos dowtyr sche was," but overwrites her answer by identifying her as a "fals strumpet" (113–14). Margery's femaleness, obscured under *creatur*, reemerges continually in the identities others inscribe upon her. The oscillation between the two (creature vs. woman/daughter/mother/wife, even strumpet) underscores rather than underplays Margery's gender.

Furthermore, Margery does not consistently refer to herself as *creatur* throughout the *Book*.[104] At two significant junctures already discussed, *creatur* is replaced by words that define Margery in relation to her husband and son. Chapter 76 relates how her husband was seriously injured and so "the sayd creatur, hys wife, was sent for," and for the rest of the chapter, the word *creatur* is not used (172).[105] Similarly, in the first and second chapter of the second book—when Margery is interacting with her grown son—the *creatur* becomes "the modyr" or "hys modyr" (207–10). She is a *creatur* again only after her son and husband have died (211). In part, these deviations are attributable to the fact that readers are seeing Margery through the eyes of others (beyond the scribe): the people of Lynn in the first case, and her son and daughter-in-law in the second. Nonetheless, these two moments illustrate the ways in which Margery is at odds with the roles of wife and mother as they are traditionally imagined: her community criticizes her for failing to care for her husband and for causing her son's illness. These moments also illuminate Margery's desire to transform those roles (and, possibly, her reluctance to label herself with them). In this context, we can see *creatur* as an empowering identity; it is constantly reinscribed as female, but the new ways in which Margery imagines what it means to be a woman, wife, and mother contribute to her power and authority rather than compromising them. She is able to shed the expectations of these roles and return to being a female *creatur*.

Despite its careful tailoring to Margery's particular experience, the *Book* does have implications for our understanding of gender and sexuality in the Middle Ages. Margery suggests that physical motherhood is valuable not only socially but also spiritually, and that spiritual value is not solely dependent upon chastity or virginity but is accessible through other means. To that extent, she—like Julian—is recuperating the fleshly aspects of femininity. In medieval texts, sex is often portrayed as earthly and negative whereas spiritual devotion is metaphorical and positive, but Margery refuses to abide by that distinction. Can we really tell the difference between her intimacy with her husband and her intimacy with Christ, except that she prefers the latter? Margery's discussions of earthly sex—and how she would rather eat muck or let her husband be beheaded than engage in it—certainly put it in a negative light, but these descriptions might be read as an attempt to enforce a difference between earthly and spiritual intimacy that otherwise barely seems to exist in the *Book*.

Margery Kempe has many eccentricities: she wears a hair shirt during the conception of at least some of her fourteen children without her husband noticing, she is tortured by visions of men's "members" and bargains with her husband for her chastity, she wears white clothes and cries loudly and (it sometimes seems) incessantly, and she has visions in which Christ invites her to kiss his toes and talks her into marrying God, among other things. But these are not random oddities; they are part of a pattern that Margery, as the author of her *Book,* creates by manipulating maternal, sexual, and—above all—Marian imagery in order to license her speech, text, and life as a religious figure. *The Book of Margery Kempe* highlights Mary as a human mother and wife who provides a specifically female form of spiritual authority that Margery closely, if selectively, shadows. In the end, her imitation of Mary surpasses its model; Margery the creature creates herself as a more powerful spiritual mother, a more influential intercessor, and a more intimate lover of Christ.

Both Julian and Margery are manipulating ideas about womanhood. Although neither woman uses that term, their reinvention of motherhood closely parallels the invention of womanhood; each draws on vernacular language, each connects the holy to the human (taking the Virgin Mary as the touchstone), each mediates between conflicting categories, and each investigates the same central questions about the nature of femininity and its relationship to authority. These women writers may not be part of the poetic tradition that created and used *womanhood,* but they are certainly part of the social and literary culture from which it emerged and which it influenced. As this chapter has shown, the enterprise of experimenting with language to express new ideas about gender was not restricted to male authors or to Middle English poetry. Nor was the enterprise solely dependent on neologisms: Julian's innovative redefinitions of extant terms and Margery's highly individual collage of established precedents both work to similar ends (and with many of the same materials) as the coinages identified in earlier chapters.

Although I have paid close attention to the changes that gendered terms underwent from the fourteenth through the fifteenth centuries, the different methods and concerns in these female-authored devotional texts paradoxically highlight the aspects that persisted through that evolution. Beyond the fundamental effort to manipulate the language to accommodate changing conceptions of gender, those similarities include a concern with issues of power and authority, an interest in what might be called the limit cases (female figures who experienced extreme or unusual circumstances), and the search for a representative or paragon of the developing category of womanhood. In comparison with male poets, Julian and Margery explored a closely related branch of—or, we might say, an alternative path through—the possibilities for gendered language that were arising and undergoing such significant shifts in the late Middle Ages. As this historical moment passed, however, those words began to become more capacious, losing or combining many of their specific definitions. Moving toward the early modern period, *womanhood*—like *motherhood*—moves very close to its general modern meaning.

THE EVOLUTION OF WOMANHOOD IN FIFTEENTH-CENTURY DISCOURSE

W hat happens to womanhood as both the historical conditions that prompted new ideas about women and the gendered language that expressed such ideas continue to evolve? The previous chapters have examined how fourteenth-century writers—most notably, Geoffrey Chaucer, John Gower, and Julian of Norwich—fashioned or expanded concepts of womanhood and how some fifteenth-century writers, including John Lydgate, Robert Henryson, and Margery Kempe, reimagined those concepts in response to their own aesthetic and social concerns. In tracing that dynamic, this book has moved from focusing on the earliest occurrences of some gendered terms to later uses that were particularly significant in the development of their meanings. Over the course of the fifteenth century, however, changing notions about womanhood and the language employed to signify those notions appeared in a wide range of discourses and texts, from the rolls of Parliament to courtly love lyrics and from royal correspondence to hagiography. In this broader context, we can see the rapid evolution of these terms and ideas as they continued to take on individual and even idiosyncratic constructions but ultimately expanded to become more general abstractions (as we have seen with Henryson's use of *womanhood* in the *Testament*).

By looking at many texts over a long range of time, we can identify larger-scale trends in the evolution of gendered language. The previous chapters examined fewer texts in greater detail, providing close looks at particular takes on and manipulations of womanhood. This conclusion surveys usage more broadly, exploring both the range of possibilities these terms represented (including which meanings are most common and which appear as outliers, and which discourses tend to use this language more often or in particular ways) and how the terms evolved over time (including when the popularity of a word waxes and wanes; how denotations expand, contract, or shift; and how various lines of influence converge or become distinct). Most of the texts I consider here do not foreground gendered language in the same way the texts examined earlier did; however, these later texts do make significant use of different notions of and concerns about femininity. The terms receive less emphasis partly because they are becoming more familiar as they become more widely used: writers no longer need to attend as carefully to specifying meanings, even though they continue to use the concepts being denoted in innovative and significant ways.

The increasing use of gendered vocabulary testifies to the social and aesthetic utility of the terms; the fact that newly coined words denoting femininity not only persist but also evolve and spread indicates that they were indeed filling the conceptual and lexical gaps described in the introduction. Recent scholarship by James Simpson, Nancy Bradley Warren, and others has reevaluated the fifteenth century and renewed attention to its aesthetic and intellectual developments; it is now recognized as a significant period in its own right (measured in part by the quality of literary and devotional texts that it produced).[1] Writers' adaptations of terms like *womanhood* and *femininity* during this period indicate that gendered language was another area in which they built on their fourteenth-century inheritance rather than merely imitating it.

Not surprisingly, the fundamental dynamic of gendered language in the fifteenth century was one of broadening meanings.[2] This phenomenon happened in different ways with different words; while *motherhood* became broader as it was increasingly used to denote a human relationship in addition to a spiritual one, for instance, *sisterhood* grew to include the relationship between nuns in a convent as well as a familial connection. Even as terms like *womanhood* and *femininity* become more general, however, they do not entirely collapse into synonyms. Chaucer's single use of *femininity*—the first recorded appearance of this term, which is of French and Latin extraction—offers negative connotations. In the *Man of Law's Tale,* the narrator apostrophizes the Sultan's mother, Constance's first evil mother-in-law: "O serpent under femynynytee, / Lik to the serpent depe in helle ybounde!"[3] About a century later, the Digby *Mary Magdalene* manipulates such connotations in order to highlight the dual nature of its title character; the first half of the play employs *feminité* to present women as fleshly, shallow, and changeable but, by the second half, the term develops a positive association with the Virgin Mary. The dramatist reserves *womanhood* for the invocation that inspires Mary Magdalene's one miracle: when the queen of Marseilles appeals to Mary as the "flower of wommanned," she saves both the queen and her child.[4] The term is not only positive but also—as we have seen in previous chapters—closely associated with exercises of feminine power.

The etymological components of *womanhood* set it up to function as a broad term, denoting the condition of being a woman; its association with prominent concerns (such as feminine authority) may also have contributed to its popularity. This combination of factors means that *womanhood* remains a critical signal of when new ideas about women are at stake in a text. Like other examples of gen-dered vocabulary in the fifteenth century, it can still carry specific meanings but the overall move is toward generalization. One of the more unusual occurrences, for instance, is in a Middle English version of the *Secretum Secretorum,* a popular text that belonged to the mirrors for princes tradition but also included an encyclopedic collection of information on various topics.[5] The section on physiognomy explains the significance of physical features in men, such as hairy eyebrows, large nos-trils, short necks, fleshy feet, and broad toes, and interprets different types of male voices: "Who þat has a grete voyce and wele souned, he es batus and eloquent, þat es to say pertly spekynge. To smalle voyce tokenes foly and wommanhede."[6] This text seems to use *womanhood* to indicate effeminacy rather than a more straightfor-ward womanliness.[7] But this usage, which comes right around 1400, still suggests collectivity since it implies that certain characteristics are common to women and are correspondingly inappropriate or undesirable for men.

The tendency toward generality becomes more pronounced over time. A later appearance of *womanhood* in the rolls of Parliament from 1472–73 demonstrates how far the term has moved along the spectrum from individual quality to shared condition. A complaint from Sir John Ashton describes how his house came under assault; perhaps to lend pathos, Ashton details his wife's fear, explaining that she had recently given birth and "was in right grete dispare of hir lyfe, and by grete space then after so contynued, and in like wyse the said gentilwomen then with hir accordyng to the lawes of God and womanhode as is aforeseid accompayned were in grete dispare of their lyves."[8] The phrase "the lawes of . . . womanhode" seems to refer to the practice of a group of women accompanying a new mother—a literal kind of collectivity, but also a reference to how women as a whole behave or what customs they observe among themselves.

Ashton portrays womanhood in a positive light; a large subset of texts associ-ated it even more directly with a feminine ideal and the term became widely used to signify that ideal, especially in romantic contexts. Middle English love lyrics—a genre that became widespread during the fifteenth century[9]—made copious use of the term, sometimes on its own and sometimes within the conventional phrase "flower of womanhood" (which we have seen Henryson exploit to memorable effect).[10] "Thair sall no vþir in-to þis warld, but dreid, / Depairt me fra þe flour of womanheid," proclaims the lover in "Sweet Enslavement."[11] And the speaker from "The Parliament of Love" instructs, "Go, thow litle songe, thow hast a blisfull day; / For sche þat is the floure of wommanhode / At her oown leyser schall the syng and rede."[12] Most often—and in far too many cases to cite individually here—we find poets using the word independently to convey the same sense of beauty, virtue, and all-around excellence. In "To His Mistress, Root of Gentleness," the lover describes his beloved as possessing "Bounte, beaute, and perfyte whomanhode."[13] Similarly, the speaker in "To His Mistress, Flower of Womanhood" says to his lady, "And sethe that ye are floure of bewte, / Constreyned y am, magrie myn hede, / hartely to loue youre womanhede."[14] "An Envoy to His Mistress" opens with this plea: "O Bewtie pereles, and right so womanhod, / ffor the grete honour and vertue in you I see."[15] Perhaps most general of all is Lydgate's "A Ballade, Of Her that Hath All Virtues," which inquires, "What shoulde I more reherce of wommanhede? / Yee beon þe myrrour and verray exemplayre."[16] While the concept of ideal femininity existed before the term *womanhood* was coined, its ability to signify so many different aspects in such a compressed space made the relatively new term well suited for this rising genre.

The most interesting uses of gendered language during the fifteenth century, however, continue to be those associated with new or unusual models of womanhood and particularly those that involve questions of female power. In the York cycle plays, for example, Pilate's wife both symbolizes and contributes to his power and her self-portrait invokes new notions of womanhood in that problematic context: "I am dame precious Percula, of prynces þe prise, / Wiffe to ser Pilate here, prince withouten pere. / All welle of all womanhede I am, wittie and wise, / Consayue nowe my countenaunce so comly and clere."[17] This usage crosses genres: Percula is a secular character in a biblical drama, manipulating notions of feminine excellence most frequently found in courtly love lyrics to assert her authority in a political and religious context. Queen Margaret is another female figure whose claims to authority were contentious and who recast concepts of femininity.[18] The incapacity of her husband, King Henry VI, and her son's young age led her to seek the regency in 1454 (albeit unsuccessfully) and to become a forceful advocate for and later leader of the Lancastrian cause.[19] In her correspondence, she argues that other kings should consider themselves injured by the actions against her deposed and now fugitive husband, just as "wymmen, whanne any thynge is done to the dishonoure of wymmenhode."[20] Margaret's critics cast her as power hungry and masculine,[21] but this letter hints at her attempts to reconcile the political demands of her royal status with the cultural demands of gender stereotypes: womanhood, like kinghood, is an honorable condition that requires vigorous defense.

While they present womanhood in a positive light, both Percula and Margaret might carry negative associations; however, other texts invoked new models of womanhood that incorporated substantial power in relation to more admirable figures. The anonymous romance *Ipomadon,* preserved in a late fifteenth-century manuscript and one of several Middle English versions of the twelfth-century Anglo-Norman romance *Ipomedon* by Hue de Rotelande, makes a notable departure from its source by portraying the central female character more positively.[22] After the heroine is orphaned as a young girl, the lords decide that an unnamed but highly virtuous man will raise her: "The moste worthely man and wyse / Shuld kepe this lady mekyll of pryse, / And teche hur womanhoode."[23] The enterprise is successful insofar as she grows up to be a typically lovely and honorable romance heroine, but she also departs from type by becoming "the Fere," or the proud one, and openly insisting that she will only marry "the best knyghte."[24] The original poem appears to critique the Fere, treating both women and courtly love ironically; while the Middle English version retains the nickname, the anonymous poet introduces it in the midst of a catalogue of the Fere's excellent qualities and discourages any scrutiny of her upbringing by making it impossible to discern which of those qualities were inherent and which the wise and worthy guardian instilled in her. Rather than problematizing or interrogating womanhood, the English text mitigates Hue's sharper depiction of the Fere by both drawing attention to her womanhood and encouraging us to accept it as exemplary.

John Capgrave's depiction of Katherine of Alexandria is even more exemplary and, because it struggles directly with different conceptions of womanhood, even more intriguing. Katherine was "the most important saint in late medieval England" and Capgrave's version of her life was the most detailed and among the most popular.[25] In the context of ongoing reevaluations of the fifteenth century and the growing interest in hagiographic and religious texts among feminists in particular, both Capgrave and Katherine are attracting more scholarly attention, with his *Life of Saint Katherine* at the conjunction of those larger concerns.[26] The text merits substantial consideration here because it is preoccupied by contrary models of womanhood, secular and religious, and it stages an explicit search for a new and more expansive model that can accommodate the unusual experiences and desires of Katherine. In the process, Capgrave shows both how many things have changed since *womanhood* and its sister terms were coined and how useful that language and the narrative strategies associated with it continue to be. He must draw on fourteenth- and fifteenth-century innovations in this area because Katherine is such an extraordinary female character: a queen who is also a scholar; a maiden whose desire for virginity predates her conversion;[27] and a woman who becomes Christ's wife, a martyr, and a saint in short order.

Ideas of femininity are at issue in the two major debate scenes, the marriage debate between Katherine and her advisors and the theological debate between Katherine and the philosophers. As the ruler of Alexandria, Katherine challenges her council's notion of femininity by insisting that she wishes to remain single and is capable of ruling without a husband. "It is full perlyous," argues an earl, "to be a mayde / And eke a qwene," hinting that these two female identities, as Katherine embodies them, are incompatible.[28] "Why hate ye now that ilk lady must have?" an admiral asks in exasperation, trying simultaneously to comprehend and undermine her insistent rejection of convention (2.884). Later, as a Christian martyr, Katherine undermines her persecutor's idea of maidenhood by refusing to be seduced by persuasive speeches and appeals to her vanity. This strategy is his last-ditch effort; he reasons, "There is non othir botte / Onto this mayden whech is so stedfast / But fayre wordes, whech draw womanhoode / And makith hem often othir thingis to tast / Than thei shulde do if thei wold be chast" (5.330–36). He fails to recognize that his concept of womanhood does not apply to Katherine.

There is only one paradigm of womanhood that does pertain: the Virgin Mary's. By chronicling Katherine's pre-conversion life in unusual detail, Capgrave shows her remarkable characteristics and accomplishments in a secular as well as a spiritual context; they not only make more sense but also take on more meaning in the latter, where the model of the Virgin Mary renders them legible. When Mary sends the monk Adrian to convert Katherine, he catches her attention by insinuating that his faith can offer her a new model of womanhood. He tells Katherine that he knows a woman who is greater, more beautiful, and more powerful than she is: "I may thee more boldely mak this commendyng: / Sche paseth yow, certeyn, in all maner thing" (3.454–55). This claim, which directly contradicts the flattery of her lords as well as Katherine's own sense of her status, makes a profound impression. Astounded, she marvels at Adrian's statement "More than sche dyd evyr hir lyve before / Of ony mater" (3.464–65).

When she finally brings herself to speak, Katherine first responds as if she has been insulted but soon reveals an intense curiosity about this new exemplar of femininity. The complex passage is worth quoting at length:

How may youre Lady be so worthy woman

As ye commende now in your tale to me,
Of hir hye worchepe and also of hir wytte?
The worthyest of all women we wene that we be—
We herd nevyr of non worthyere yytte!
Wher lygthte hir londe? We wold fayn know itte.
Who is hir lorde—or wheyther is sche lordelees?
Ye telle us thingys whech we holde but lees!

Wheythyr is that dame lyvyng in spousayle
Or levyth sche sool as we do now?
If sche be weddyd, sykyrly sche may fayle
Mych of hir wyll, for sche mote nedys bowe
Onto hir lord, loke he nevyr so row;
And if sche lyve be hirself alone,
Than may sche make full oft mech mone,

Ryght for vexacyoun of hir lordes aboute—
This know we well; we are used ther-to!
Therfor, goodeman, put us oute of doute:
Tell us the sothe, be it joye or woo,

Whech that this lady most is used too,
And we wyll thank and rewarde yow eke
With swech plenté that it schall yow leke! (3.483–504)

Although Katherine begins her speech defensive and suspicious, her words betray a growing excitement by the end. She finds it hard to believe that such a woman exists, but she is intrigued by the possibility. The mystery woman (who turns out to be Mary) might be not only a peer but also a model for Katherine, who wonders whether the woman has resolved the dilemmas that Katherine herself has encountered in trying to live out this unusual form of womanhood. This passage resembles Knighton's description of the troop of cross-dressing women discussed in the introduction in that both reveal the need for new models of womanhood; by the fifteenth century, however, linguistic, literary, and social precedents provide Capgrave with the necessary material to fashion such a model in his text.

The *Life of Saint Katherine* brings together some of the gendered terms favored by Chaucer, Gower, and their male followers with tactics utilized by Julian and Margery for constructing feminine authority in the mode of the Virgin Mary to create a version of womanhood that is both particularly Capgrave's and particularly appropriate for the saint's life he is writing. He stages a collision between spiritual and secular notions of womanhood, associating the term itself more strongly with the latter (and thus recalling its origins as secular rather than religious) while suggesting that the idea must be enlarged to accommodate more meanings and interpretations. This text is consistent with the fifteenth-century tendency to relate *womanhood* to an ideal femininity, but it also deals squarely with issues of feminine power. As a result, it illustrates how the two primary sets of meanings during the period could be combined and suggests that the capacious nature of *womanhood* and its related terms allows the bridging rather than the calcifying of differences. The *Life of Saint Katherine* also reaches back to the fourteenth-century emphasis on the mediating power of womanhood, which offered a conceptual space for bringing together and working through divergent definitions of women's roles. Chaucer's Griselda had to reconcile the competing demands of wifehood and motherhood, making her spiritual virtues signify in a secular context; Capgrave's Katherine struggles with precedents and expectations for maidenhood and womanhood, discovering that her secular virtues fit more comfortably in a spiritual context. In both cases, the conflict can only be mediated within and by ideas of womanhood.

The examples in this study show the interdependent evolution of concepts of gender and gendered language; I have suggested both that the experiences of women and ideas about femininity outstripped the available vocabulary and that the creation of new vocabulary enabled writers to experiment with new ways of thinking about womanhood. Such experimentation was all the more possible because the terms on which I have focused were collective as well as abstract; they allowed for the consideration of relationships between central and marginal characteristics or cases of femininity and between otherwise incompatible precedents or stereotypes. By positing broad categories, these terms invited explorations of how much might be encompassed and where the borders might be drawn. The process of evolution is never simple or unidirectional, of course; even as denotations are broadening in the fifteenth century, for example, there are two divergent strands of association (with ideal femininity and with questions of female power). Indeed, the ability to contain divergent meanings must have been part of what made these gendered terms so useful and widely adopted.

By looking at Middle English texts, we can see the heterogeneous origins of some of our most important gendered vocabulary and the variety of meanings such terms held from their earliest usages. Recent studies and theories have examined the important function of language in gender construction, but scholars have not attended as deeply to the history of the vocabulary—*womanhood, manhood, femininity, masculinity,* etc.—that allows us fundamentally to describe gender. Experimenting with representations of women outside of the conventional identities dependent on relationships to masculine authority, Middle English writers confront a variety of challenges—not the least of which is the problem of how to reconcile feminine virtue and authority. At the same time, the gendered language writers now have to describe women in new ways continues to evolve, accumulating different meanings but becoming progressively broader. The invention of womanhood is not the work of a single moment, a single author, or a single word but instead a lengthy and complex process furthered both by women whose lives incorporated expanding opportunities and challenging circumstances, like Margery Kempe and Queen Margaret, and by the writers, male as well as female, who sought fresh ways of representing women and their experiences.

NOTES

Introduction

1. Illis diebus ortus est rumor et ingens clamor in populo eo quod ubi hastiludia prose-
quebantur, quasi in quolibet loco dominarum cohors affuit, quasi comes interludii in diuerso
et mirabili apparatu uirili, ad numerum quandoque quasi .xl. quandoque .i. dominarum, de
speciosioribus et pulcrioribus, non melioribus tocius regni, in tunicis partitis scilicet una parte
/ de una secta, et altera de alia secta, cum capuciis breuibus et liripiis ad modum cordarum
circa capud aduolutis, et 3onis argento uel auro bene circumstipatis in extransuerso uentris sub
umbilico habentes cultellos quos daggerios wlgaliter dicunt, in powchiis desuper impositis. Et
sic procedebant in electis dextrariis uel aliis equis bene comptis de loco ad locum hastiludiorum.
Et tali modo expendebant et deuastabant bona sua, et corpora sua ludibriis et scurilosis lasciuiis
uexitabant, ut rumor populi personabat.

Et sic nec Deum uerebantur, nec uerecundam populi uocem erubescebant, laxato matrimonialis pudicie freno. . . . Sed Deus in hiis sicud in cunctis aliis affuit mirabili remedio, eorum
dissipando dissolucionem. Nam loca et tempora ad hec uana assignata, imbrium resolucione
tonitrui et fulguris coruscacione, et uariarum tempestatum mirabili uentilacione preocupauit.
(Henry Knighton, *Knighton's Chronicle, 1337–1396*, ed. and trans. G. H. Martin [Oxford: Clarendon Press; New York: Oxford University Press, 1995], 92–95).

2. My interest in gendered language thus separates this project from Catherine Cox's *Gender and Language in Chaucer* (Gainesville: University Press of Florida, 1997), which is focused on
gender and textuality or, in other words, on the more symbolic deployment of the feminine.

3. This argument is also supported by the term *womankind,* which—although first used
in the thirteenth century—also began to appear more widely in the fourteenth and fifteenth
centuries.

4. Sarah Salih, *Versions of Virginity in Late Medieval England* (Cambridge: D. S. Brewer,
2001); and Jennifer Summit, *Lost Property: The Woman Writer and English Literary History, 1380–
1589* (Chicago: University of Chicago Press, 2000). Other critics often explore broader topics or
themes related to gender, however; see, for example, Emma Lipton's treatment of sacramental
marriage in *Affections of the Mind: The Politics of Sacramental Marriage in Late Medieval English Literature* (Notre Dame, IN: University of Notre Dame Press, 2007); and Susan Phillips's
consideration of gossip in *Transforming Talk: The Problem with Gossip in Late Medieval England*

(University Park: Pennsylvania State University Press, 2007).

5. Davis, *Writing Masculinity in the Later Middle Ages* (Cambridge: Cambridge University Press, 2007); and Crocker, *Chaucer's Visions of Manhood* (New York: Palgrave Macmillan, 2007). See also Clare Lees, *Medieval Masculinities: Regarding Men in the Middle Ages* (Minneapolis: University of Minnesota Press, 2004); Derek G. Neal, *The Masculine Self in Late Medieval England* (Chicago: University of Chicago Press, 2008); and a number of edited collections on the topic, such as Peter G. Beidler, ed., *Masculinities in Chaucer: Approaches to Maleness in the* Canterbury Tales *and* Troilus and Criseyde (Rochester, NY: D. S. Brewer, 1998); Jeffrey Cohen and Bonnie Wheeler, eds., *Becoming Male in the Middle Ages* (New York: Garland, 1997); and Tison Pugh and Marcia Smith Marzec, eds., *Men and Masculinities in Chaucer's* Troilus and Criseyde (Rochester, NY: D. S. Brewer, 2008).

6. Crocker, *Chaucer's Visions of Manhood*, 9.

7. Although Seth Lerer's *Inventing English: A Portable History of the Language* (New York: Columbia University Press, 2007) appeared after I had titled this project, both titles reflect this sense of English as a language that is not simply evolving but also being created consciously through a variety of specific texts and circumstances.

8. Mary Erler, *Women, Reading, and Piety in Late Medieval England* (Cambridge: Cambridge University Press, 2002); Rebecca Krug, *Reading Families: Women's Literate Practice in Late Medieval England* (Ithaca, NY: Cornell University Press, 2002); Catherine Sanok, *Her Life Historical: Exemplarity and Female Saints' Lives in Late Medieval England* (Philadelphia: University of Pennsylvania Press, 2007); Nancy Bradley Warren, *Spiritual Economies: Female Monasticism in Later Medieval England* (Philadelphia: University of Pennsylvania Press, 2001) and *Women of God and Arms: Female Spirituality and Political Conflict, 1380–1600* (Philadelphia: University of Pennsylvania Press, 2005); and Claire Waters, *Angels and Earthly Creatures: Preaching, Performance, and Gender in the Later Middle Ages* (Philadelphia: University of Pennsylvania Press, 2004). Elizabeth Scala has recently critiqued "the institutional hegemony of historicism in medieval studies" as inherently patriarchal, but these scholars demonstrate that historicist approaches can still provide fresh and significant insights into gender in the Middle Ages (Scala, "The Gender of Historicism," in *The Post-Historical Middle Ages,* ed. Scala and Sylvia Federico [New York: Palgrave Macmillan, 2009], 194).

9. Theresa Coletti, *Mary Magdalene and the Drama of Saints: Theater, Gender, and Religion in Late Medieval England* (Philadelphia: University of Pennsylvania Press, 2004).

10. Susan Crane, *Gender and Romance in Chaucer's* Canterbury Tales (Princeton: Princeton University Press, 1994); Carolyn Dinshaw, *Chaucer's Sexual Poetics* (Madison: University of Wisconsin Press, 1989); Elaine Tuttle Hansen, *Chaucer and the Fictions of Gender* (Berkeley: University of California Press, 1992); and Jill Mann, *Feminizing Chaucer* (Cambridge: D. S. Brewer, 2002; originally published as *Geoffrey Chaucer*, 1991).

11. Especially significant in this regard are Mary Erler, *Women, Reading, and Piety;* D. H. Green, *Women Readers in the Middle Ages* (Cambridge: Cambridge University Press, 2008)*;* Krug, *Reading Families;* and Sanok, *Her Life Historical.*

12. Nicole Rice foregrounds the connections between religious and secular texts in *Lay Piety and Religious Discipline in Middle English Literature* (Cambridge: Cambridge University Press, 2008), but it also figures significantly in Sanok, *Her Life Historical;* Warren, *Spiritual Economies;* and Waters, *Angels and Earthly Creatures.*

13. Warren's work has been particularly important in this regard.

14. As David Burnley points out, there is a relationship between language and perception specifically associated with these three female roles: "The triplet *maiden, wife, widow,* which

is a frequent collocation in the works of Chaucer and Gower, became a collocational set from frequent repetition in discourse reflecting contemporary Christian perceptions of the role of women" (Burnley, "Lexis and Semantics," in *The Cambridge History of the English Language,* vol. II, ed. Norman Blake [New York: Cambridge University Press, 1992], 452).

15. The historical changes in fourteenth and fifteenth centuries affected not only gendered language but also the language and imagery needed to describe political power; see Lynn Staley, *Languages of Power in the Age of Richard II* (University Park: Pennsylvania State University Press, 2005); and Paul Strohm, *Politique: Languages of Statecraft between Chaucer and Shakespeare* (Notre Dame, IN: University of Notre Dame Press, 2005).

16. Judith Bennett, *Ale, Beer, and Brewsters in England: Women's Work in a Changing World* (New York: Oxford University Press, 1996), 6. For more general studies on late medieval English society, see P. J. P. Goldberg, *Medieval England: A Social History, 1250–1550* (London: Arnold, 2004); Maurice Keen, *English Society in the Later Middle Ages, 1348–1500* (New York: Penguin, 1990); and S. H. Rigby, *English Society in the Later Middle Ages: Class, Status, and Gender* (New York: St. Martin's Press, 1995).

17. The spread of the plague throughout England actually occurred from multiple fronts; for a detailed discussion, see Ole J. Benedictow, *The Black Death, 1346–1353: The Complete History* (Rochester, NY: Boydell Press, 2004), ch. 5. For a general overview, see Joseph P. Byrne, *The Black Death* (Westport, CT: Greenwood Press, 2004); and for a popular medical perspective, see John Kelly, *The Great Mortality: An Intimate History of the Black Death, the Most Devastating Plague of All Time* (New York: HarperCollins, 2005).

18. The critical studies on women's post-plague economic opportunities are Bennett and Goldberg. See Bennett's *Ale, Beer, and Brewsters;* and P. J. P. Goldberg, *Women, Work and Life Cycle in a Medieval Economy: Women in York and Yorkshire, c.1300–1520* (New York: Oxford University Press, 1992). Goldberg also examines the effect on marriage patterns, especially on pp. 272 and 336–37, and in *Women in England, c.1275–1525* (Manchester: Manchester University Press, 1995), 11.

19. Shannon McSheffrey has persuasively argued that Lollardy drew more men than women because "Lollards most virulently attacked precisely those aspects of late medieval Catholicism that . . . were both attractive to, and to a large extent created by, women," such as the cult of saints (*Gender and Heresy: Women and Men in Lollard Communities, 1420–1530* [Philadelphia: University of Pennsylvania Press, 1995], 138). The claim that heresy empowered women rests on the Lollard argument that any good person could be a priest; however, because the Lollards rejected transubstantiation, the priestly role did not have the same significance in their view that it had in Catholicism. Rather than valuing women more highly, the Lollard position on female priests devalued the role of priests. Furthermore, although there were Lollard female preachers, there is no definitive evidence that there were female priests. See Margaret Aston, *Lollards and Reformers: Images and Literacy in Late Medieval Religion* (London: Hambledon Press, 1984).

20. See, e.g., Caroline Barron, "The 'Golden Age' of Women in Medieval London," *Reading Medieval Studies* 15 (1989): 35–58; and Norman F. Cantor, *In the Wake of the Plague: The Black Death and the World It Made* (New York: The Free Press, 2001), 130. For a more nuanced study— focused on London—of women's access to wealth through marriage, see Barbara A. Hanawalt, *The Wealth of Wives: Women, Law, and Economy in Late Medieval London* (Oxford: Oxford University Press, 2007).

21. See, for instance, Judith Bennett, *Women in the Medieval English Countryside: Gender and Household in Brigstock before the Plague* (New York: Oxford University Press, 1987), 195–96.

22. Burnley goes on to note that "The same situation may, however, arise more slowly as the

product of cultural evolution, and in either case, if the deficit occurs in some highly structured area of the lexis, it is often referred to as a 'lexical gap'" ("Lexis and Semantics," 489).

23. Chaucer and Gower are also the first known writers in English to use *Femenie* (to name the land of the Amazons) and among the first to use *feminine*. Chaucer has the earliest recorded usage of *wifehood* and *wifely*, while Gower has the first of *sisterhood*. "Wommanhede," "femininite," "Femenie," "feminine," "wifhode," "wifli," and "susterhede," *Middle English Dictionary* (*Middle English Compendium*), <http://ets.umdl.umich.edu/m/med>. All subsequent references to the *MED* will be to this version unless otherwise noted.

24. Ardis Butterfield, *The Familiar Enemy: Chaucer, Language, and Nation in the Hundred Years War* (Oxford: Oxford University Press, 2009); Christopher Cannon, *The Making of Chaucer's English: A Study of Words* (Cambridge: Cambridge University Press, 1998); Ralph Hanna, "Chaucer and the Future of Language Study," *Studies in the Age of Chaucer* 24 (2002): 309–15; Simon Horobin, *The Language of the Chaucer Tradition* (Cambridge: D. S. Brewer, 2003); Wendy Scase, "Tolkien, Philology, and *The Reeve's Tale:* Towards the Cultural Move in Middle English Studies," *Studies in the Age of Chaucer* 24 (2002): 325–34; and Karla Taylor, "Language in Use," in *Chaucer: Contemporary Approaches,* ed. Susanna Fein and David Raybin (University Park: Pennsylvania State University Press, 2009). Tim William Machan undertakes a sociolinguistic study of Middle English more generally in *English in the Middle Ages* (Oxford: Oxford University Press, 2003). Both Hanna and Taylor advocate for attending to usage more carefully, which is what I attempt to do here. Butterfield argues persuasively for the necessity of considering Middle English's entanglements with French; these gendered terms, however, are interesting because many of them—including *womanhood*—appear to be characteristically English inventions.

25. Cannon, *Making of Chaucer's English,* especially pp. 55, 77, and 120.

26. Warren, *Women of God and Arms;* Coletti, *Mary Magdalene;* and Carolyn P. Collette, *Performing Polity: Women and Agency in the Anglo-French Tradition, 1385–1620* (Turnhout, Belgium: Brepols, 2006).

27. "Manhede," "moderhede," and "faderhod," *MED.*

Chapter One

1. For a more detailed consideration of feminism in late medieval literary studies, see Tara Williams, "Fragments and Foundations: Medieval Texts and the Future of Feminism," *Literature Compass* 4 (May 2007): 1003–16.

2. See, for example, Catherine Sanok's exploration of Chaucer and hagiographic exemplarity in *Her Life Historical: Exemplarity and Female Saints' Lives in Late Medieval England* (Philadelphia: University of Pennsylvania Press, 2007), chs. 2 and 6; and Claire Waters's consideration of Chaucer in relation to medieval preaching in *Angels and Earthly Creatures: Preaching, Performance, and Gender in the Later Middle Ages* (Philadelphia: University of Pennsylvania Press, 2004), chs. 2 and 7. Susan Phillips is interested in Chaucer's adaptation of gossip as a literary strategy as well as his representations of the concept in *Transforming Talk: The Problem with Gossip in Late Medieval England* (University Park: Pennsylvania State University Press, 2007), ch. 2.

3. In his latest book, *Chaucer, Ethics, and Gender* (Oxford: Oxford University Press, 2006), Alcuin Blamires suggests that "what is needed now is a period of consolidation, defining gender formulations in Chaucer's poetry with greater precision in relation to the various medieval discourses through and against which his formulations are positioned" (3). This chapter advances that aim by considering "gender formulations" through the lens of gendered language.

4. Paul Strohm, "Queens as Intercessors," *Hochon's Arrow: The Social Imagination of Fourteenth-Century Texts* (Princeton: Princeton University Press, 1992), 96.

5. Charles Muscatine, *Chaucer and the French Tradition: A Study in Style and Meaning* (Berkeley: University of California Press, 1957), 190. See also Robert M. Stein, "The Conquest of Femenye: Desire, Power, and Narrative in Chaucer's *Knight's Tale*," in *Desiring Discourse: The Literature of Love, Ovid through Chaucer,* ed. James J. Paxson and Cynthia A. Gravlee (Selinsgrove, PA: Susquehanna University Press, 1998); Winthrop Wetherbee, "Romance and Epic in Chaucer's *Knight's Tale*," *Exemplaria* 11.1 (1990): 303–28; and, for a recent reconsideration of this theme, Joshua R. Eyler and John P. Sexton, "Once More to the Grove: A Note on Symbolic Space in the *Knight's Tale*," *Chaucer Review* 40.4 (2006): 433–39.

6. Geoffrey Chaucer, *The Riverside Chaucer,* ed. Larry Benson (Boston: Houghton Mifflin, 1987). All future references will be parenthetical by line number.

7. The project of defining womanhood is an interesting corollary to an investigation of knighthood, which many critics have read as the purpose of the tale. See Laurel Amtower, "Mimetic Desire and the Misappropriation of the Ideal in the *Knight's Tale*," *Exemplaria* 8.1 (1996): 125–44; and Lee Patterson, *Chaucer and the Subject of History* (Madison: University of Wisconsin Press, 1991), ch. 3.

8. Ilse Kirk, "Images of Amazons: Marriage and Matriarchy," *Images of Women in Peace and War: Cross-Cultural and Historical Perspectives,* ed. Sharon Macdonald, Pat Holden, and Shirley Ardener (Basingstoke, UK: Macmillan Education in association with the Oxford University Women's Studies Committee, 1987), 30–31 (emphasis in the original).

9. Batya Weinbaum, *Islands of Women and Amazons: Representations and Realities* (Austin: University of Texas Press, 1999), 82.

10. "Femenie," *Middle English Dictionary* (*Middle English Compendium*), <http://ets.umdl.umich.edu/m/med>. All subsequent references to the *MED* will be to this version unless otherwise noted. Gower also uses this term.

11. The Knight does use the term "Amazones" once (880), but it seems to refer to the land or the people as a whole (syntactically equivalent to "Atthenes") rather than to the sisters specifically.

12. This contrasts sharply with the tale's epigraph from Statius's *Thebeid,* which describes the "Scithian folk," lacking any specific gender reference.

13. Elaine Tuttle Hansen, *Chaucer and the Fictions of Gender* (Berkeley: University of California Press, 1992), 217–18. For a discussion of how "Femenye" is subjugated by the duke and the Knight through discourse, see Mark A. Sherman, "The Politics of Discourse in Chaucer's *Knight's Tale*," *Exemplaria* 6.1 (1994): 87–114.

14. Abby Wettan Kleinbaum argues that "in the hands of Chaucer and Boccaccio . . . [the Amazons'] image was even further weakened: they were shorn of their warrior determination and prowess." She goes on to say that in the *Knight's Tale,* Hippolyta "is only incidentally an Amazon. It is her sister Emily who is a beauty and neither woman has formidable strength. Hippolyta is just the woman whom Theseus happened to marry, and she is hardly noticeable. Her Amazon past is far behind her, and she is a dutiful and obedient helpmeet" (*The War against the Amazons* [New York: New Press, 1983], 61).

15. Christine de Pizan, *The Book of the City of Ladies,* trans. Earl Jeffrey Richards (New York: Persea Books, 1998), 46.

16. Sir John Mandeville, *The Bodley Version of Mandeville's Travels,* ed. M. C. Seymour, EETS 253 (New York: Oxford University Press, 1963), 83–85. He does also describe it as the "Maydelond," reflecting the fact that women live and rule there without men (83).

17. This is a common feature of Amazon stories: "solitary images were passed on rather than

the image of a collective horde of women who could have conquered men or held their own as peers" (Weinbaum, *Islands of Women,* 11).

18. N. R. Havely, *Chaucer's Boccaccio: Sources for* Troilus *and the* Knight's *and* Franklin's Tales *(Translations from the* Filostrato, Teseida, *and* Filocolo*)* (Cambridge: D. S. Brewer, 1980), 106. "Dico, e brievemente, che l'autore a niuno altro fine queste cose scrisse, se non per mostrare onde Emilia fosse venuta ad Attene; e perciò che la materia, cioè li costumi delle predette donne amazone, è alquanto pellegrina alle più genti, e perciò piu piacevole, la volle alquanto più distesamente porre che per avventura non bi sognava" (Giovanni Boccaccio, *Teseida Delle Nozze di Emilia,* ed. Alberto Limentani, in *Tutte le opere di Giovanni Boccaccio,* ed. Vittorio Branca, vol. II [Milan: Mondadori, 1964], 255–56 n6 on I.6).

19. Fowler, "Chaucer's Hard Cases," in *Medieval Crime and Social Control,* ed. Barbara A. Hanawalt and David Wallace (Minneapolis: University of Minnesota Press, 1999). Fowler is interested in some of the same textual gaps in the Amazons' portrayals that I discuss, but she considers them in the context of political philosophy.

20. Hansen, *Fictions of Gender,* 223. For a discussion of Emelye's role in allegorical terms, see William F. Woods, "'My Sweete Foo': Emelye's Role in the *Knight's Tale,*" *Studies in Philology* 88.3 (1991): 276–306.

21. This does not discount the possibility that the tale is more interested in the relationship between these two suitors than in their love for Emelye; see John M. Bowers, "Three Readings of the *Knight's Tale:* Sir John Clanvowe, Geoffrey Chaucer, and James I of Scotland," *Journal of Medieval and Early Modern Studies* 34.2 (Spring 2004): 279–307.

22. See line 1452. In Chaucer, there are two suitors, but in Boccaccio there are three.

23. Mandeville explains that the women have "lemanys to whom they may gon to whan they lestyn to haue bodily lykynge of hem" and that sons are killed or given to their fathers while daughters are raised as Amazons (*Mandeville's Travels,* 85).

24. Elizabeth Robertson considers the different meanings of virginity in pagan and Christian cultures, suggesting that "Emelye wishes to make such a choice of [Christian contemplative] religious life, but that choice has no practical legitimacy in the world of Athens" ("Marriage, Mutual Consent, and the Affirmation of the Female Subject in the *Knight's Tale,* the *Wife of Bath's Tale,* and the *Franklin's Tale,*" in *Drama, Narrative, and Poetry in the Canterbury Tales,* ed. Wendy Harding [Toulouse, France: Presses Universitaires du Mirail, 2003], 183).

25. Elizabeth B. Edwards reads Emelye and Palamon's marriage as accomplishing the work of mourning in the *Knight's Tale;* their marriage also supplants the mourning and Emelye's participation in the more recognizable rituals of mourning is obscured ("Chaucer's *Knight's Tale* and the Work of Mourning," *Exemplaria* 20.4 [Winter 2008]: 361–84).

26. Havely, *Chaucer's Boccaccio,* 148. "Emilia, la quale ancor piangea" (*Teseida,* XII.4).

27. Similar descriptions of Emelye wounding the men reappear later in her absence, part of the prelude to violence between Palamon and Arcite (1567–68).

28. Susan Crane, *Gender and Romance in Chaucer's* Canterbury Tales (Princeton: Princeton University Press, 1994), 81.

29. Havely, *Chaucer's Boccaccio,* 112–13. "Piacere," "sospesi e attenti," and "l'angelica bellezza" (*Teseida,* III.13 and 15).

30. Havely, *Chaucer's Boccaccio,* 113. " . . . e in man dui / istral dorati tene" and "Sì, e' m'ha piagato in guisa tal che di dolor m'acora" (*Teseida,* III.16 and 17).

31. Havely, *Chaucer's Boccaccio,* 113. "Io non so che nel cor quel fiero arcieri / m'ha saettato, che mi to' la vita" and "sì m'è fissa nel cor la sua figura, / e sì mi sta nell'animo piacente" (*Teseida,* III.20 and 21).

32. Havely, *Chaucer's Boccaccio,* 143. "A Dio, Emilia!" (*Teseida,* X.113).

33. Havely, *Chaucer's Boccaccio,* 143. "del mio cor disio, / . . . da me sola amata, / . . . cuor del corpo mio" (*Teseida,* X.104).

34. David Wallace, *Chaucerian Polity: Absolutist Lineages and Associational Forms in England and Italy* (Stanford, CA: Stanford University Press, 1997), 119.

35. Wallace, *Chaucerian Polity,* 106.

36. Quoted in Wallace, *Chaucerian Polity,* 106–7.

> Ipolita era a maraviglia bella;
> e di valore accesa nel coraggio;
> ella sembiava matutina stella
> o fresca rosa del mese di maggio;
> giovine assai e ancora pulcella,
> ricca d'avere, e di real legnaggio,
> savia e ben costumata, e per natura
> nell'armi ardita e fiera oltre misura. (*Teseida,* I.125)

37. The Knight expends more lines commenting on the length of his tale than covering the events he will not describe, ten total (875–76, 885–92) versus eight total (877–83).

38. Crane, *Gender and Romance,* 80.

39. The problem is complicated, of course, by the fact that most of Chaucer's female fictional characters are upper class and others (like Alison in the *Miller's Tale* or the Wife of Bath) are presented in contexts or genres where feminine virtue is less directly invoked.

40. Hansen points out that "the Theban widows, who are represented as proper, submissive, defeated, and dependent . . . thus serve as a crucial part of the narrative strategy that defines Woman." She also notes the parallel between the widows' scene and the intercession scene that I discuss here, though not in the same detail or to the same end (*Fictions of Gender,* 218 and 220).

41. Wallace argues that the *Knight's Tale* presents a version of polity in which the autocratic ruler does not allow himself to be counseled by a consort (*Chaucerian Polity,* 107 and Chapter 4: "No Felaweshipe": Thesian Polity, *passim*). While this is true to a large extent, it is also true that several of the decisions in the story—including the decisions to battle Creon and to spare Arcite and Palamon—are influenced by the interventions of women. Similarly, Fowler contends that the tale implicitly critiques the model of conquest by showing how it endangers the social bonds—especially marriage—that would be formed through consent ("Chaucer's Hard Cases," 132–33). Jill Mann, on the other hand, argues that Chaucer presents the quality of pity—exhibited by Theseus as well as by the women—as an heroic virtue appropriate to both men and women (*Feminizing Chaucer* [Rochester, NY: D. S. Brewer, 2002], 134–42).

42. The intercession scene is frequently discussed by critics. See, for example, Wallace's discussion of Hippolyta's silence and Thesian polity (*Chaucerian Polity,* 104–5 and 119) and Crane's discussion of the scene (*Gender and Romance,* 22).

43. Havely, *Chaucer's Boccaccio,* 121. "Non piaccia a Dio che sia / ciò che dimandi, ben che meritato / l'aggiate per la vostra gran follia" (*Teseida,* V.91).

44. Wallace, *Chaucerian Polity,* 116. Invoking postcolonial theory, Keiko Hamaguchi reads this scene as an instance of mimicry and also suggests that such mimicry indicates that the Amazons' assimilation is incomplete ("Domesticating Amazons in *The Knight's Tale,*" *Studies in the Age of Chaucer* 26 [2004]: 342–46).

45. David Herlihy, *Medieval Households* (Cambridge: Harvard University Press, 1985), 121.

46. Strohm, "Queens as Intercessors," *Hochon's Arrow,* 95 (emphasis in original).

47. See, for example, Deborah S. Ellis, "Domestic Treachery in the *Clerk's Tale,*" in *Ambiguous Realities: Women in the Middle Ages and Renaissance,* ed. Carole Levin and Jeanie Watson (Detroit, MI: Wayne State University Press, 1987); Michaela Paasche Grudin, "Chaucer's *Clerk's Tale* as Political Paradox," *Studies in the Age of Chaucer* 11 (1989): 63–92; and Charlotte C. Morse, "The Exemplary Griselda," *Studies in the Age of Chaucer* 7 (1985): 51–86.

48. See, for example, Elaine Tuttle Hansen, *Chaucer and the Fictions of Gender,* ch. 7; Mann, *Feminizing Chaucer,* 114–25; and Carolynn Van Dyke, "The Clerk's and the Franklin's Subjected Subjects," *Studies in the Age of Chaucer* 17 (1995): 45–68.

49. Carolyn Dinshaw, *Chaucer's Sexual Poetics* (Madison: University of Wisconsin Press, 1989), 133.

50. David Wallace has argued that Chaucer exploited the contradictions in Petrarch's version of the story in order to critique the tyranny Chaucer associated with Petrarch; here I read some of the same aspects of the tale as allowing Chaucer's examination of the category of womanhood (*Chaucerian Polity,* ch. 10). Mark Miller also examines these extremes through a philosophical lens (*Philosophical Chaucer: Love, Sex, and Agency in the* Canterbury Tales [Cambridge: Cambridge University Press, 2004], ch. 6).

51. Hansen and, to a lesser extent, Dinshaw and Wallace see Walter as primarily a reactionary, while those who focus on the marquis and his possible motivations, such as Kathryn L. Lynch, "Despoiling Griselda: Chaucer's Walter and the Problem of Knowledge in *The Clerk's Tale,*" *Studies in the Age of Chaucer* 10 (1988): 41–70; Andrew Sprung, "'If It Youre Wille Be': Coercion and Compliance in Chaucer's *Clerk's Tale,*" *Exemplaria* 7.2 (1995): 345–69; and Thomas A. Van, "Walter at the Stake: A Reading of Chaucer's *Clerk's Tale,*" *Chaucer Review* 22.3 (1988): 214–24, tend to flatten out the complexities in Chaucer's portrayal of Griselda. Many of these readings have been influenced by Robert O. Payne's early interpretation of the tale as a "sentimental experiment" in which Chaucer seems to be "working toward a . . . moral statement which will be immediately apprehensible emotionally and nearly incomprehensible by any rational or intellectual faculty" (*The Key of Remembrance: A Study of Chaucer's Poetics* [New Haven: Yale University Press, 1963], 164). In such a reading, there is no need to seek intelligibility in either Walter or Griselda. By contrast, I will argue that Walter plays a vital role in the construction of Griselda's exemplary womanhood; if Griselda is a mediating figure, then Walter necessarily becomes slightly more rational or at least intelligible.

52. Barbara Newman, *From Virile Woman to WomanChrist: Studies in Medieval Religion and Literature* (Philadelphia: University of Pennsylvania Press, 1997), 93.

53. Newman, *Virile Woman,* 84.

54. Newman, *Virile Woman,* 97.

55. Karen A. Winstead, ed. and trans., *Chaste Passions: Medieval English Virgin Martyr Legends* (Ithaca, NY: Cornell University Press, 2000), 4, and her *Virgin Martyrs: Legends of Sainthood in Late Medieval England* (Ithaca, NY: Cornell University Press, 1997), 14.

56. Winstead, *Virgin Martyrs,* especially pp. 83 and 85.

57. "Cujus condicionis es?" in the *Legenda Aurea* and "Cuius conditionis es?" in *In Festo Sancte Cecilie Virginis et Martyris,* both in Sherry L. Reames, "The Second Nun's Prologue and Tale," in *Sources and Analogues of the* Canterbury Tales, ed. Robert M. Correale and Mary Hamel, vol. 1 (Rochester, NY: D. S. Brewer, 2002), 515 and 523. Chaucer amends both the question and the answer to include "woman."

58. For example, Morse observes that Chaucer was "the first to set her [Griselda] against the antifeminist type of woman, perhaps in the translation itself, certainly in the responses he invents to the tale at its end" ("The Exemplary Griselda," 55).

59. Susan Crane observes that "Griselda's imagined performance of marriage articulates

social understandings of wifehood" and that "Chaucer's version sharply interrogates women's place in marriage. Chaucer took that cue from the French versions of the tale, which are particularly concerned to model conduct for women" (*The Performance of Self: Ritual, Clothing, and Identity during the Hundred Years War* [Philadelphia: University of Pennsylvania Press, 2002], 29). I agree, but would add that Chaucer also takes his cue from contemporary hagiography, from which the tale draws.

60. See the preface of *Le Livre Griseldis* in J. Burke Severs, *The Literary Relationships of Chaucer's* Clerkes Tale (New Haven: Yale University Press, 1942; Hamden, CT: Archon Books, 1972), 255; or the same preface in Thomas J. Farrell and Amy W. Goodwin, "The Clerk's Tale," in *Sources and Analogues of the* Canterbury Tales, vol. 1, ed. Robert M. Correale and Mary Hamel (Rochester, NY: D. S. Brewer, 2002), 141.

61. For the history of the tale, see Judith Bronfman, *Chaucer's* Clerk's Tale: *The Griselda Story Received, Rewritten, Illustrated* (New York: Garland Publishing, 1994); Farrell and Goodwin, "The Clerk's Tale"; Dudley David Griffith, *The Origin of the Griselda Story* (Seattle: University of Washington Press, 1931); and Severs, *Literary Relationships.*

62. Petrarch, *Epistola,* in Severs, *Literary Relationships,* 288; for an alternate version, see Farrell and Goodwin, "The Clerk's Tale," 129 and 26n. In the *Decameron,* the story is addressed to women but has a mixed audience and is on the topic of governance. De Mézières follows Petrarch in offering Griselda as a female and human model. *Le Ménagier* presents the story in a conduct book for a young wife, but the writer asks his wife not to take it as an example for herself (Severs, *Literary Relationships,* 22). The play is written "in order that people can use [it] as a mirror, and in order that those ladies who are visited by adversity can bear it with patience" (Brownlee, 876; see full reference below). Note that all of the French versions rely (directly or indirectly) on Petrarch rather than Boccaccio. For a discussion of the differences between some of these versions, see Kevin Brownlee, "Commentary and the Rhetoric of Exemplarity: Griseldis in Petrarch, Philippe de Mézières, and the *Estoire,*" *South Atlantic Quarterly* 91.4 (Fall 1992): 865–90.

63. This is particularly interesting because one possible antecedent of the tale, Cupid and Psyche folktales, could involve human protagonists of either sex/gender. However, this proposed precursor (Griffith's) is no longer widely accepted; William E. Bettridge and Francis L. Utley suggest "The Patience of a Princess," which does depend on a female protagonist, instead ("New Light on the Origin of the Griselda Story," *Texas Studies in Literature and Language* 13.2 [Summer 1971]: 153–208).

64. Bronfman, *Chaucer's* Clerk's Tale, 17.

65. See, for example, Mann: "the most obvious testimony to Griselda's strength is the tale's ending. . . . For it is not Griselda who gives way under the pressures of her trial, but Walter. . . . [T]he story does not simply illustrate the virtue of patience; it shows that patience *conquers*" (*Feminizing Chaucer,* 119; emphasis in original).

66. Dante Alighieri, *La Vita Nuova,* ed. and trans. Dino S. Cervigni and Edward Vasta (Notre Dame, IN: University of Notre Dame Press, 1995), 46–47: "In quello punto dico veracemente che lo spirito de la vita, lo quale dimora ne la secretissima camera de lo cuore, cominciò a tremare sì fortemente, che apparia ne li menimi polsi orribilmente; e tremando disse queste parole: 'Ecce deus fortior me, qui veniens dominabitur michi.'"

67. Francesco Petrarch, *Petrarch's Lyric Poems: The* Rime sparse *and Other Lyrics,* ed. and trans. Robert M. Durling (Cambridge: Harvard University Press, 1976), 38–39: " . . . i' fui preso, et non me ne guardai, / ché i be' vostr' occhi, Donna, mi legaro."

68. Havely, *Chaucer's Boccaccio,* 113.

69. See especially Morse, "Exemplary Griselda."

70. Giovanni Boccaccio, *The Decameron,* trans. G. H. McWilliam (New York: Penguin,

1972), 785. " . . . [E] parendogli bella assai, estimò che con costei dovesse potere aver vita assai consolata" (Giovanni Boccaccio, *Il Decamerone,* ed. Angelo Ottolini [Milan: Ulrico Hoepli, (1948)], 665). The *Decameron* is now being more seriously considered as an influence, if not a direct source, for Chaucer's *Clerk's Tale.* See Helen Cooper, "The Frame," in *Sources and Analogues of the* Canterbury Tales, ed. Robert M. Correale and Mary Hamel, vol. 1 (Rochester, NY: D. S. Brewer, 2002), 1–22.

71. McWilliam, *Decameron,* 785. "Io ho trovata una giovane secondo il cuor mio, assai presso di qui" (Ottolini, *Il Decamerone,* 666).

72. Petrarch, *Epistola,* in Farrell and Goodwin, "The Clerk's Tale," 114–15: "virilis senilisque animus virgineo latebat in pectore" and "virtutem eximiam supra sexum supraque etatem."

73. Walter's first sight of Griselda seemed to validate her "wommanhede," since it was the basis of his choice. However, he insists on excessive submission from her as a condition, which suggests that her behavior may be in doubt.

74. For instance, Dinshaw grounds her reading in the trope of *translatio,* titling the relevant chapter "Griselda Translated" (*Sexual Poetics,* ch. 5). Wallace also makes important use of the trope in his reading of the tale (*Chaucerian Polity,* ch. 10), as does Emma Campbell in "Sexual Poetics and the Politics of Translation in the Tale of Griselda," *Comparative Literature* 55.3 (Summer 2003): 191–216. Crane is an exception; in *The Performance of Self,* she investigates Griselda's clothing as a material expression of identity and its role in the ritual of marriage (29–37). Andrea Denny-Brown also considers the material aesthetics of the Clerk through this scene and the tale's general preoccupation with clothing in "*Povre* Griselda and the All-Consuming *Archewyves,*" *Studies in the Age of Chaucer* 28 (2006): 77–115.

75. Christiane Klapisch-Zuber, "The Griselda Complex: Dowry and Marriage Gifts in the Quattrocento," in her *Women, Family and Ritual in Renaissance Italy,* trans. Lydia Cochrane (Chicago: University of Chicago Press, 1985), 245. Consciously or not, Chaucer's emphasis on clothing and dowry echoes some of the issues in medieval Italian wedding customs, which are appropriate to the story's Italian setting and provenance.

76. Klapisch-Zuber, "Griselda Complex," 219 and 224.

77. Crane goes on to argue that this reclothing "leaves visible a residual self that remains unincorporated" (*Performance of Self,* 33).

78. Klapisch-Zuber, "Griselda Complex," 218–24.

79. Klapisch-Zuber, "Griselda Complex," 224.

80. The undoing of the translation does not work; as she walks home, her father tries to cover her with her old coat "But on hire body myghte he it nat brynge, / For rude was the clooth, and moore of age / By dayes fele than at hire mariage" (915–17).

81. Hansen, *Fictions of Gender,* ch. 7; Lynch, "Despoiling Griselda," *passim;* and Sprung, "Coercion and Compliance," *passim.*

82. "Lust" is reiterated as the term for Walter's self-interested desires; Griselda is grieved to leave her husband but does so, "abidynge evere his lust and his plesance" (757) and when she returns to prepare for the new wife, Walter directs Griselda to array the chambers "in ordinaunce / After my lust" (961–62).

83. The son was two years old when he was taken away (617) and is seven when he returns (780).

84. Dyan Elliott, *Spiritual Marriage: Sexual Abstinence in Medieval Wedlock* (Princeton: Princeton University Press, 1993), 220.

85. Morse sees the people not as a crucial part of Griselda's testing, as I argue, but as themselves subject to a similar test: "The testing of Griselda proves to be also the testing of the people,

which shows the people less strong in their faith to Walter than Griselda is" (Morse, "Griselda Reads Philippa de Coucy," *Speaking Images: Essays in Honor of V. A. Kolve,* ed. R. F. Yeager and Charlotte C. Morse [Asheville, NC: Pegasus, 2001], 352–53). Lynn Staley also argues that Chaucer places particular emphasis on the role of the people in his version of the tale ("Chaucer and the Postures of Sanctity," in *The Powers of the Holy: Religion, Politics, and Gender in Late Medieval Culture,* ed. David Aers and Lynn Staley [University Park: Pennsylvania State University Press, 1996]).

86. Alcuin Blamires, the only other critic to have paid substantial attention to this phrase, reads the meaning of "wommanheede" in this scene differently:

> Womanhood remains unexplained here and seems at first sight peculiar. In conventional Middle English, a test of someone's *manhode* would signify a test of his courage. There was no broadly agreed complementary significance for *wommanheede.* However, from a question asked at 698–9, about what more a stern husband could do "to preeve hir wyfhod and hir stedefastnesse", it seems that in *The Clerk's Tale* Griselda's "wifehood" and her "steadfastness" are symbiotic: one might conjecture that her womanhood and her steadfastness are similarly meant to be symbiotic in this tale. That is to say, in "assaying" (investigating the quality of) Griselda's womanhood, Walter is investigating the degree of *stabilitas* in her, he is determining the level of unchangeability in her because this was the supreme criterion for assessing women in a culture obsessed with feminine "weakness." (Blamires, *The Case for Women in Medieval Culture* [Oxford: Oxford University Press, 1998], 167–68)

The question of Griselda's womanhood is broader, however; it is not only about her *stabilitas,* but also about her ability to combine different models of femininity while maintaining appropriate feminine virtues to an exemplary degree.

87. "Let those who believed the opposite know me painstaking and testing, not impious. I have proved my wife rather than condemning her [Sciant qui contrarium crediderunt me curiosum atque experientem esse, non [impium]; probasse coniugem, non dampnasse]" and "I did what I did only to test and try you [moy avoir fait ce que j'ay fait pour toy approuver et essaier tant seulement]" (Farrell and Goodwin, "The Clerk's Tale," 128–29 and 164–65). See also Severs, *Literary Relationships,* 286 and 287.

88. Laura Ashe argues that Griselda actually transforms Walter through her reading of her husband as good and his love for her as powerful: "Ultimately, Griselda's reading of Walter is powerful enough to become his salvation. . . . [S]he reads him as beneficent and just: and so he is saved from himself" ("Reading Like a Clerk in the *Clerk's Tale,*" *Modern Language Review* 101.4 (October 2006), 942–43).

89. These multiple endings of the tale have invited multiple interpretations. Many critics have discussed the envoy in response to Muscatine's view of it as a comic strategy (*French Tradition,* 197). For the connections to (and distinctions from) Petrarch that Chaucer constructs, see Wallace, *Chaucerian Polity,* 293; and Campbell, "Politics of Translation," especially pp. 211–14. The multiple endings have also produced divergent interpretations of the tale's treatment of women (and specifically Griselda). Dinshaw suggests that the Clerk "addresses himself, finally, not to another man—he does not pass his text on from clerk to clerk—but to women" (*Sexual Poetics,* 152), while Hansen argues that "the Clerk's humorous ending deflates rather than protects Griselda's virtue. . . . [He] devalues and dismisses the feminine powers of silence without liberating women from the complementary myths of absence or excess" (*Fictions of Gender,* 205). For an overview of the polyvalent morality of the tale, see J. Allan Mitchell, "Chaucer's *Clerk's Tale* and

the Question of Ethical Monstrosity," *Studies in Philology* 102.1 (Winter 2005): 1–26.

90. We might read "secte" as "sex" or as a more exclusive subset of that sex. The latter reading is best supported by the text and by the later address to "archewyves," another Chaucerian coinage that seems to describe a particular group of women (1195).

Chapter Two

1. My reading participates in the rehabilitation of Gower that characterizes much recent work. Such rehabilitation has tended to praise his style and technique; here, I connect Gower's skillful manipulation of language to his development of womanhood. The classic treatment of Gower's style is C. S. Lewis, "Gower," in *Gower's* Confessio Amantis: *A Critical Anthology*, ed. Peter Nicholson (Cambridge: D. S. Brewer, 1991). For more recent studies, see Tim William Machan, "Medieval Multilingualism and Gower's Literary Practice," *Studies in Philology* 103.1 (Winter 2006): 1–25; and Jeremy J. Smith, "John Gower and London English," in *A Companion to Gower*, ed. Sian Echard (Rochester, NY: D. S. Brewer, 2004). On Gower's technical skills, see, R. F. Yeager, *John Gower's Poetic: The Search for a New Arion* (Cambridge: D. S. Brewer, 1990), especially ch. 1.

2. For a comparison of morality and ethics in Chaucer and Gower, see J. Allan Mitchell, *Ethics and Exemplary Narrative in Chaucer and Gower*, Chaucer Studies XXXIII (Rochester, NY: D. S. Brewer, 2004).

3. Judith Butler, *Gender Trouble* (New York: Routledge, 1990; rpt. 1999), xv.

4. Butler, *Gender Trouble*, xxiii.

5. Choosing to write the *Confessio Amantis* in English, Gower manipulates the vernacular to achieve both precision and ambiguity. Götz Schmitz contends that Gower's "main concern is with the ambiguity of words and with the danger inherent in the fact that words can be used to both good and evil ends" ("Rhetoric and Fiction: Gower's Comments on Eloquence and Courtly Poetry," in *Gower's* Confessio Amantis: *A Critical Anthology*, ed. Peter Nicholson [Cambridge: D. S. Brewer, 1991], 128). However, in constructing an idea of womanhood that is performative rather than innate, Gower exploits ambiguity in language to reflect ambiguity in nature. On this issue, ambiguity is productive as well as dangerous.

6. In the *Confessio, wommanhiede* variously signifies virtue, an association with maidenhead, a contrast to manhood (manly courage contrasted with womanly dread, for example), a tempting quality of sinfulness, and, most broadly, possession of a feminine nature. An important pattern of usage develops, however, as Gower employs womanhood as a focus for his ideas about the multiple manifestations of human nature.

7. Watt contends that the *Confessio Amantis* "deliberately encourages its audience to take risks in interpretation, to experiment with meaning, and to offer individualist readings. Indeed, insofar as it does not always give satisfactory answers to the moral questions it raises, and at times obfuscates rather than clarifies, it can be seen to pursue a negative critique of ethical poetry" (*Amoral Gower: Language, Sex, and Politics* [Minneapolis: University of Minnesota Press, 2003], xii). In a larger sense, this is certainly true, but in the specific case of his treatment of female victims, I believe that Gower takes an important—and unusual—approach toward their suffering as an index of immoral behavior. My interpretation comes closer to Elizabeth Allen's view that Gower's "moral poetry does not simply strive to legislate or 'correcte' human behavior, but seeks to engage his readers in the experience of conscious and deliberate moral choice" ("Chaucer Answers Gower: Constance and the Trouble with Reading," *ELH* 64.3 (Fall 1997), 627–28).

8. There are eleven appearances in the frame versus thirteen in the tales. A large number of the tales discussed in this chapter, however, come from Book V of the *Confessio;* the adaptation of financial sins to love relationships creates interesting disjunctions that hint at the "value" of womanhood and its significance to both romance and the concept of manhood.

9. John Gower, *The English Works of John Gower,* ed. G. C. Macaulay, EETS Extra Series 81 and 82, 2 vols. (1900; London: Oxford University Press, 1957), I, 1501–3. All future references will be parenthetical.

10. Geoffrey Chaucer, *Wife of Bath's Tale,* in *The Riverside Chaucer,* ed. Larry Benson (Boston: Houghton Mifflin, 1987), 1026–29.

11. *Wife of Bath's Tale,* 1043–44.

12. This may be because Chaucer envisions the word as having a definition beyond the Wife of Bath's own ideas or experiences or because he does not want her to be one of the speakers who contribute to defining the term. Her ideas about what it means to be a woman certainly contrast with the characteristics and virtues Chaucer associates with *womanhood* elsewhere in the *Canterbury Tales.*

13. *Wife of Bath's Tale,* 998, 1000, and 1005. The word "wyf" is being used in the general sense of "goodwife," meaning "woman" rather than designating marital status.

14. Interestingly, the knight himself is originally described as "wifles"—this descriptor occurs even before his name is given (I, 1411).

15. Genius applies it to the Sirens, for example (I, 495).

16. Although it is difficult to ascertain how a pun like this would have worked in a primarily oral literary culture, it certainly exists in the written text and might have been conveyed through pronunciation or enjoyed by readers or the writer himself.

17. In Chaucer's version of the story, it is at this moment that the loathly lady appeals to the queen to enforce the knight's promise and announces her wish that he marry her. In the *Confessio Amantis,* Florent leaves the court to return to the woman, already knowing that he must marry her.

18. *Wife of Bath's Tale,* 999–1000.

19. Gower also compares her to a Moor (I, 1686), another method of dehumanizing her and emphasizing that she inhabits the border between human and creature.

20. In his edition of the *Confessio Amantis,* Russell Peck glosses this line as a pun. At this point, however, the "best woman" reading seems less viable—there has been no evidence either of the knight's feelings or of the woman's nature that would justify that interpretation as anything more than a distinctly secondary alternative. The pun is stronger in its earlier appearance (which Peck does not note). John Gower, *Confessio Amantis,* ed. Russell A. Peck (Toronto, Canada: University of Toronto Press, 1980), 67n.

21. Susan Crane, *Gender and Romance in Chaucer's* Canterbury Tales (Princeton: Princeton University Press, 1994), 88.

22. In making the jump to the fifth book, I pass over ten intervening occurrences of *womanhood* (including some that will be explored later in this chapter), but I trace a trajectory of usage that has its own coherence.

23. Here I disagree with Karma Lochrie, who claims that Genius "trivializes rape and the woman's suffering in particular" (*Covert Operations: The Medieval Uses of Secrecy* [Philadelphia: University of Pennsylvania Press, 1999], 218). His representation of suffering is crucial to the text, although Amans fails to read and react to it.

24. The shape of the narrative as the Tale of Tereus rather than the Tale of Philomena reveals Gower's focus on male behavior rather than female characters in this and other stories. By con-

trast, it is The Legend of Philomela in Chaucer's *Legend of Good Women.*

25. Chaucer's version of the story in the *Legend of Good Women* includes quite similar animal imagery in describing the rape—an event that was perhaps more comfortably and more effectively described by way of a predator–prey simile—but only at this moment rather than throughout the story as in Gower's version.

26. Carolyn Dinshaw argues that "making the rape seem unusual, the result of a single, even inhuman, desire" protects the patriarchal system from analysis and "keeps us from seeing other victimizations of women" ("Quarrels, Rivals, and Rape: Gower and Chaucer," in *A Wyf Ther Was: Essays in Honour of Paule Mertens-Fonck,* ed. Juliette Dor [Liège, Belgium: University of Liège Press, 1992], 119 and 118). While I agree that Tereus's beastliness protects manhood from critique, I believe it also heightens readers' sense of the women's victimization.

27. As in the *Manciple's Tale,* there is a pun here on bird/bride.

28. Dinshaw, "Quarrels, Rivals, and Rape," 119 and 120.

29. The Legend of Philomela, in the *Legend of Good Women,* in *Riverside Chaucer,* 2328–29.

30. The revenge also points up Tereus's unkind and unnatural behavior by forcing him to do something against "kinde" (V, 5905).

31. Pity was also the crucial characteristic by which Hippolyta validated her womanhood in the *Knight's Tale,* as discussed in the previous chapter.

32. Interestingly, Genius's description of the vice includes not only rape (deluding and having sex with a woman as if she were a shepherdess, "For other mennes good is swete" [V, 6118]) but also concealing the rape from one's unsuspecting wife. The husband or father is often figured as the victim of this crime; rape takes something away from the man who "owns" the woman by diminishing her "value." Gower's perspective on rape as robbery is unusually woman-centered, first in identifying the raped woman as a true victim of the crime, but, more remarkably, by considering the wife of the rapist rather than the husband or father of the raped woman.

33. See also Nicola F. McDonald, "Avarice and the Economics of the Erotic in Gower," in *Treasure in the Medieval West,* ed. Elizabeth M. Tyler (York, UK: York Medieval Press, 2000), especially pp. 152–53. This article contains an interesting discussion of Book V to which much of my thinking is indebted, although McDonald focuses on the disjunction Book V creates between "Christian and erotic codes of conduct" (152).

34. Genius clearly declares Cornix as the winner, saying, "The faire Maide him hath ascaped, / Wherof for evere he was bejaped" (V, 6215–16).

35. Ovid, *Ovid's Metamorphoses Books I–VIII,* ed. and trans. Frank Justus Miller (Cambridge: Harvard University Press, 1994), 93–95.

36. Genius then tells the tale of the Chastity of Valentinian, which is a more conventional treatment of male chastity. Although it is difficult to be certain, Gower's use of "maidehiede" rather than "maidenhiede" or "maydenhede," which consistently appear elsewhere in the text, may represent a lexical distinction between masculine and feminine states of virginity.

37. Watt considers some of these same tales in her examination of "transgressive genders" such as effeminacy and female masculinity, but she does not go so far as to suggest that these identities show the basic categories of manhood and womanhood as performative rather than innate, nor does she consider their overlap with beastliness (*Amoral Gower,* ch. 6).

38. Achilles does so by practicing "Honour, servise, and reverence" and adopting a "sobre and goodli contenance" (V, 3001 and 3005).

39. For *hert,* see earlier in this same tale (IV, 1978 and 1991) as well as I, 371 and 2299; V, 7401; and VIII, 2160. For *herte,* see Prologue 111, 155, and 184 and examples throughout the remainder of the text.

40. Lochrie, *Covert Operations,* 217. Rosemary Woolf also suggests that Gower has created more "sexual indeterminacy" than exists in his sources, but still believes that "he shows Achilles's masculinity asserting itself in both amatory and martial instincts" ("Moral Chaucer and Kindly Gower," in *J. R. R. Tolkien, Scholar and Storyteller,* ed. Mary Salu and Robert T. Farrell [Ithaca, NY: Cornell University Press, 1979], 224).

41. Here Gower, like Butler, challenges the idea that "certain kinds of gendered expressions were found to be false or derivative, and others, true and original" and seeks "to open up the field of possibility for gender" (*Gender Trouble,* vii–viii).

42. Lochrie believes that even after they have had sex, "Achilles is still identified with his cross-dressed womanliness" and "there is no suggestion by Genius that the sexual act changes Achilles's identity" (*Covert Operations,* 216–17). Although Achilles still demonstrates womanhood by day, I would argue that this passage suggests a change in his identity at some level—and perhaps recalls the similar proposed conditions of the loathly lady's transformation in the Tale of Florent.

43. Deidamia's son by Achilles is mentioned but is born outside the bounds of this tale. In addition to the interesting ambiguities it raises, this incident may reassure the reader that Achilles's womanliness is a social performance and that his sexual performance, by contrast, is indisputably masculine. He may be acting like a woman but, as this scene demonstrates, he is not becoming one.

44. If we read this tale as one in which Achilles's manly nature cannot be suppressed, then that nature is tied to war—he chooses the battle gear and this choice leads to his involvement in the Trojan War. Given Genius's negative comments on war and violence elsewhere in the *Confessio Amantis,* this vision of manly nature appears problematic.

45. Elizabeth Allen suggests that Gower manipulates the representation of incest in Book VIII to encourage readers to construct their own moral code rather than simply identifying with and imitating moral characters or behavior; here, same-sex desire may work similarly. Allen, "Newfangled Readers in Gower's 'Apollonius of Tyre,'" *Studies in the Age of Chaucer* 29 (2007): 419–64.

46. Diane Watt argues that Iphis is an example of how Genius "does not exclude women from masculinity, but rather allows the masculine woman to exist as a positive exemplary model and distinct gender category" ("Gender and Sexuality in *Confessio Amantis,*" in *A Companion to Gower,* ed. Sian Echard [Rochester, NY: D. S. Brewer, 2004], 207). In this case, however, that category is collapsed back into traditional ones.

47. Lochrie, *Covert Operations,* 215.

48. Amans refers to the unnamed lady in this way in III, 541.

49. For a fuller discussion of Gower's critique of romance through his use of exempla, see Larry Scanlon, *Narrative, Authority, and Power: The Medieval Exemplum and the Chaucerian Tradition* (Cambridge: Cambridge University Press, 1996), 267–82.

50. Winthrop Wetherbee, "John Gower," in *The Cambridge History of Medieval English Literature,* ed. David Wallace (New York: Cambridge University Press, 2002), 602.

51. Kurt Olsson argues that Amans, responding to the tales of Iphis and Araxarathen and Pygmalion, "refashions his lady accordingly, fitting her variously to the types of gentle woman presented in these two tales" ("Aspects of *Gentilesse* in John Gower's *Confessio Amantis,* Books III–V," in *John Gower: Recent Readings,* ed. R. F. Yeager [Kalamazoo, MI: Medieval Institute Publications, 1989], 260). In my reading, Amans responds to these stories by recognizing the possibility of blaming the lady for her behavior; he does not change his view of her, only the way in which he is willing to express it.

52. Crane, *Gender and Romance,* 65.

53. Jenny Rebecca Rytting, for example, identifies the *Confessio* as a marriage manual but does not explore the implications of this for Amans or his lady. Rytting, "In Search of the Perfect Spouse: John Gower's *Confessio Amantis* as a Marriage Manual," *Dalhousie Review* 82.1 (2002): 113–26.

54. J. A. Burrow suggests that Gower's depiction of Amans is stereotypical and "delicately shaded and touched with naturalistic detail, but not individualized." Burrow, "The Portrayal of Amans in *Confessio Amantis,*" in *Gower's* Confessio Amantis: *Responses and Reassessments,* ed. A. J. Minnis (Cambridge: D. S. Brewer, 1983), 10. I argue that both characters exceed conventions.

55. G. C. Macaulay, "The *Confessio Amantis,*" in *Gower's* Confessio Amantis: *A Critical Anthology,* ed. Peter Nicholson (Cambridge: D. S. Brewer, 1991), 13.

56. The Tale of Rosiphelee is frequently mentioned in the criticism for its beauty of expression but, to my knowledge, no one has remarked on its unusual nature as a female example. For discussions of this tale, see: J. A. W. Bennett, "Gower's 'Honeste Love,'" in *Gower's* Confessio Amantis: *A Critical Anthology*; María Bullón-Fernández, *Fathers and Daughters in Gower's* Confessio Amantis: *Authority, Family, State, and Writing* (Cambridge: D. S. Brewer, 2000), ch. 5; and Arno Esch, "John Gower's Narrative Art," trans. Linda Barney Burke, in *Gower's* Confessio Amantis: *A Critical Anthology,* especially pp. 83–90.

57. James T. Bratcher suggests that Gower revises his sources to include a pun on *brydel* that "deepens the pathos of the lady's fate, the price of her having tarried too long before seeking marriage." If this is the case, then it resembles Gower's use of the *beste* pun in the Tale of Florent. Bratcher, "The Function of the Jeweled Bridle in Gower's 'Tale of Rosiphelee,'" *Chaucer Review* 40.1 (2005), 110.

58. Conor McCarthy argues that Gower "offers marriage primarily as a remedy for lust, as something that can make love *honeste,* rather than as something good in itself"; in my view, these tales suggest that marriage is a virtuous responsibility ("Love and Marriage in the *Confessio Amantis,*" *Neophilologus* 84 [2000], 495).

59. For a different view of this tale, focusing on Iphis as a Christ-like figure, see David G. Allen, "God's Faithfulness and the Lover's Despair: The Theological Framework of the Iphis and Araxarathen Story," in *John Gower: Recent Readings,* ed. R. F. Yeager (Kalamazoo, MI: Medieval Institute Publications, 1989).

60. One exception is McDonald, who notes in regard to a later passage, "Amans's deep-seated desire to hold the lady fast, to wield her according to his own will, is one of the more unpleasant, even disturbing aspects of the lover's character. It is also one aspect of his myopic pursuit that is explicitly condemned by Genius as sinful, avaricious behavior" ("Economics of the Erotic," 151).

61. McDonald, "Economics of the Erotic," 145.

62. These accusations differ significantly from Amans's earlier suggestion that the lady might be guilty of homicide, which was couched in terms of potentiality rather than actuality and hewed closer to romantic rhetoric. His accusations in Book V are direct and disturbing, distant from romantic convention.

63. In the tale of King, Wine, Woman and Truth in Book VII, the argument that woman is strongest runs thus: "The king and the vinour also / Of wommen comen bothe tuo; / And . . . manhede / Thurgh strengthe unto the wommanhede / Of love, wher he wole or non, / Obeie schal" (VII, 1875–80). Here again, the ambiguity of the language suggests both that men are subject to women in love and that a man's manhood becomes like womanhood in the process.

64. Genius will explain in Book VIII that men who do not obey the laws of marriage are like

beasts (VIII, 159–63). Although most of the book will be devoted to the specific issue of incest, this comment is part of the more general introduction to the book.

65. In the *Romance of the Rose,* Reason urges the lover to rule his heart rather than letting it rule him, but Reason is overthrown. Venus's intervention contains the same message but is more successful: reason is restored and both the text and Amans are lifted out of romance.

66. Peck points out in the introduction to his abridged edition of the text that the question recalls Boethius's *Consolation* and that this is the proper answer ("Introduction," *Confessio Amantis,* xiii).

67. Alceste was also a paragon of womanhood in Chaucer's *Legend of Good Women.*

Chapter Three

1. I have come across the term in Hoccleve's "Balade to the Duke of York" (l. 30) and in the final envoy to Lady Westmoreland in the Durham ms. of the *Series.* It also occurs in the *Kingis Quair* (l. 814).

2. See Robert Meyer-Lee, *Poets and Power from Chaucer to Wyatt* (Cambridge: Cambridge University Press, 2007); Nigel Mortimer, *John Lydgate's Fall of Princes: Narrative Tragedy in Its Literary and Political Contexts* (Oxford: Oxford University Press, 2005); Maura Nolan, *John Lydgate and the Making of Public Culture* (Cambridge: Cambridge University Press, 2005); Lisa H. Cooper and Andrea Denny-Brown, eds., *Lydgate Matters: Poetry and Material Culture in the Fifteenth Century* (New York: Palgrave Macmillan, 2008); and Larry Scanlon and James Simpson, eds., *John Lydgate: Poetry, Culture, and Lancastrian England* (Notre Dame, IN: University of Notre Dame Press, 2006).

3. There has been some work on Lydgatian gender portrayals, including Julia Boffey, "Lydgate, Henryson, and the Literary Testament," *Modern Language Quarterly* 53.1 (1992): 41–56; and Anna Torti, "John Lydgate's *Temple of Glas:* 'Atwixen Two so Hang I in Balaunce,'" in *Intellectuals and Writers in Fourteenth-Century Europe,* ed. Piero Boitani and Torti (Cambridge: D. S. Brewer, 1986).

4. This epithet is the knight's description of the lady (John Lydgate, *Temple of Glas,* ed. J. Schick, EETS Extra Series 60 [1891; London: Oxford University Press, 1924], l. 766). All subsequent references to this text will be parenthetical by line number.

5. Scanlon and Simpson's "Introduction" provides an excellent overview of the critical history (*John Lydgate,* ed. Scanlon and Simpson, 1–11).

6. Derek Pearsall, *John Lydgate* (Charlottesville: University Press of Virginia, 1970), 238.

7. Two exceptions are J. Allan Mitchell, "Queen Katherine and the Secret of Lydgate's *Temple of Glas,*" *Medium Aevum* 77.1 (2008), 64–66; and Larry Scanlon, "Lydgate's Poetics: Laureation and Domesticity in the *Temple of Glass,*" in *John Lydgate,* ed. Scanlon and Simpson, 87. Mitchell argues that the poem alludes to the clandestine marriage of Henry V's widow, Katherine of Valois, and so the unnamed restriction is her delicate political position; Scanlon points out that the constraint is unspecified.

8. C. S. Lewis, *The Allegory of Love: A Study in Medieval Tradition* (New York: Oxford University Press, 1958), 241.

9. Pearsall, *John Lydgate,* 107.

10. The modern adoption of this assumption dates from Pearsall; previous critics were not as uniform in reading the lady as married. Alain Renoir, for example, believed that the lady was complaining against the conventions of courtly love, which would not allow her to demonstrate

her feelings. Arguing that Lydgate held a kind of protohumanist attitude toward women, Renoir claims that in the *Temple of Glas,* Lydgate "shows us the woman suffering . . . because she is an individual human being who bruises herself against a convention which expects her to pretend aloofness before her lover, while every emotional impulse in her urges immediate submission to the flesh" (Renoir, *The Poetry of John Lydgate* [London: Routledge, 1967], 93).

11. Bryan Crockett, "Venus Unveiled: Lydgate's *Temple of Glas* and the Religion of Love," in *New Readings of Late Medieval Love Poems,* ed. David Chamberlain (Lanham, MD: University Press of America, 1993), 79.

12. Pearsall, *John Lydgate,* 107. This group of stanzas is present only in one group of manuscripts. See *Temple of Glas,* p. 14. Pearsall believes this version to be an earlier one but, in his "Introduction," Schick identifies this interpolation as a corruption rather than an original section of the poem (xlix) because these stanzas seem inconsistent with the lady's voice (1). These variations suggest that this passage, which describes the subject of the lady's complaint, is a problematic section for scribes/readers.

13. Pearsall, *John Lydgate,* 108. Even if we accept this as an earlier version, it does not directly mention a husband; however, the hint of marriage is stronger.

14. There are seven instances of *womanhed* (266, 288, 766, 931, 975, 1117, and 1386) and four of *womanhede* (746, 875, 1065, and 1207).

15. The dreamer describes the lady's

> . . . gret semelines,
> Hir womanhed, hir port, & hir fairnes,
> It was a meruaile, hou euer þat nature
> Coude in hir werkis make a creature
> So aungellike, so goodli on to se,
> So femynyn or passing of beaute. (265–70)

The dreamer describes the knight similarly:

> Me þou3t he was, to speke of semelynes,
> Of shappe, of fourme, & also of stature,
> The most passing þat euir 3it nature
> Made in hir werkis, & like to ben a man;
> And þerwith-al, as I reherse can,
> Of face and chere þe most gracious. (556–61)

The resemblances are apparent, but the first passage is only a small part of the representation of the lady while the second passage is the majority of the knight's.

16. This may be a sign of Gower's influence, although the *Confessio* does not present Venus as an overt model of womanhood.

17. See also Crockett, "Venus Unveiled," 77–81, for an ironic reading of the religious symbolism.

18. Theresa Tinkle, *Medieval Venuses and Cupids: Sexuality, Hermeneutics, and English Poetry* (Stanford, CA: Stanford University Press, 1996), 49. Tinkle argues that poets, like mythographers, work with these various possible meanings. She specifically discusses Lydgate's deployment of Venus in the *Temple of Glas* and elsewhere:

> [T]he *Temple of Glass* initially refers to Venus, quite sketchily, as the *anadyomene:* "she sate fleting in the se" (53). The lovers in the poem describe her as a planet, a star of comforting light. The narrator eventually depicts Venus as a unified carnal and

spiritual force, a planetary goddess holding tightly to the fiery chain of eternal love. None of these descriptions gains a mythographic commentary, and each complicates the deity's import. The Venuses of *Troybook, Reason and Sensuality,* and *Temple of Glass* exemplify once again the range of refigurations and reinterpretations possible even for one writer. . . . Lydgate continually describes and deciphers the deities anew, combining and revising traditions to suit his immediate purposes. (132)

19. Nor is a husband or marriage directly invoked when the two lovers are joined at the close of the vision.

20. See note 10.

21. As Torti points out, by focusing on the lady's perspective, Lydgate creates a new vision of love, "not to be looked at only from the point of view of the man imploring a woman made of ice, but from the woman's point of view as well" (Torti, "Atwixen Two," 229).

22. The knight begins his complaint, "Allas! what þing mai þis be, / That nou am bound, þat whilom was so fre, / And went at laarge, at myn eleccioun: / Nou am I cauȝt vnder subieccioun" (567–70).

23. This is my primary point of disagreement with Scanlon, who argues that Lydgate empowers the lady by prioritizing her desire ("Lydgate's Poetics," 86 and 91).

24. It is uncertain here whether womanhood would constrain any woman's response in this situation or whether it is the lady's class position (as a "quene of womanhed") or even her earlier exchange with Venus that binds the lady specifically.

25. In fact, part of the lady's response to the knight is physical: her "femyny[ni]te" is revealed in her face (1045). The knight's plea literally brings forth her femininity. This suggests that the lady may be responding according to social convention—ideals of femininity—rather than personal desire.

26. Accepting the adultery reading of the poem, Tinkle interprets this final scene differently: "Venus's chain binding these lovers together contrasts with another chain binding the woman, an image of her present unavailability. The two chains picture an opposition between natural desire and legal duty, between natural and human law. Venus takes the side of natural desire, and nature here accords with eternal love" (*Medieval Venuses,* 154).

27. This interpretation brings us back to the Petrarchan take on Griselda. We might view women as traditional/archetypal subjects and hence read their situations as that of any subject— i.e., constrained by subjecthood rather than specifically womanhood. However, because the poem is so focused on the lady and on womanhood, and on the differences between the constraints experienced by the lady and those experienced by the knight, I read the *Temple of Glas* as focusing on the more specific issue of womanhood.

28. A. C. Spearing, *Medieval Dream Poetry* (Cambridge: Cambridge University Press, 1976), 173; Pearsall, *John Lydgate,* 104.

29. Robert Henryson, *Poems of Robert Henryson,* ed. Denton Fox (New York: Oxford University Press, 1981), 1. 608. All future references to this text will be parenthetical by line number.

30. As Douglas Gray reminds us, Henryson had diverse influences, including Lydgate, James I, and the alliterative tradition. Douglas Gray, *Robert Henryson* (Leiden, The Netherlands: E. J. Brill, 1979), 18. On the nature of Chaucer's influence on Henryson, see also Fox's "Introduction" in Henryson, *Poems,* xxiii.

31. John Lydgate, *Lydgate's Troy Book, Part II: Book III and Part III: Books IV–V,* ed. Henry Bergen, EETS Extra Series 103 and 106 (1908 and 1910; Millwood, NY: Kraus Reprint Company, 1973) III, 4438, 4639, 4646, and 4836; and IV, 2132 and 2148.

32. *Troilus and Criseyde* in *Riverside Chaucer,* ed. Larry D. Benson (Boston: Houghton Mif-

flin, 1987), I, 283; III, 1302 and 1740; IV, 1462; and V, 473.

33. Fox notes that Henryson's use of the word may recall Chaucer's use of the word to describe Criseyde, but he does not explore the significance of this connection (Henryson, *Poems,* p. 346 n88). C. David Benson notes another usage by Henryson that expands on rather than critiques Chaucer's meaning: the term "parliament" (Benson, "Critic and Poet: What Lydgate and Henryson Did to Chaucer's *Troilus and Criseyde,*" in *Writing After Chaucer: Essential Readings in Chaucer and the Fifteenth Century,* ed. Daniel J. Pinti [New York: Garland, 1998], 236).

34. For a view that connects the feminine to the spiritual rather than the corporeal, see Sarah M. Dunnigan, "Feminizing the Text, Feminizing the Reader?: The Mirror of 'Feminitie' in the *Testament of Cresseid,*" *Studies in Scottish Literature* 33–34 (2004): 107–23.

35. Previous critics have argued that Henryson is commenting on or critiquing Chaucer, but that Henryson is exposing Chaucer's portrayal of Criseyde as unsympathetic is a new claim. See, for example, Fox's "Introduction" in Henryson, *Poems,* lxxxiii; John MacQueen, "The Literature of Fifteenth-Century Scotland," in *Scottish Society in the Fifteenth Century,* ed. Jennifer M. Brown (New York: St. Martin's Press, 1977), 206; and MacQueen, "Poetry—James I to Henryson," in *The History of Scottish Literature, Volume 1: Beginnings to 1660 (Medieval and Renaissance),* ed. R. D. S. Jack (Aberdeen, UK: Aberdeen University Press, 1988), 66.

36. Derek Pearsall provides a typical formulation: Henryson is "determined that Chaucer's heroine should be brought to the bar of judgment. He plucks her out of the kindly oblivion in which Chaucer had left her, makes a spiteful insinuation about her subsequent career, loads her with infamy, punishes her, and then, as if under challenge to prove that humanity is never irredeemable, redeems her" (Pearsall, "'Quha Wait Gif All That Chauceir Wrait Was Trew?': Henryson's *Testament of Cresseid,*" in *New Perspectives on Middle English Texts: A Festschrift for R. A. Waldron,* ed. Susan Powell and Jeremy J. Smith [Cambridge: D. S. Brewer, 2000], 173). Felicity Riddy argues that "Henryson's version of the harlot's ruin is not simply antifeminist but is used to shore up one kind of femininity against another: the 'worthie women' of the final stanza against the 'giglot'" ("'Abject Odious': Feminine and Masculine in Henryson's *Testament of Cresseid,*" in *The Long Fifteenth Century,* ed. Helen Cooper, Sally Mapstone, and Joerg O. Fichte [Oxford: Clarendon, 1997], 242). Lee Patterson sees Cresseid as "sluttish" ("Christian and Pagan in *The Testament of Cresseid,*" *Philological Quarterly* 52 [1973]: 698) while R. James Goldstein describes Henryson as "misogynistic" ("Writing in Scotland, 1058–1560," in *The Cambridge History of Medieval English Literature,* ed. David Wallace [New York: Cambridge University Press, 2002], 241). At best, Henryson's narrator is echoing Chaucer's. After various comments on this subject (see pp. 163, 169–70, and 174, for example), Gray concludes his study of the poem by stating that "*Pite,* that great expression of love, is continually present—in the comments of the narrator, in the kindness shown to her by the human characters in the story . . . [L]ove and human affection assert themselves" (*Robert Henryson,* 207–8). Fox argues that Henryson "understood and imitated Chaucer's narrator" in his vacillation from condemnation to sympathy and that Henryson's narrator is "impassioned by sympathy for the wronged Cresseid" ("Introduction" in Henryson, *Poems,* xciii and 346 n89–91).

37. Summit, *"Troilus and Criseyde,"* in *The Yale Companion to Chaucer,* ed. Seth Lerer (New Haven: Yale University Press, 2006), 214.

38. See, for example, MacQueen "Poetry—James I to Henryson," 70; Patterson, "Christian and Pagan," especially pp. 698, 700, and 704; and Edwin D. Craun, "Blaspheming Her 'Awin God': Cresseid's 'Lamentatioun' in Henryson's *Testament,*" *Studies in Philology* 82.1 (1985), especially p. 27.

39. Elizabeth Allen, *False Fables and Exemplary Truth in Later Middle English Literature*

(New York: Palgrave Macmillan, 2005), 134, 158, and 143.

40. Benson argues that "Lydgate approached Chaucer's story of *Troilus and Criseyde* as a scholarly commentator ready to annotate, reinforce, and provide his readers with the historical context to Chaucer's work; Henryson's response is to exploit in his own original way Chaucer's innovative literary devices, including the characterization of Criseyde. It is as if each were attempting to rectify a different absence in *Troilus*" ("Critic and Poet," 228). I agree with the broad outline of Benson's argument, but whereas Benson sees Henryson as straightforwardly giving Cresseid's side of the story, I see him using the depiction of Cresseid to critique Chaucer. Benson argues, "Henryson's Cresseid not only transcends Lydgate's antifeminist cliché but also becomes in some ways more interesting and certainly braver than Chaucer's heroine" ("Critic and Poet," 239).

41. At one point, Troilus even comments on the difficulty of interpreting Criseyde's beautiful face: "Though ther be mercy writen in youre cheere, / God woot, the text ful hard is, soth, to fynde!" (III, 1356–57).

42. III, 4436–38 and 4441–43.

43. It is the second, non-Chaucerian account of "the fatall destenie / Of fair Cresseid, that endit wretchitlie," which the narrator picks up after Chaucer's "quair," that prompts the narrator to ponder the veracity of Chaucer's version (62–63).

44. Pearsall claims this lament is "famously queasy" and the narrator's "professed sympathy is deeply suspect" ("Quha Wait Gif," 174). Gray suggests that in this passage Henryson is "echoing Chaucer's words on Criseyde (V, 1093–99)," which were referred to above (*Robert Henryson*, 173). Rather than echoing Chaucer's words, however, Henryson is illustrating where and how they fell short.

45. Gray, *Robert Henryson*, 170. Henryson connected the epithet with Chaucer's version of Criseyde when he named "fair Creissid and worthie Troylus" (42) as the subjects of Chaucer's "quair" (40).

46. Chaucer, Gower, and Lydgate also used this specific phrase, so it has been connected to the idea of womanhood from its inception. See, for example, Chaucer's "Womanly Noblesse" (28); Gower's *Confessio Amantis* (V, 6182); and Lydgate's *Life of Our Lady* (I, 182; and V, 383) and *Temple of Glas* (1207).

47. Riddy, "Abject Odious," 246. It is not entirely clear whether Cresseid exchanged her femininity for filth or whether she changed it with filth, but the context favors the latter interpretation.

48. This phrasing recalls the more positive translation of Griselda in the *Clerk's Tale*.

49. This sets up a situation parallel to that of Chaucer's narrator, who hid behind his sources to excuse his inability to explain what happened to Criseyde more fully. Because her blasphemy is the immediate cause of her punishment, it is true that if she hadn't blasphemed then she might not have been punished by the gods. But Henryson's narrator has encouraged readers to see Criseyde's treatment as so unfair that she can hardly help crying out against it.

50. Boffey claims that "The projection of her disfigured self as a 'mirror' to warn others of the physical decay that awaits them is also here perhaps not entirely altruistic; Cresseid seems partly to seek consolation in anticipating the fragility of others' beauty" ("Literary Testament," 55).

51. See Patterson, "Christian and Pagan," for example.

52. See Fox, "Introduction," in Henryson, *Poems,* xciii; and Patterson, "Christian and Pagan," 705. The form does vary slightly (in the antistrophe, for example), but this is the dominant stanza type.

53. The text ends just after Anelida concludes her complaint and it may be that Chaucer has written himself into a situation from which it is difficult to imagine what the next step would be. What might a woman like Anelida do after making this complaint, having rejected the traditional alternatives of pleading with her lover or telling her story to others?

54. Lesley Johnson argues that Cresseid's "leprosy, which literally produces the conditions of old age, gives Cresseid the privileged position of 'advanced time' from which, detached from, yet still inside the worldly frame, she may undercut the heroic sweep of epic history with more mundane insights into worldly mutability" ("Whatever Happened to Criseyde? Henryson's *Testament of Cresseid*," in *Courtly Literature: Culture and Context,* ed. Keith Busby and Erik Kooper (Amsterdam: Benjamins, 1990), 314. We might read Cresseid's death as a kind of ultimate extension of this position.

55. The epitaph is usually read as significant primarily because it effectively shuts the door on Cresseid's life and story. See, for example, Boffey, "Literary Testament," 53 ("[Troilus's epitaph] stresses at once Cresseid's physical degeneration and the possibility that her story, given visible form in the written letters, may have some kind of salutary afterlife in the minds of its readers."); Craun, "Blaspheming," 39 ("[The epitaph] records not her infidelity in love but the bare facts of her physical degradation and death."); and Johnson, "Whatever Happened," 317 ("Cresseid's epitaph . . . provides no further clue to what should be made of Cresseid's history other than restating her story in its most abbreviated form").

56. *Womanhood* is also used by other Scottish writers of the same period; for instance, it appears in the *Kingis Quair* (814), *Hary's Wallace* (V, 691), and several of Dunbar's works (*The Twa Mariit Wemen and the Wedo,* 77 and 315; "[In Prays of Woman]," 11; and "[To a Ladye.] Quhone He List to Feyne," 9 and 39).

57. *The Tragedy of Troilus and Cressida* (V.ii.152).

Chapter Four

1. Mary C. Erler, *Women, Reading, and Piety in Late Medieval England* (Cambridge: Cambridge University Press, 2002); Rebecca Krug, *Reading Families: Women's Literate Practice in Late Medieval England* (Ithaca, NY: Cornell University Press, 2002); Catherine Sanok, *Her Life Historical: Exemplarity and Female Saints' Lives in Late Medieval England* (Philadelphia: University of Pennsylvania Press, 2007); and Claire M. Waters, *Angels and Earthly Creatures: Preaching, Performance, and Gender in the Later Middle Ages* (Philadelphia: University of Pennsylvania Press, 2004).

2. Nicholas Watson, "'Yf Women Be Double Naturelly': Remaking 'Woman' in Julian of Norwich's *Revelation of Love*," *Exemplaria* 8.1 (Spring 1996): 8.

3. Theresa Coletti, *Mary Magdalene and the Drama of Saints: Theater, Gender, and Religion in Late Medieval England* (Philadelphia: University of Pennsylvania Press, 2004); and Nancy Bradley Warren, *Spiritual Economies: Female Monasticism in Later Medieval England* (Philadelphia: University of Pennsylvania Press, 2001), and *Women of God and Arms: Female Spirituality and Political Conflict, 1380–1600* (Philadelphia: University of Pennsylvania Press, 2005).

4. Jennifer Summit, *Lost Property: The Woman Writer and English Literary History, 1380–1589* (Chicago: University of Chicago Press, 2000).

5. Caroline Walker Bynum, *Jesus as Mother: Studies in the Spirituality of the High Middle Ages* (Berkeley: University of California Press, 1984), 131.

6. Nicholas Watson makes a similar point, though more broadly, in "The Middle English

Mystics," in *The Cambridge History of Medieval English Literature,* ed. David Wallace (New York: Cambridge University Press, 2002), 539–40. Denise Baker cautions against seeing the *Shewings* as too tightly related to other mystical texts, while Diane Watt positions Julian within an explicitly female visionary community. See Baker, "Julian of Norwich and the Varieties of Middle English Mystical Discourse," and Watt, "Saint Julian of the Apocalypse," both in *A Companion to Julian of Norwich,* ed. Liz Herbert McAvoy (Cambridge: D. S. Brewer, 2008).

7. Nicholas Watson and Jacqueline Jenkins, "Introduction," in *The Writings of Julian of Norwich,* ed. Watson and Jenkins (University Park: Pennsylvania State University Press, 2006), 3. Watson also argues elsewhere that the text "functions on a number of levels as a sophisticated response to and critique of the misogynistic tradition which viewed women as a sign of doubleness" ("Remaking Woman," 15).

8. No fewer than three essays in the new *Companion to Julian of Norwich,* edited by Liz McAvoy (Cambridge: D. S. Brewer, 2008), examine this poeticity: Vincent Gillespie, "'[S]he Do the Police in Different Voices': Pastiche, Ventriloquism, and Parody in Julian of Norwich"; Ena Jenkins, "Julian's *Revelation of Love:* A Web of Metaphor"; and McAvoy, "'For We Be Doubel of God's Making': Writing, Gender and the Body in Julian of Norwich."

9. This language also found its way into the Church as an institution; Jeremy Catto notes, "In the new occasional offices [in the fifteenth century] of the Five Wounds, the Crown of Thorns (*Corona Domini*), or the Compassion of the Virgin, meditations on the Passion of Christ were given liturgical expression, drawing on the same fund of religious feeling and sometimes on the same language as the *Revelations* of Julian of Norwich" ("Religious Change under Henry V," in *Henry V: The Practice of Kingship,* ed. G. L. Harriss [Oxford: Oxford University Press, 1985], 109).

10. On theology, see, for example, David Aers, *Salvation and Sin: Augustine, Langland, and Fourteenth-Century Theology* (Notre Dame, IN: Notre Dame University Press, 2009), ch. 5; Denise Nowakowski Baker, *Julian of Norwich's* Showings*: From Vision to Book* (Princeton: Princeton University Press, 1994); and Grace Jantzen, *Julian of Norwich: Mystic and Theologian* (New York: Paulist Press, 2000). On short versus long, see, for example, Felicity Riddy, "Julian of Norwich and Self-Textualization," in *Editing Women,* ed. Ann Hutchison (Toronto, Canada: University of Toronto Press, 1998); Nicholas Watson, "The Composition of Julian of Norwich's *Revelation of Love,*" *Speculum* 68.3 (1993): 637–84, and "Censorship and Cultural Change in Late Medieval England: Vernacular Theology, the Oxford Translation Debate, and Arundel's Constitutions of 1409," *Speculum* 70.4 (1995): 822–64; and Barry Windeatt, "Julian of Norwich and Her Audience," *Review of English Studies* 28 (1977): 1–17.

11. Baker, *From Vision to Book,* 164. There have been studies that treated the language of the text in order to draw conclusions about how and where different manuscripts originated (see, e.g., Riddy "Self-Textualization"), but Julian's methods of expression and articulation are more recently coming to the forefront in work by critics such as Watson and Jenkins in *The Writings of Julian of Norwich* and Jennifer Bryan in *Looking Inward: Devotional Reading and the Private Self in Late Medieval England* (Philadelphia: University of Pennsylvania Press, 2008), ch. 4. In their edition of *A Book of Showings,* Edmund Colledge and James Walsh do provide a brief appendix listing rhetorical figures employed by Julian (Julian of Norwich, *A Book of Showings to the Anchoress Julian of Norwich,* ed. Colledge and Walsh, 2 vols., Studies and Texts 35 [Toronto, Canada: Pontifical Institute of Medieval Studies, 1978], 735–48). Robert Stone's *Middle English Prose Style: Margery Kempe and Julian of Norwich* (The Hague: Mouton, 1970) compares the styles of Julian and Margery, but is dated in its attitude toward the latter.

12. Julian's ideas have also been privileged over her language in popular reception (literary as well as religious); for considerations of this largely postmedieval history, see Sarah Salih and

Denise N. Baker, eds., *Julian of Norwich's Legacy: Medieval Mysticism and Post-Medieval Reception* (New York: Palgrave Macmillan, 2009).

13. These and all future parenthetical references are to the Watson and Jenkins edition.

14. R. N. Swanson comments on this problem: "The 'mystical' writers, such as Richard Rolle, Walter Hilton, and Julian of Norwich, grappled with the problem of expressing a tradition of Latin spirituality in English, and had to stretch the language considerably (although in less mystical treatises the writers worked largely within the extant vocabulary)" (Swanson, *Church and Society in Late Medieval England* [Oxford: Basil Blackwell, 1989], 263).

15. McAvoy, "For We Be Doubel of God's Making," 180.

16. For a discussion of the possible social and/or collaborative nature of the text, see Riddy, "Self-Textualization" and "'Publication' Before Print: The Case of Julian of Norwich," in *The Uses of Script and Print, 1300–1700*, ed. Julia Crick and Alexandra Walsham (Cambridge: Cambridge University Press, 2004).

17. "Fulhede," *Middle English Dictionary* (*Middle English Compendium*), <http://ets.umdl. umich.edu/m/med>. All subsequent references to the *MED* will be to this version unless otherwise noted.

18. By contrast, Margery Kempe uses only a few *-hed(e)* words, and those seem to be established terms rather than of her own coining. Generally speaking, the language of Margery's *Book* is less inventive and varied than Julian's. Margery uses *Godheed* and *manhood* most often; *childhod* several times; and *maydenhed, wedewhode,* and *presthoode* twice each. As an interesting aside, none of the terms appears prior to the seventeenth chapter, the one that precedes the chapter in which Margery describes her visit with Julian. The terms do not appear in clusters, as they do in the *Shewings,* but *Godheed* often appears with references to the *manhood* or *childhod* of Christ. Most of Margery's *-hed(e)* words are religious by denotation or connotation.

19. See Watson and Jenkins, "Introduction," 36.

20. The Sloane manuscript was the basis for two modern critical editions of the long text: Julian of Norwich, *The Shewings of Julian of Norwich,* ed. Georgia Crampton, TEAMS Middle English Texts Series (Kalamazoo, MI: Medieval Institute Publications, 1993); and *Julian of Norwich: A Revelation of Love,* ed. Marion Glasscoe (1976; Exeter, UK: University of Exeter, 1989). In the newest edition, Watson and Jenkins combine features from multiple manuscripts but argue convincingly for the linguistic accuracy of Sloane: "There is thus much to be said for following many of Sloane's word choices, which tend to be more consistent than Paris's, are generally northeastern in character, and are often supported by Additional, sometimes by Westminster, and sometimes by irregular forms in Paris. . . . In matters of diction, the analysis clearly favors S's readings over those of P" ("Introduction," 37). Colledge and Walsh's earlier critical edition, however, used the Paris manuscript. The linguistic patterns I note here are also present in Paris, although somewhat less pronounced. Colledge and Walsh even note that "throughout, Julian shows marked preference for abstract nouns in '-head'" (*A Book of Showings,* 309n). The primary difference between the two versions is that in the Paris manuscript some of the *-head* words have the *-ness* suffix instead (particularly the more unusual and isolated words, such as "irkehede" and "bolnehed"); this difference may be dialectical or a modernization imposed by the Paris scribe. The patterns I note here apply generally to both manuscripts.

21. See, for example, "plentuoushede" (147) versus "plentous" (149) or "irkehede" (123) versus "irkenes" (175). Some of this may be attributable to scribes, but the substantial number of appearances of *-hed(e)* forms at the moments I note later and the appearances of other forms at other moments suggest that the choice of forms has significance beyond being a purely personal or regional pattern of usage.

22. There are a number of common terms with the *-hede* ending, including *fatherhood, man-*

hood, widowhood, and *maidenhood,* but it is less common to create adjectives or abstract nouns by pinning the *-hede* suffix onto a word rather than, for example, *-ness.*

23. See "-head [suffix]," and "-ness [suffix]," *Oxford English Dictionary Online,* <http://dictionary.oed.com>.

24. Bynum, *Jesus as Mother,* especially pp. 110–69.

25. In what seems to be an earlier usage, Gower employs the term in his *Confessio Amantis.* Chaucer does not use it.

26. Cf. Julian of Norwich, *Shewings,* ed. Crampton, 124.

27. Bynum, *Jesus as Mother,* 168.

28. Jantzen, *Mystic and Theologian,* 119.

29. Bryan, *Looking Inward,* 164–70.

30. We might also see Julian's revisions as maternal—she nurtures and shapes the text.

31. Sarah Beckwith, "Problems of Authority in Late Medieval Mysticism: Language, Agency, and Authority in *The Book of Margery Kempe,*" *Exemplaria* 4.1 (1992), 182.

32. The long text appears to have been written about twenty years after the short text, although Watson has argued for a reversal of this chronology in "Composition."

33. For the scribal headings, see Julian of Norwich, *Shewings,* ed. Crampton, 49. On male and female anchorites, see Crampton, "Introduction," in Julian of Norwich, *Shewings,* ed. Crampton, 7.

34. Sister Benedicta [Ward], "Julian the Solitary," in *Julian Reconsidered,* by Kenneth Leech and Sister Benedicta (Oxford: SLG Press, 1988).

35. Riddy, "Self-Textualization," 106.

36. Both Julian and Margery also invoked Mary Magdalene (and leveraged her connection to the corporeal) to develop their spiritual authority, as Theresa Coletti has shown in *Mary Magdalene,* 77–84.

37. Because the visit seems to have taken place in 1412 or 1413, it is unlikely that Margery influenced Julian's thinking in or writing of her *Shewings,* even if we accept Watson's later date of composition for the long text.

38. For the critical and manuscript history of the *Book,* see Marea Mitchell, *The Book of Margery Kempe: Scholarship, Community, and Criticism* (New York: Peter Lang, 2005). For sociohistorical and religious contexts, see Santha Bhattacharji, *God Is an Earthquake: The Spirituality of Margery Kempe* (London: Darton, Longman and Todd, 1997); and Anthony Goodman, *Margery Kempe and Her World* (London: Longman, 2002).

39. Margery Kempe, *The Book of Margery Kempe,* ed. Lynn Staley, TEAMS Middle English Texts Series (Kalamazoo, MI: Medieval Institute Publications, 1998), 26. Hereafter referred to parenthetically.

40. Caroline Walker Bynum negotiates this problem more carefully than most, admitting that Margery "takes such [sexual and maternal] images to heights of literalism" but rejecting the view that her "cuddling with Christ in bed is simply a case of an uneducated woman taking literally metaphors from the Song of Songs" (Bynum, *Fragmentation and Redemption: Essays on Gender and the Human Body in Medieval Religion* [New York: Zone Books, 1991], 41 and 44). For Bynum, however, these images from affective piety reveal Margery's conventional interest in the humanity of Christ; they are not original or strategic because "Margery, for all her fervor, her courage, her piety, her mystical gifts and her brilliant imagination, cannot write her own script" (41).

41. Lynn Staley, *Margery Kempe's Dissenting Fictions* (University Park: Pennsylvania State University Press, 1994).

42. A. C. Spearing, "*The Book of Margery Kempe;* or, The Diary of a Nobody," *The Southern Review* 38.3 (Summer 2002): 625–35.

43. Nicholas Watson, "The Making of *The Book of Margery Kempe*," and Felicity Riddy, "Text and Self in *The Book of Margery Kempe*," both in *Voices in Dialogue: Reading Women in the Middle Ages*, ed. Linda Olson and Kathryn Kerby-Fulton (Notre Dame, IN: University of Notre Dame Press, 2005).

44. Virginia Burrus, *The Sex Lives of Saints: An Erotics of Ancient Hagiography* (Philadelphia: University of Pennsylvania Press, 2004), 1. Burrus does suggest that this eroticism was the product of particular historical circumstances, perhaps explaining why Margery's case is uncommon among medieval devotional writers: "The ascetics of late antiquity cultivated purposeful disciplines of embodiment and textuality, pedagogy and prayer, which freed desire from the constraining and often violently oppressive structures of familial, civic, and imperial domination" (161). It is also worth noting that none of Burrus's texts was the product of women; perhaps it was easier for men to use this kind of concrete sexual imagery.

45. See John Bugge, *Virginitas: An Essay in the History of a Medieval Ideal* (The Hague: Martinus Nijhoff, 1975), ch. 4; Wolfgang Riehle, *The Middle English Mystics,* trans. Bernard Standring (Boston: Routledge & Kegan Paul, 1981), chs. 3 and 7; Elizabeth Robertson, *Early English Devotional Prose and the Female Audience* (Knoxville: University of Tennessee Press, 1990); and Deborah Kuller Shuger, *The Renaissance Bible: Scholarship, Sacrifice, and Subjectivity* (Berkeley: University of California Press, 1994), ch. 5.

46. Janette Dillon offers a typical interpretation of such metaphors: "The language of women's revelations often suggests sublimated sexual desire, but we must remember that such language is usually the product of collaboration between the female speaker and the male scribe" ("Holy Women and Their Confessors or Confessors and Their Holy Women? Margery Kempe and Continental Tradition," in *Prophets Abroad: The Reception of Continental Holy Women in Late-Medieval England,* ed. Rosalynn Voaden [Cambridge: Cambridge University Press, 1996], 127). For a different reading of Margery's use of sexuality, see Kathy Lavezzo, "Sobs and Sighs between Women: The Homoerotics of Compassion in *The Book of Margery Kempe,*" in *Premodern Sexualities,* ed. Louise Fradenburg and Carla Freccero (New York: Routledge, 1996).

47. Margery nonetheless uses the discourse of virginity. See Sarah Salih, *Versions of Virginity in Late Medieval England* (Cambridge: D. S. Brewer, 2001), ch. 5. Warren shows that Margery also draws on the traditions of female monasticism (*Spiritual Economies,* 92–108).

48. For more on "mother saints" or "holy mothers," see Anneke B. Mulder-Bakker, ed., *Sanctity and Motherhood: Essays on Holy Mothers in the Middle Ages* (New York and London: Garland, 1995).

49. This tradition dates back to at least the twelfth century; see, for example, Luigi Gambero, *Mary in the Middle Ages: The Blessed Virgin Mary in the Thought of Medieval Latin Theologians,* trans. Thomas Buffer (San Francisco: Ignatius Press, 2005), 169, 178–79, and 186–88; and, for a popular study, Marina Warner, *Alone of All Her Sex: The Myth and Cult of the Virgin Mary* (New York: Vintage Books, 1976), ch. 8.

50. Carolyn Dinshaw, *Getting Medieval: Sexualities and Communities, Pre- and Post-Modern* (Durham, NC: Duke University Press, 1999), 149.

51. Cf. Daniele Alexandre-Bidon and Didier Lett, *Children in the Middle Ages: Fifth–Fifteenth Centuries,* trans. Jody Gladding (Notre Dame, IN: University of Notre Dame Press, 1999), 54–58 and 61; Barbara A. Hanawalt, *Growing Up in Medieval London: The Experience of Childhood in History* (New York: Oxford University Press, 1993), 69–72; David Herlihy, *Medieval Households* (Cambridge: Harvard University Press, 1985), 120–27; John Carmi Parsons and Bonnie Wheeler, "Introduction: Medieval Mothering, Medieval Motherers," in *Medieval Mothering,* ed. Parsons and Wheeler (New York: Garland, 1996); and Shulamith Shahar, *Childhood in the Middle Ages,*

trans. Chaya Galai (London: Routledge, 1990), 115–17.

52. For an exception, see Liz Herbert McAvoy, *Authority and the Female Body in the Writings of Julian of Norwich and Margery Kempe* (Cambridge: Boydell Press, 2004), ch. 1. She notes the importance of motherhood in the *Book* but does not examine how Margery uses her own physical motherhood to create authority for herself nor how she mixes maternal with sexual imagery (although McAvoy separately discusses images of prostitution in the text).

53. Clarissa Atkinson, *The Oldest Vocation: Christian Motherhood in the Middle Ages* (Ithaca, NY: Cornell University Press, 1991), 188. See also Atkinson, *Mystic and Pilgrim: The Book and the World of Margery Kempe* (Ithaca, NY: Cornell University Press, 1983); and Gayle Margherita, *The Romance of Origins: Language and Sexual Difference in Middle English Literature* (Philadelphia: University of Pennsylvania Press, 1994), 36–38.

54. Goodman, *Margery Kempe and Her World,* 67.

55. Wendy Harding, "Medieval Women's Unwritten Discourse on Motherhood: A Reading of Two Fifteenth-Century Texts," *Women's Studies* 21.2 (1992), 205.

56. Critics consistently classify this unspecified sin as sexual. For a discussion of it as incest, see Nancy F. Partner, "Reading *The Book of Margery Kempe,*" *Exemplaria* 3.1 (1991): 29–66; as masturbation, see Barrie Ruth Straus, "Freedom through Renunciation?: Women's Voices, Women's Bodies, and the Phallic Order," in *Desire and Discipline: Sex and Sexuality in the Premodern West,* ed. Jacqueline Murray and Konrad Eisenbichler (Toronto, Canada: University of Toronto Press, 1996); as part of a more general sexual guilt, see David Aers, *Community, Gender, and Individual Identity: English Writing, 1360–1430* (New York: Routledge, 1988), 83–87.

57. By undergoing churching, Mary conformed to the Jewish practice of undergoing purification forty days after childbirth. See Gail McMurray Gibson, "Blessing from Sun and Moon: Churching as Women's Theater," in *Bodies and Disciplines: Intersections of Literature and History in Fifteenth-Century England,* ed. Barbara A. Hanawalt and David Wallace (Minneapolis: University of Minnesota Press, 1996), 139 and 142–43.

58. "Semper te cubiculi tui secreta custodiant, semper tecum sponsus ludat intrinsecus" (Jerome, *Select Letters of St. Jerome,* ed. and trans. F. A. Wright [Cambridge: Harvard University Press, 1954], 108–9).

59. Bridget of Sweden does experience a difficult childbirth, but Mary appears and takes away the pain so that Bridget's experience of giving birth mirrors Mary's own painless labor (Bridget of Sweden, *Birgitta of Sweden: Life and Selected Revelations,* ed. Marguerite Tjader Harris and trans. Albert Ryle Kezel [New York: Paulist Press, 1990], 76).

60. Staley, *Dissenting Fictions,* 89.

61. Bridget of Sweden, *Birgitta of Sweden,* 148 (see also pp. 77–78).

62. Bynum suggests that the dangers of marriage and motherhood were serious enough to explain some women's desire for chastity and continence (*Holy Feast and Holy Fast: The Religious Significance of Food to Medieval Women* [Berkeley: University of California Press, 1988], 226). Dyan Elliott terms the impulse toward chastity "a revolt against the reproductive imperative" (*Spiritual Marriage: Sexual Abstinence in Medieval Wedlock* [Princeton: Princeton University Press, 1993], 5).

63. See "privete (n.)" in the *MED.*

64. Such figurative interpretations are also orthodox. See Margery Kempe, *The Book of Margery Kempe,* trans. and ed. Lynn Staley (New York: W. W. Norton, 2001), 89 n5.

65. This interpretation is reinforced by Christ's comment earlier in the text that it is "no synne" for Margery to continue to have sex with her husband because "I wyl that thow bryng me forth mor frwte" (59).

66. Margery's suggestion that both physical and spiritual offspring are desirable and that the latter is somehow dependent on the former departs from typical representations. *Hali Meidhad,* for instance, sharply contrasts the experience of physically bearing children (which involves "sore sorhfule angoise") with producing spiritual offspring (which is restricted to a virgin, who "ne swinke[eth] ne ne pineo[eth]") (Bella Millett, ed., *Hali Meidhad,* EETS 284 [Oxford: Oxford University Press, 1982], 18 and 20).

67. Herlihy, *Medieval Households,* 123. Geoffrey Chaucer's *Prioress's Tale* provides one example of a mother in this role and also draws comparisons with Mary; see Bruce Holsinger, "Pedagogy, Violence, and the Subject of Music: Chaucer's *Prioress's Tale* and the Ideologies of 'Song,'" *New Medieval Literatures* 1 (1997): 157–92.

68. While Julian of Norwich is also interested in both motherhood and Mary, and also uses these concerns as authorizing strategies, critics have most heavily emphasized the former in her text. See, for example, Ritamary Bradley, "The Motherhood Theme in Julian of Norwich," *Fourteenth-Century English Mystics Newsletter* 2.4 (1976): 25–30; McAvoy, *Authority and the Female Body,* ch. 2; and Maud Burnett McInerney, "'In the Meydens Womb': Julian of Norwich and the Poetics of Enclosure," and Andrew Sprung, "The Inverted Metaphor: Earthly Mothering as *Figura* of Divine Love in Julian of Norwich's *Book of Showings,*" both in *Medieval Mothering,* ed. John Carmi Parsons and Bonnie Wheeler (New York: Garland, 1996). For more general discussion of how both male and female mystics made use of maternal imagery, see Bynum, *Jesus as Mother,* ch. 4.

69. Bynum, *Holy Feast,* 269. Gambero notes, however, that the human aspects of Mary were becoming more emphasized near the end of the Middle Ages; he suggests that the faithful imagined Mary "as a Mother, smiling as her Holy Child embraces her" and, during the Passion, as "a Mother who cannot bear the overwhelming sorrow that has befallen her" (*Mary in the Middle Ages,* 255–56).

70. Critics who have discussed *imitatio Mariae* in the *Book* include Gail McMurray Gibson, *The Theater of Devotion: East Anglian Drama and Society in the Late Middle Ages* (Chicago: University of Chicago Press, 1994), 49–50; Karma Lochrie, *Margery Kempe and Translations of the Flesh* (Philadelphia: University of Pennsylvania Press, 1994), ch. 1; Ute Stargardt, "The Beguines of Belgium, the Dominican Nuns of Germany, and Margery Kempe," in *The Popular Literature of Medieval England,* ed. Thomas Heffernan (Knoxville: University of Tennessee Press, 1985), 291–92; Rosalynn Voaden, *God's Words, Women's Voices: The Discernment of Spirits in the Writing of Late-Medieval Women Visionaries* (Suffolk, UK: York Medieval Press, 1999), 140; and Hope Phyllis Weissman, "Margery Kempe in Jerusalem: *Hysterica Compassio* in the Late Middle Ages," in *Acts of Interpretation: The Text in Its Contexts, 700–1600,* ed. Mary J. Carruthers and Elizabeth D. Kirk (Norman, OK: Pilgrim Books, 1982).

71. Dante Alighieri, *The Divine Comedy: Paradiso, Vol. III, Part 1: Text,* trans. with commentary by Charles S. Singleton (Princeton: Princeton University Press, 1975), Canto XXXIII; and Geoffrey Chaucer, "An ABC" and *Canterbury Tales,* in *Riverside Chaucer,* ed. Larry Benson (Boston: Houghton Mifflin, 1987), hereafter referred to parenthetically by line number. Jaroslav Pelikan notes that these two aspects of Mary—as *Mediatrix* and as *Mater Dolorosa*—were the most important contributions of the later Middle Ages to Christian teachings about Mary; he observes "a close correlation between the subjectivity of the devotion to Mary as the Mater Dolorosa and the objectivity of the doctrine of Mary as the Mediatrix" (*Mary through the Centuries: Her Place in the History of Culture* [New Haven: Yale University Press, 1996], 125–26 and 136).

72. For more on the varied paradoxes mobilized in portrayals of the Virgin Mary in medieval literature, see Teresa P. Reed, *Shadows of Mary: Reading the Virgin Mary in Medieval Texts*

(Cardiff: University of Wales Press, 2003).

73. Dante Alighieri, *The Divine Comedy: Paradiso,* 371. As Charles Singleton notes, such "characteristic antitheses" belong to "liturgical style" (Dante Alighieri, *The Divine Comedy: Paradiso, Vol. III, Part 2: Commentary,* trans. with commentary by Charles S. Singleton [Princeton: Princeton University Press, 1975], 560).

74. Eamon Duffy, *The Stripping of the Altars: Traditional Religion in England, c.1400–c.1580* (New Haven: Yale University Press, 1994), 256–57. For a discussion of the possible psychological reasons for the development of the Marian cult, see Michael P. Carroll, *The Cult of the Virgin Mary: Psychological Origins* (Princeton: Princeton University Press, 1986).

75. Bynum, *Jesus as Mother,* 115.

76. Warner, *Alone of All Her Sex,* 202.

77. Bynum, *Holy Feast,* 274.

78. Sarah Beckwith, *Christ's Body: Identity, Culture, and Society in Late Medieval Writings* (New York: Routledge, 1993), 89. Other female spiritual figures, such as Marie d'Oignies, were also associated with excessive weeping, but their tears and suffering are not connected with Mary's. For Marie's case, see Jennifer N. Brown, *Three Women of Liège: A Critical Edition of and Commentary on the Middle English Lives of Elizabeth of Spalbeek, Christina Mirabilis, and Marie d'Oignies* (Turnhout, Belgium: Brepols, 2008), 93–95.

79. Duffy, *Altars,* 258.

80. Poem 37, *Middle English Marian Lyrics,* ed. Karen Saupe, TEAMS Middle English Texts Series (Kalamazoo, MI: Medieval Institute Publications, 1998), ll. 7–10.

81. Alternatively, Jeffrey Cohen suggests that Margery's cries represent "vocalizations [that] might be understood as a bodily response to the inadequacies of language, communicating on her behalf what words might or could not" (*Medieval Identity Machines,* Medieval Cultures, vol. 35 [Minneapolis: University of Minnesota Press, 2003], 162).

82. Beckwith, *Christ's Body,* 81. Beckwith does also suggest that this embodied strategy ultimately provides a way to move past the body: "By approximating herself to Christ, misrecognising herself in him, by living a life which is itself a mimesis and remembrance of the Passion, the female mystic may gain access to the Word" ("A Very Material Mysticism: The Medieval Mysticism of Margery Kempe," in *Medieval Literature: Criticism, Ideology, and History,* ed. David Aers [New York: St. Martin's Press, 1986], 54).

83. Lochrie, *Translations of the Flesh,* 169–70.

84. Herlihy, *Medieval Households,* 122.

85. Bridget of Sweden has a similar episode with one of her sons, Charles, but it is narrated by the Virgin Mary as she tells how she attended his judgment after death; there is no direct discussion of Bridget's concern for Charles beforehand or of how her community perceived this (although, according to Mary, a devil does colorfully decry Bridget as a "cursed sow . . . who had a belly so expansive that so much water poured into her that her belly's every space was filled with liquid for tears!") (*Birgitta of Sweden,* 187).

86. The vow of chastity Margery takes is an important part of this process, as are her various mentions of how she is revolted by the prospect of sex with her husband or other men. Her recurring fear of rape as she travels signals her desire to preserve the transition she has made while also indicating that this is not completely under her control.

87. Dinshaw, *Getting Medieval,* 149.

88. Margery's literalism might also be read in the context of the particular kind of spiritual life she develops, rejecting enclosure in favor of wandering the world. Beckwith points out that "Margery's book is a devotional work which does not exclude the material context of its

piety. . . . Margery was a religious woman who refused the space traditionally allotted to religious women—the sanctuary (or imprisonment) provided by the anchoress's cell or the nunnery. Her lack of circumspection, her insistence on living in the world, enables the social dimension which makes her mysticism distinctive" ("A Very Material Mysticism," 37). See also Beckwith, *Christ's Body,* ch. 4.

89. See note 40.

90. Elsewhere I have argued that Margery's deployment of widowhood and wifehood represents a similar manipulation of female roles and similarly signals her active role in shaping the *Book.* Williams, "'As Thu Wer a Wedow': Margery Kempe's Wifehood and Widowhood," *Exemplaria* 21.4 (Winter 2009): 345–62.

91. See, for example, Barry Windeatt, "Introduction," in *The Book of Margery Kempe,* trans. Windeatt (New York: Penguin, 1985), 20–21; and, in a broader context, Bynum, *Holy Feast,* 246–48 and 153–60.

92. Hadewijch, *Hadewijch: The Complete Works,* trans. Mother Columbia Hart, O.S.B. (New York: Paulist Press, 1980), 281.

93. Angela of Foligno, *Angela of Foligno: Complete Works,* trans. Paul Lachance, O.F.M. (New York: Paulist Press, 1993), 182. Further page references in the text.

94. See, for example, Julia Bolton Holloway, "Bride, Margery, Julian, and Alice: Bridget of Sweden's Textual Community in Medieval England," in *Margery Kempe: A Book of Essays,* ed. Sandra J. McEntire (New York: Garland, 1992); and Nanda Hopenwasser and Signe Wegener, "Vox Matris: The Influence of St. Birgitta's *Revelations* on *The Book of Margery Kempe:* St. Birgitta and Margery Kempe as Wives and Mothers," in *Crossing the Bridge: Comparative Essays on Medieval European and Heian Japanese Women Writers,* ed. Barbara Stevenson and Cynthia Ho (New York: Palgrave, 2000).

95. Claire L. Sahlin, "Gender and Prophetic Authority in Birgitta of Sweden's Revelations," in *Gender and Text in the Later Middle Ages,* ed. Jane Chance (Gainesville: University Press of Florida, 1996).

96. This is a dominant theme in the *Book* and is also observed by others; one clerk affirms, "he had nevyr herd of non sweche in this worlde levyng for to be so homly wyth God be lofe and homly dalyawnce as sche was" (85).

97. These problematic characteristics of Margery and her text may be partly responsible for Sarah Rees Jones's provocative contention that the text was a fiction "written by men, for men, and about men." Jones argues for locating the text not in the tradition of female autobiography but instead "within the general tradition of clerical chastisement through the medium of lives of holy women" ("'A Peler of Holy Church': Margery Kempe and the Bishops," in *Medieval Women: Texts and Contexts in Late Medieval Britain,* ed. Jocelyn Wogan-Browne et al. [Turnhout, Belgium: Brepols, 2000], 391 and 382).

98. Aers, *Community, Gender and Individual Identity,* 106.

99. Hanna, "Some Norfolk Women and Their Books," in *The Cultural Patronage of Medieval Women,* ed. June Hall McCash (Athens: University of Georgia Press, 1996), 295 and 296.

100. Beckwith, *Christ's Body,* 84–85.

101. Aers, *Community, Gender and Individual Identity,* 97–99.

102. While references to mystics as mothers of Christ, and to God or Christ as mother, occurred elsewhere—most famously in Julian's *Shewings*—Margery's role as mother of God is unusual. On the distinction between God as mother and Christ as mother, see Ricki Jean Cohn, "God and Motherhood in *The Book of Margery Kempe,*" *Studia Mystica* 9.1 (1986): 26–35.

103. Bynum argues that gender and gendered characteristics are relatively fluid for medieval

writers (*Jesus as Mother,* 162).

104. Previous studies have paid little attention to this, but Staley does note that Margery slips from third to first person pronouns during her visit with her husband to the Bishop of Lincoln (*Dissenting Fictions,* 79).

105. When Margery negotiates with her husband over chastity, she is referred to as "hys wyfe" (37), but this is a more isolated example and she is the "creatur" for the rest of that chapter.

Conclusion

1. See especially James Simpson, *Oxford English Literary History, Volume 2, 1350–1457: Reform and Cultural Revolution* (Oxford: Oxford University Press, 2004); and Nancy Bradley Warren, *Women of God and Arms: Female Spirituality and Political Conflict, 1380–1600* (Philadelphia: University of Pennsylvania Press, 2005). Other critics have participated in this broader reevaluation by reconsidering particular authors, such as Thomas Hoccleve (see Ethan Knapp, *The Bureaucratic Muse: Thomas Hoccleve and the Literature of Late Medieval England* [University Park: Pennsylvania State University Press, 2001]), John Lydgate (see Lisa H. Cooper and Andrea Denny-Brown, eds., *Lydgate Matters: Poetry and Material Culture in the Fifteenth Century* [New York: Palgrave Macmillan, 2008]; Maura Nolan, *John Lydgate and the Making of Public Culture* [Cambridge: Cambridge University Press, 2005]; and Larry Scanlon and James Simpson, eds., *John Lydgate: Poetry, Culture, and Lancastrian England* [Notre Dame, IN: University of Notre Dame Press, 2006]), and John Capgrave (see Karen Winstead, *John Capgrave's Fifteenth Century* [Philadelphia: University of Pennsylvania Press, 2007]).

2. One exception to this trend is *Femenie,* which retains its narrow primary meaning as a name for the land of the Amazons.

3. Geoffrey Chaucer, *The Riverside Chaucer,* ed. Larry Benson (Boston: Houghton Mifflin, 1987), 360–61.

4. *The Digby Plays with an Incomplete "Morality" of Wisdom, Who Is Christ,* ed. F. J. Furnivall, EETS Extra Series 70 (London: Oxford University Press, 1967), 121.

5. For more on the history of the text in its Latin version, see Steven J. Williams, *The Secret of Secrets: The Scholarly Career of a Pseudo-Aristotelian Text in the Latin Middle Ages* (Ann Arbor: University of Michigan Press, 2003). For more on how the *Secretum Secretorum* fits into the mirrors for princes tradition, see Judith Ferster, *Fictions of Advice: The Literature and Politics of Counsel in Late Medieval England* (Philadelphia: University of Pennsylvania Press, 1996), especially chs. 3–4.

6. *Secretum Secretorum: Nine English Versions,* ed. M. A. Manzalaoui, EETS 276 (Oxford: Oxford University Press, 1977), 12–13. This usage of *womanhood* is unusual not only in relation to other occurrences of the term but also in relation to other Middle English translations of the *Secretum Secretorum.* See, for instance, the parallel sections in the "Ashmole" version (106–7) and the translations by Johannes de Caritate (200–1) and Robert Copland (380–81). In each case, small voices have negative connotations and are associated with lying, but they are neither characterized as feminine nor connected to womanhood.

7. The *MED* makes this distinction in its second set of definitions for "wommanhede," which include "the qualities belonging to or characteristic of a woman, womanliness, femininity; ?also, effeminacy [quot. ?c1400]." The single quote offered as evidence of usage for "effeminacy" is this one from *Secretum Secretorum. Middle English Dictionary* (*Middle English Compendium*), <http://ets.umdl.umich.edu/m/med>.

8. *The Parliament Rolls of Medieval England, 1275–1504,* ed. Chris Given-Wilson, vol. XIV: Edward IV, 1472–1483, ed. Rosemary Horrox (London: Boydell Press, 2005), 113.

9. On the status of these lyrics as a genre, see William D. Paden, "Introduction," in *Medieval Lyric: Genres in Historical Context,* ed. Paden (Urbana: University of Illinois Press, 2000). Rosemary Woolf attributes the scarcity of such lyrics in earlier periods to the fact that "English was a depressed vernacular" and may have seemed impoverished in comparison with French love poetry (*The English Religious Lyric in the Middle Ages* [Oxford: Oxford University Press, 1968], 2).

10. This convention can be traced back to the fourteenth century, when Chaucer also employed it (and prefigured the more general usage of *womanhood* that it later entails) by naming a lady "Soveraigne of beautee, floure of wommanhede" in the envoy to "Womanly Noblesse" (*Riverside Chaucer,* ed. Larry D. Benson [Boston: Houghton Mifflin, 1987], 28).

11. *Secular Lyrics of the XIVth and XVth Centuries,* ed. Rossell Hope Robbins, 2nd ed. (Oxford: Clarendon Press, 1955), 130–32, ll. 20–21.

12. *Political, Religious, and Love Poems,* ed. Frederick James Furnivall, EETS 15 (Oxford: Oxford University Press, 1965), 76–79, ll. 106–8.

13. *Secular Lyrics,* 200–2, l. 33.

14. *Secular Lyrics,* 190–91, ll. 5–7. A very similar usage occurs in "La Belle Dame sans Merci" (*Political, Religious, and Love Poems,* 80–111, l. 241).

15. *Secular Lyrics,* 206, ll. 1–2.

16. *The Minor Poems of John Lydgate, Part II: Secular Poems,* ed. Henry Noble MacCracken, EETS 192 (Oxford: Oxford University Press, 1934), 379–81, ll. 29–30. Lydgate uses the term with varying degrees of generality in other courtly poems, including "The Complaint of the Black Knight" (l. 501); "The Floure of Curtesye" (l. 154); "A Gentlewoman's Lament" (l. 4); "A Lover's New Year's Gift" (l. 29); "The Servant of Cupyde Forsaken" (l. 37); and "Beware of Doublenesse" (l. 5).

17. *The York Plays,* ed. Richard Beadle (London: Edward Arnold, 1982), 255.

18. As Helen Maurer observes, Margaret's "experience pushed the limits of the gender system that she and her contemporaries accepted and acknowledged" (*Margaret of Anjou: Queenship and Power in Late Medieval England* [Woodbridge, UK: Boydell Press, 2003], 4). Margaret was not the only woman in her family whose experiences pushed those limits, however; see p. 23. Nancy Bradley Warren has linked Margaret to Christine de Pizan and Joan of Arc (both also often seen as problematically powerful) (*Women of God and Arms,* ch. 3).

19. Anthony Gross suggests that Margaret's attempt to gain the regency may have been heavily influenced—even instigated—by her advisors (*The Dissolution of the Lancastrian Kingship: Sir John Fortescue and the Crisis of Monarchy in Fifteenth-Century England* [Stamford, UK: Paul Watkins, 1996], 51–57).

20. Her letter appears in the "Life of Sir John Fortescue," put together by his nineteenth-century descendant, Lord Clermont, as the preface to *The Works of Sir John Fortescue, Knight, Chief Justice of England and Lord Chancellor to King Henry the Sixth.* The "Life" collects a number of letters to and from Fortescue, including one from December 1463 or 1464 that he wrote to the Earl of Ormond with directions for a trip to Portugal to seek assistance for Henry VI. This letter encloses a second missive with instructions to the earl from Queen Margaret (Thomas Fortescue Clermont, "Life of Sir John Fortescue," in *The Works of Sir John Fortescue, Knight, Chief Justice of England and Lord Chancellor to King Henry the Sixth* [London: Printed for private distribution, 1869], 26).

21. A 1456 letter in the Paston collection from John Bocking to Sir John Fastolfe famously describes Margaret as "a grete and strong labourid woman, for she spareth noo peyne to sue hire

thinges to an intent and conclusion to hir power" (James Gairdner, ed., *The Paston Letters, A.D. 1422–1509,* New Complete Library Edition, 6 vols. [New York: AMS Press, 1965], III, 75). For more on the development of Margaret's image in this direction, see Patricia-Ann Lee, "Reflections of Power: Margaret of Anjou and the Dark Side of Queenship," *Renaissance Quarterly* 39.2 (Summer 1986): 204–17.

22. For more on the changes made by the *Ipomadon* poet, see Susan Crane, *Insular Romance: Politics, Faith, and Culture in Anglo-Norman and Middle English Literature* (Berkeley: University of California Press, 1986), 202–11; and Rosalind Field, "*Ipomedon* to *Ipomadon A:* Two Views of Courtliness," in *The Medieval Translator: The Theory and Practice of Translation in the Middle Ages,* ed. Roger Ellis (Cambridge: D. S. Brewer, 1989).

23. *Ipomadon,* ed. Rhiannon Purdie, EETS 316 (Oxford: Oxford University Press, 2001), ll. 88–90. The Anglo-Norman original lacks even this brief discussion of the arrangements for the child's minority, noting only that she gained her inheritance after becoming very wise. "E la meschine ot le heritage / Ke a merveille devint sage" (*Ipomedon, poème de Hue de Rotelande,* ed. A. J. Holden [Paris: Éditions Klincksieck, 1979], ll. 103–4).

24. *Ipomadon,* l. 118.

25. Katherine J. Lewis, *The Cult of St. Katherine of Alexandria in Late Medieval England* (Rochester, NY: Boydell Press, 2000), 2.

26. The most significant recent treatment of Capgrave, Winstead's *John Capgrave's Fifteenth Century,* includes substantial analysis of the *Life* and its representations of intellectualism, sovereignty, and virginity.

27. For more on this aspect of the *Life,* see Paul Price, "I Want to Be Alone: The Single Woman in Fifteenth-Century Legends of St. Katherine of Alexandria," in *The Single Woman in Medieval and Early Modern England: Her Life and Representation,* ed. Laurel Amtower and Dorothea Kehler (Tempe: Arizona Center for Medieval and Renaissance Studies, 2003); and Karen Winstead, "Capgrave's Saint Katherine and the Perils of Gynecocracy," *Viator* 25 (1994): 361–76.

28. John Capgrave, *The Life of Saint Katherine,* ed. Karen A. Winstead, TEAMS Middle English Texts Series (Kalamazoo, MI: Medieval Institute Publications, 1999), 2.452–53. Hereafter referred to parenthetically.

WORKS CITED

Primary

Alighieri, Dante. *La Vita Nuova.* Edited and translated by Dino S. Cervigni and Edward Vasta. Notre Dame, IN: University of Notre Dame Press, 1995.

———. *The Divine Comedy: Paradiso, Vol. III, Part 1: Text.* Translated with commentary by Charles S. Singleton. Princeton: Princeton University Press, 1975.

———. *The Divine Comedy: Paradiso, Vol. III, Part 2: Commentary.* Translated with commentary by Charles S. Singleton. Princeton: Princeton University Press, 1975.

Angela of Foligno. *Angela of Foligno: Complete Works.* Translated by Paul Lachance, O.F.M. New York: Paulist Press, 1993.

Boccaccio, Giovanni. *The Decameron.* Translated by G. H. McWilliam. New York: Penguin, 1972.

———. *Il Decamerone.* Edited by Angelo Ottolini. Milan: Ulrico Hoepli, [1948].

———. *Teseida Delle Nozze di Emilia.* Edited by Alberto Limentani. In *Tutte le opere di Giovanni Boccaccio,* edited by Vittorio Branca, vol. II. Milan: Mondadori, 1964.

Bridget of Sweden. *Birgitta of Sweden: Life and Selected Revelations.* Edited by Marguerite Tjader Harris and translated by Albert Ryle Kezel. New York: Paulist Press, 1990.

Capgrave, John. *The Life of Saint Katherine.* Edited by Karen A. Winstead. TEAMS Middle English Texts Series. Kalamazoo, MI: Medieval Institute Publications, 1999.

Chaucer, Geoffrey. *The Riverside Chaucer.* Edited by Larry Benson. 3rd ed. Boston: Houghton Mifflin, 1987.

Clermont, Thomas Fortescue. "Life of Sir John Fortescue." In *The Works of Sir John Fortescue, Knight, Chief Justice of England and Lord Chancellor to King Henry the Sixth,* 1–52. London: Printed for private distribution, 1869.

de Pizan, Christine. *The Book of the City of Ladies.* Translated by Earl Jeffrey Richards. New York: Persea Books, 1998.

de Rotelande, Hue. *Ipomedon, poème de Hue de Rotelande.* Edited by A. J. Holden. Paris: Éditions Klincksieck, 1979.

The Digby Plays with an Incomplete "Morality" of Wisdom, Who Is Christ. Edited by F. J. Furnivall. EETS Extra Series 70. London: Oxford University Press, 1967.

Gower, John. *Confessio Amantis,* with an introduction by Russell A. Peck. Edited by Peck.

Toronto, Canada: University of Toronto Press, 1980.

———. *The English Works of John Gower.* Edited by G. C. Macaulay. EETS Extra Series 81 and 82. 2 vols., 1900; London: Oxford University Press, 1957.

Hadewijch. *Hadewijch: The Complete Works.* Translated by Mother Columbia Hart, O.S.B. New York: Paulist Press, 1980.

Hali Meidhad. Edited by Bella Millett. EETS 284. London: Oxford University Press, 1982.

Henryson, Robert. *Poems of Robert Henryson*, with an introduction by Denton Fox. Edited by Fox. New York: Oxford University Press, 1981.

Ipomadon. Edited by Rhiannon Purdie. EETS 316. Oxford: Oxford University Press, 2001.

Jerome. *Select Letters of St. Jerome.* Edited and translated by F. A. Wright. Cambridge: Harvard University Press, 1954.

Julian of Norwich. *A Book of Showings to the Anchoress Julian of Norwich.* Edited by Edmund Colledge and James Walsh. 2 vols. Studies and Texts 35. Toronto, Canada: Pontifical Institute of Medieval Studies, 1978.

———. *Julian of Norwich: A Revelation of Love.* Edited by Marion Glasscoe. 1976; Exeter, UK: University of Exeter, 1989.

———. *The Shewings of Julian of Norwich*, with an introduction by Georgia Crampton. Edited by Crampton. TEAMS Middle English Texts Series. Kalamazoo, MI: Medieval Institute Publications, 1993.

———. *The Writings of Julian of Norwich*, with an introduction by Nicholas Watson and Jacqueline Jenkins. Edited by Watson and Jenkins. University Park: Pennsylvania State University Press, 2006.

Kempe, Margery. *The Book of Margery Kempe,* with an introduction by Barry Windeatt. Translated by Windeatt. New York: Penguin, 1985.

———. *The Book of Margery Kempe.* Edited by Lynn Staley. TEAMS Middle English Texts Series. Kalamazoo, MI: Medieval Institute Publications, 1998.

———. *The Book of Margery Kempe.* Translated and edited by Lynn Staley. New York: W. W. Norton, 2001.

Middle English Marian Lyrics. Edited by Karen Saupe. TEAMS Middle English Texts Series. Kalamazoo, MI: Medieval Institute Publications, 1998.

Knighton, Henry. *Knighton's Chronicle, 1337–1396.* Edited and translated by G. H. Martin. Oxford: Clarendon Press; New York: Oxford University Press, 1995.

Lydgate, John. *Temple of Glas,* with an introduction by J. Schick. Edited by Schick. EETS Extra Series 60. 1891; London: Oxford University Press, 1924.

———. *The Minor Poems of John Lydgate, Part II: The Secular Poems.* Edited by Henry Noble MacCracken. EETS 192. Oxford: Oxford University Press, 1934.

———. *Lydgate's Troy Book, Part II: Book III and Part III: Books IV-V.* Edited by Henry Bergen. EETS Extra Series 103 and 106. 1908 and 1910; Millwood, NY: Kraus Reprint Company, 1973.

Mandeville, Sir John. *The Bodley Version of Mandeville's Travels.* Edited by M. C. Seymour. EETS 253. New York: Oxford University Press, 1963.

Ovid. *Ovid's Metamorphoses Books I–VIII.* Edited and translated by Frank Justus Miller. Cambridge: Harvard University Press, 1994.

The Parliament Rolls of Medieval England, 1275–1504. Edited by Chris Given-Wilson. Vol. XIV: Edward IV, 1472–1483. Edited by Rosemary Horrox. London: Boydell Press, 2005.

The Paston Letters, A.D. 1422–1509. Edited by James Gairdner. New Complete Library Edition, 6 vols. New York: AMS Press, 1965.

Petrarch, Francesco. *Petrarch's Lyric Poems: The* Rime sparse *and Other Lyrics.* Edited and translated by Robert M. Durling. Cambridge: Harvard University Press, 1976.

Political, Religious, and Love Poems. Edited by Frederick James Furnivall. EETS 15. Oxford: Oxford University Press, 1965.

Secretum Secretorum: Nine English Versions. Edited by M. A. Manzalaoui. EETS 276. Oxford: Oxford University Press, 1977.

Secular Lyrics of the XIVth and XVth Centuries. Edited by Rossell Hope Robbins. 2nd ed. Oxford: Clarendon Press, 1955.

The York Plays. Edited by Richard Beadle. London: Edward Arnold, 1982.

Secondary

Aers, David. *Community, Gender, and Individual Identity: English Writing, 1360–1430.* New York: Routledge, 1988.

———. *Salvation and Sin: Augustine, Langland, and Fourteenth-Century Theology.* Notre Dame, IN: Notre Dame University Press, 2009.

Alexandre-Bidon, Daniele, and Didier Lett. *Children in the Middle Ages: Fifth–Fifteenth Centuries.* Translated by Jody Gladding. Notre Dame, IN: University of Notre Dame Press, 1999.

Allen, David G. "God's Faithfulness and the Lover's Despair: The Theological Framework of the Iphis and Araxarathen Story." In *John Gower: Recent Readings,* edited by R. F. Yeager, 209–23. Kalamazoo, MI: Medieval Institute Publications, 1989.

Allen, Elizabeth. "Chaucer Answers Gower: Constance and the Trouble with Reading," *ELH* 64.3 (Fall 1997): 627–55.

———. *False Fables and Exemplary Truth in Later Middle English Literature.* New York: Palgrave Macmillan, 2005.

———. "Newfangled Readers in Gower's 'Apollonius of Tyre.'" *Studies in the Age of Chaucer* 29 (2007): 419–64.

Amtower, Laurel. "Mimetic Desire and the Misappropriation of the Ideal in the *Knight's Tale.*" *Exemplaria* 8.1 (1996): 125–44.

Ashe, Laura. "Reading Like a Clerk in the *Clerk's Tale.*" *Modern Language Review* 101.4 (October 2006): 935–44.

Aston, Margaret. *Lollards and Reformers: Images and Literacy in Late Medieval Religion.* London: Hambledon Press, 1984.

Atkinson, Clarissa. *Mystic and Pilgrim: The Book and the World of Margery Kempe.* Ithaca, NY: Cornell University Press, 1983.

———. *The Oldest Vocation: Christian Motherhood in the Middle Ages.* Ithaca, NY: Cornell University Press, 1991.

Baker, Denise Nowakowski. *Julian of Norwich's* Showings*: From Vision to Book.* Princeton: Princeton University Press, 1994.

———. "Julian of Norwich and the Varieties of Middle English Mystical Discourse." In *A Companion to Julian of Norwich,* edited by Liz Herbert McAvoy, 53–63. Cambridge: D. S. Brewer, 2008.

Barron, Caroline. "The 'Golden Age' of Women in Medieval London." *Reading Medieval Studies* 15 (1989): 35–58.

Beckwith, Sarah. "A Very Material Mysticism: The Medieval Mysticism of Margery Kempe." In *Medieval Literature: Criticism, Ideology, and History,* edited by David Aers, 34–57. New York:

St. Martin's Press, 1986.

———. "Problems of Authority in Late Medieval Mysticism: Language, Agency, and Authority in *The Book of Margery Kempe.*" *Exemplaria* 4.1 (1992): 172–99.

———. *Christ's Body: Identity, Culture, and Society in Late Medieval Writings.* New York: Routledge, 1993.

Beidler, Peter G., ed. *Masculinities in Chaucer: Approaches to Maleness in the* Canterbury Tales *and* Troilus and Criseyde. Rochester, NY: D. S. Brewer, 1998.

Benedictow, Ole J. *The Black Death, 1346–1353: The Complete History.* Rochester, NY: Boydell Press, 2004.

Bennett, J. A. W. "Gower's 'Honeste Love.'" In *Gower's* Confessio Amantis: *A Critical Anthology,* edited by Peter Nicholson, 49–61. Cambridge: D. S. Brewer, 1991.

Bennett, Judith. *Women in the Medieval English Countryside: Gender and Household in Brigstock before the Plague.* New York: Oxford University Press, 1987.

———. *Ale, Beer, and Brewsters in England: Women's Work in a Changing World.* New York: Oxford University Press, 1996.

Benson, C. David. "Critic and Poet: What Lydgate and Henryson Did to Chaucer's *Troilus and Criseyde.*" In *Writing after Chaucer: Essential Readings in Chaucer and the Fifteenth Century,* edited by Daniel J. Pinti, 227–42. New York: Garland, 1998.

Bettridge, William E., and Francis L. Utley. "New Light on the Origin of the Griselda Story." *Texas Studies in Literature and Language* 13.2 (Summer 1971): 153–208.

Bhattacharji, Santha. *God Is an Earthquake: The Spirituality of Margery Kempe.* London: Darton, Longman and Todd, 1997.

Blamires, Alcuin. *The Case for Women in Medieval Culture.* Oxford: Oxford University Press, 1998.

———. *Chaucer, Ethics, and Gender.* Oxford: Oxford University Press, 2006.

Boffey, Julia. "Lydgate, Henryson, and the Literary Testament." *Modern Language Quarterly* 53.1 (1992): 41–56.

Bowers, John M. "Three Readings of the *Knight's Tale:* Sir John Clanvowe, Geoffrey Chaucer, and James I of Scotland." *Journal of Medieval and Early Modern Studies* 34.2 (Spring 2004): 279–307.

Bradley, Ritamary. "The Motherhood Theme in Julian of Norwich." *Fourteenth-Century English Mystics Newsletter* 2.4 (1976): 25–30.

Bratcher, James T. "The Function of the Jeweled Bridle in Gower's 'Tale of Rosiphelee.'" *Chaucer Review* 40.1 (2005): 107–10.

Bronfman, Judith. *Chaucer's* Clerk's Tale: *The Griselda Story Received, Rewritten, Illustrated.* New York: Garland Publishing, 1994.

Brown, Jennifer N. *Three Women of Liège: A Critical Edition of and Commentary on the Middle English Lives of Elizabeth of Spalbeek, Christina Mirabilis, and Marie d'Oignies.* Turnhout, Belgium: Brepols, 2008.

Brownlee, Kevin. "Commentary and the Rhetoric of Exemplarity: Griseldis in Petrarch, Philippe de Mézières, and the *Estoire.*" *South Atlantic Quarterly* 91.4 (Fall 1992): 865–90.

Bryan, Jennifer. *Looking Inward: Devotional Reading and the Private Self in Late Medieval England.* Philadelphia: University of Pennsylvania Press, 2008.

Bugge, John. *Virginitas: An Essay in the History of a Medieval Ideal.* The Hague: Martinus Nijhoff, 1975.

Bullón-Fernández, María. *Fathers and Daughters in Gower's* Confessio Amantis: *Authority, Family, State, and Writing.* Cambridge: D. S. Brewer, 2000.

Burnley, David. "Lexis and Semantics." In *The Cambridge History of the English Language,* vol. II, edited by Norman Blake, 409–99. New York: Cambridge University Press, 1992.

Burrow, J. A. "The Portrayal of Amans in *Confessio Amantis*." In *Gower's* Confessio Amantis: *Responses and Reassessments,* edited by A. J. Minnis, 5–24. Cambridge: D. S. Brewer, 1983.

Burrus, Virginia. *The Sex Lives of Saints: An Erotics of Ancient Hagiography.* Philadelphia: University of Pennsylvania Press, 2004.

Butler, Judith. *Gender Trouble.* New York: Routledge, 1990; rpt. 1999.

Butterfield, Ardis. *The Familiar Enemy: Chaucer, Language, and Nation in the Hundred Years War.* Oxford: Oxford University Press, 2009.

Bynum, Caroline Walker. *Jesus as Mother: Studies in the Spirituality of the High Middle Ages.* Berkeley: University of California Press, 1984.

———. *Holy Feast and Holy Fast: The Religious Significance of Food to Medieval Women.* Berkeley: University of California Press, 1988.

———. *Fragmentation and Redemption: Essays on Gender and the Human Body in Medieval Religion.* New York: Zone Books, 1991.

Byrne, Joseph P. *The Black Death.* Greenwood Guides to Historic Events of the Medieval World. Westport, CT: Greenwood Press, 2004.

Campbell, Emma. "Sexual Poetics and the Politics of Translation in the Tale of Griselda." *Comparative Literature* 55.3 (Summer 2003): 191–216.

Cannon, Christopher. *The Making of Chaucer's English: A Study of Words.* Cambridge: Cambridge University Press, 1998.

Cantor, Norman F. *In the Wake of the Plague: The Black Death and the World It Made.* New York: The Free Press, 2001.

Carroll, Michael P. *The Cult of the Virgin Mary: Psychological Origins.* Princeton: Princeton University Press, 1986.

Catto, Jeremy. "Religious Change under Henry V." In *Henry V: The Practice of Kingship,* edited by G. L. Harriss, 97–115. Oxford: Oxford University Press, 1985.

Cohen, Jeffrey. *Medieval Identity Machines.* Medieval Cultures, vol. 35. Minneapolis: University of Minnesota Press, 2003.

——— and Bonnie Wheeler, eds. *Becoming Male in the Middle Ages.* New York: Garland, 1997.

Cohn, Ricki Jean. "God and Motherhood in *The Book of Margery Kempe*." *Studia Mystica* 9.1 (1986): 26–35.

Coletti, Theresa. *Mary Magdalene and the Drama of Saints: Theater, Gender, and Religion in Late Medieval England.* Philadelphia: University of Pennsylvania Press, 2004.

Collette, Carolyn P. *Performing Polity: Women and Agency in the Anglo-French Tradition, 1385–1620.* Turnhout, Belgium: Brepols, 2006.

Cooper, Helen. "The Frame." In *Sources and Analogues of the* Canterbury Tales, vol. 1, edited by Robert M. Correale and Mary Hamel, 1-22. Rochester, NY: D. S. Brewer, 2002.

Cooper, Lisa H., and Andrea Denny-Brown, eds. *Lydgate Matters: Poetry and Material Culture in the Fifteenth Century.* New York: Palgrave Macmillan, 2008.

Cox, Catherine. *Gender and Language in Chaucer.* Gainesville: University Press of Florida, 1997.

Crane, Susan. *Insular Romance: Politics, Faith, and Culture in Anglo-Norman and Middle English Literature.* Berkeley: University of California Press, 1986.

———. *Gender and Romance in Chaucer's* Canterbury Tales. Princeton: Princeton University Press, 1994.

———. *The Performance of Self: Ritual, Clothing, and Identity during the Hundred Years War.* Philadelphia: University of Pennsylvania Press, 2002.

Craun, Edwin D. "Blaspheming Her 'Awin God': Cresseid's 'Lamentatioun' in Henryson's *Testament*." *Studies in Philology* 82.1 (1985): 25–41.

Crocker, Holly. *Chaucer's Visions of Manhood.* New York: Palgrave Macmillan, 2007.

Crockett, Bryan. "Venus Unveiled: Lydgate's *Temple of Glas* and the Religion of Love." In *New Readings of Late Medieval Love Poems,* edited by David Chamberlain, 67–93. Lanham, MD: University Press of America, 1993.

Davis, Isabel. *Writing Masculinity in the Later Middle Ages.* Cambridge: Cambridge University Press, 2007.

Denny-Brown, Andrea. "*Povre* Griselda and the All-Consuming *Archewyves.*" *Studies in the Age of Chaucer* 28 (2006): 77–115.

Dillon, Janette. "Holy Women and Their Confessors or Confessors and Their Holy Women? Margery Kempe and Continental Tradition." In *Prophets Abroad: The Reception of Continental Holy Women in Late-Medieval England*, edited by Rosalynn Voaden, 115–40. Cambridge: Cambridge University Press, 1996.

Dinshaw, Carolyn. *Chaucer's Sexual Poetics.* Madison: University of Wisconsin Press, 1989.

———. "Quarrels, Rivals, and Rape: Gower and Chaucer." In *A Wyf Ther Was: Essays in Honour of Paule Mertens-Fonck,* edited by Juliette Dor, 112–22. Liège, Belgium: University of Liège Press, 1992.

———. *Getting Medieval: Sexualities and Communities, Pre- and Post-Modern.* Durham, NC: Duke University Press, 1999.

Duffy, Eamon. *The Stripping of the Altars: Traditional Religion in England, c.1400–c.1580.* New Haven: Yale University Press, 1994.

Dunnigan, Sarah M. "Feminizing the Text, Feminizing the Reader?: The Mirror of 'Feminitie' in the *Testament of Cresseid.*" *Studies in Scottish Literature* 33–34 (2004): 107–23.

Edwards, Elizabeth B. "Chaucer's *Knight's Tale* and the Work of Mourning." *Exemplaria* 20.4 (Winter 2008): 361–84.

Elliott, Dyan. *Spiritual Marriage: Sexual Abstinence in Medieval Wedlock.* Princeton: Princeton University Press, 1993.

Ellis, Deborah S. "Domestic Treachery in the *Clerk's Tale.*" In *Ambiguous Realities: Women in the Middle Ages and Renaissance,* edited by Carole Levin and Jeanie Watson, 99–113. Detroit, MI: Wayne State University Press, 1987.

Erler, Mary. *Women, Reading, and Piety in Late Medieval England.* Cambridge: Cambridge University Press, 2002.

Esch, Arno. "John Gower's Narrative Art." Translated by Linda Barney Burke. In *Gower's Confessio Amantis: A Critical Anthology,* edited by Peter Nicholson, 81–109. Cambridge: D. S. Brewer, 1991.

Eyler, Joshua R., and John P. Sexton. "Once More to the Grove: A Note on Symbolic Space in the *Knight's Tale.*" *Chaucer Review* 40.4 (2006): 433–39.

Farrell, Thomas J., and Amy W. Goodwin, "The Clerk's Tale." In *Sources and Analogues of the Canterbury Tales,* vol. 1, edited by Robert M. Correale and Mary Hamel, 101–67. Rochester, NY: D. S. Brewer, 2002.

Ferster, Judith. *Fictions of Advice: The Literature and Politics of Counsel in Late Medieval England.* Philadelphia: University of Pennsylvania Press, 1996.

Field, Rosalind. "*Ipomedon* to *Ipomadon A:* Two Views of Courtliness." In *The Medieval Translator: The Theory and Practice of Translation in the Middle Ages,* edited by Roger Ellis, 135–41. Cambridge: D. S. Brewer, 1989.

Fowler, Elizabeth. "Chaucer's Hard Cases." In *Medieval Crime and Social Control,* edited by Barbara A. Hanawalt and David Wallace, 124–42. Minneapolis: University of Minnesota Press, 1999.

Gambero, Luigi. *Mary in the Middle Ages: The Blessed Virgin Mary in the Thought of Medieval Latin Theologians.* Translated by Thomas Buffer. San Francisco: Ignatius Press, 2005.

Gibson, Gail McMurray. *The Theater of Devotion: East Anglian Drama and Society in the Late Middle Ages.* Chicago: University of Chicago Press, 1994.

———. "Blessing from Sun and Moon: Churching as Women's Theater." In *Bodies and Disciplines: Intersections of Literature and History in Fifteenth-Century England,* edited by Barbara A. Hanawalt and David Wallace, 139–54. Minneapolis: University of Minnesota Press, 1996.

Gillespie, Vincent. "'[S]he Do the Police in Different Voices': Pastiche, Ventriloquism, and Parody in Julian of Norwich." In *A Companion to Julian of Norwich,* edited by Liz Herbert McAvoy, 192–207. Cambridge: D. S. Brewer, 2008.

Goldberg, P. J. P. *Women, Work and Life Cycle in a Medieval Economy: Women in York and Yorkshire, c.1300–1520.* New York: Oxford University Press, 1992.

———. *Women in England, c.1275–1525.* Manchester: Manchester University Press, 1995.

———. *Medieval England: A Social History, 1250–1550.* London: Arnold, 2004.

Goldstein, R. James. "Writing in Scotland, 1058–1560." In *The Cambridge History of Medieval English Literature,* edited by David Wallace, 229–54. New York: Cambridge University Press, 2002.

Goodman, Anthony. *Margery Kempe and Her World.* London: Longman, 2002.

Gray, Douglas. *Robert Henryson.* Leiden, The Netherlands: E. J. Brill, 1979.

Green, D. H. *Women Readers in the Middle Ages.* Cambridge: Cambridge University Press, 2008.

Griffith, Dudley David. *The Origin of the Griselda Story.* Seattle: University of Washington Press, 1931.

Gross, Anthony. *The Dissolution of the Lancastrian Kingship: Sir John Fortescue and the Crisis of Monarchy in Fifteenth-Century England.* Stamford, UK: Paul Watkins, 1996.

Grudin, Michaela Paasche. "Chaucer's *Clerk's Tale* as Political Paradox." *Studies in the Age of Chaucer* 11 (1989): 63–92.

Hamaguchi, Keiko. "Domesticating Amazons in *The Knight's Tale.*" *Studies in the Age of Chaucer* 26 (2004): 331–54.

Hanawalt, Barbara A. *Growing Up in Medieval London: The Experience of Childhood in History.* New York: Oxford University Press, 1993.

———. *The Wealth of Wives: Women, Law, and Economy in Late Medieval London.* Oxford: Oxford University Press, 2007.

Hanna, Ralph. "Some Norfolk Women and Their Books." In *The Cultural Patronage of Medieval Women,* edited by June Hall McCash, 288–305. Athens: University of Georgia Press, 1996.

———. "Chaucer and the Future of Language Study." *Studies in the Age of Chaucer* 24 (2002): 309–15.

Hansen, Elaine Tuttle. *Chaucer and the Fictions of Gender.* Berkeley: University of California Press, 1992.

Harding, Wendy. "Medieval Women's Unwritten Discourse on Motherhood: A Reading of Two Fifteenth-Century Texts." *Women's Studies* 21.2 (1992): 197–209.

Havely, N. R., ed. and trans. *Chaucer's Boccaccio: Sources for* Troilus *and the* Knight's *and* Franklin's Tales *(Translations from the* Filostrato, Teseida, *and* Filocolo*).* Cambridge: D. S. Brewer, 1980.

Herlihy, David. *Medieval Households.* Cambridge: Harvard University Press, 1985.

Holloway, Julia Bolton. "Bride, Margery, Julian, and Alice: Bridget of Sweden's Textual Community in Medieval England." In *Margery Kempe: A Book of Essays,* edited by Sandra J. McEntire, 203–22. New York: Garland, 1992.

Holsinger, Bruce. "Pedagogy, Violence, and the Subject of Music: Chaucer's *Prioress's Tale* and the Ideologies of 'Song.'" *New Medieval Literatures* 1 (1997): 157–92.

Hopenwasser, Nanda, and Signe Wegener. "Vox Matris: The Influence of St. Birgitta's *Revelations* on *The Book of Margery Kempe:* St. Birgitta and Margery Kempe as Wives and Mothers." In *Crossing the Bridge: Comparative Essays on Medieval European and Heian Japanese Women Writers,* edited by Barbara Stevenson and Cynthia Ho, 61–85. New York: Palgrave, 2000.

Horobin, Simon. *The Language of the Chaucer Tradition.* Cambridge: D. S. Brewer, 2003.

Jantzen, Grace. *Julian of Norwich: Mystic and Theologian.* New York: Paulist Press, 2000.

Jenkins, Ena. "Julian's *Revelation of Love:* A Web of Metaphor." In *A Companion to Julian of Norwich,* edited by Liz Herbert McAvoy, 181–91. Cambridge: D. S. Brewer, 2008.

Johnson, Lesley. "Whatever Happened to Criseyde? Henryson's *Testament of Cresseid.*" In *Courtly Literature: Culture and Context,* edited by Keith Busby and Erik Kooper, 313–21. Amsterdam: Benjamins, 1990.

Jones, Sarah Rees. "'A Peler of Holy Church': Margery Kempe and the Bishops." In *Medieval Women: Texts and Contexts in Late Medieval Britain,* edited by Jocelyn Wogan-Browne et al., 376–91. Turnhout, Belgium: Brepols, 2000.

Keen, Maurice. *English Society in the Later Middle Ages, 1348–1500.* New York: Penguin, 1990.

Kelly, John. *The Great Mortality: An Intimate History of the Black Death, the Most Devastating Plague of All Time.* New York: HarperCollins, 2005.

Kirk, Ilse. "Images of Amazons: Marriage and Matriarchy." In *Images of Women in Peace and War: Cross-Cultural and Historical Perspectives,* edited by Sharon Macdonald, Pat Holden, and Shirley Ardener, 27–39. Basingstoke, UK: Macmillan Education in association with the Oxford University Women's Studies Committee, 1987.

Klapisch-Zuber, Christiane. "The Griselda Complex: Dowry and Marriage Gifts in the Quattrocento." In *Women, Family and Ritual in Renaissance Italy,* translated by Lydia Cochrane, 213–46. Chicago: University of Chicago Press, 1985.

Kleinbaum, Abby Wettan. *The War against the Amazons.* New York: New Press, 1983.

Knapp, Ethan. *The Bureaucratic Muse: Thomas Hoccleve and the Literature of Late Medieval England.* University Park: Pennsylvania State University Press, 2001.

Krug, Rebecca. *Reading Families: Women's Literate Practice in Late Medieval England.* Ithaca, NY: Cornell University Press, 2002.

Lavezzo, Kathy. "Sobs and Sighs between Women: The Homoerotics of Compassion in *The Book of Margery Kempe.*" In *Premodern Sexualities,* edited by Louise Fradenburg and Carla Freccero, 175–98. New York: Routledge, 1996.

Lee, Patricia-Ann. "Reflections of Power: Margaret of Anjou and the Dark Side of Queenship." *Renaissance Quarterly* 39.2 (Summer 1986): 183–217.

Lees, Clare, ed. *Medieval Masculinities: Regarding Men in the Middle Ages.* Minneapolis: University of Minnesota Press, 2004.

Lerer, Seth. *Inventing English: A Portable History of the Language.* New York: Columbia University Press, 2007.

Lewis, C. S. *The Allegory of Love: A Study in Medieval Tradition.* New York: Oxford University Press, 1958.

———. "Gower." In *Gower's* Confessio Amantis: *A Critical Anthology,* edited by Peter Nicholson, 15–39. Cambridge: D. S. Brewer, 1991.

Lewis, Katherine J. *The Cult of St. Katherine of Alexandria in Late Medieval England.* Rochester, NY: Boydell Press, 2000.

Lipton, Emma. *Affections of the Mind: The Politics of Sacramental Marriage in Late Medieval Eng-*

lish Literature. Notre Dame, IN: University of Notre Dame Press, 2007.

Lochrie, Karma. *Margery Kempe and Translations of the Flesh.* Philadelphia: University of Pennsylvania Press, 1994.

———. *Covert Operations: The Medieval Uses of Secrecy.* Philadelphia: University of Pennsylvania Press, 1999.

Lynch, Kathryn L. "Despoiling Griselda: Chaucer's Walter and the Problem of Knowledge in The *Clerk's Tale.*" *Studies in the Age of Chaucer* 10 (1988): 41–70.

Macaulay, G. C. "The *Confessio Amantis.*" In *Gower's* Confessio Amantis: *A Critical Anthology,* edited by Peter Nicholson, 6–14. Cambridge: D. S. Brewer, 1991.

Machan, Tim William. *English in the Middle Ages.* Oxford: Oxford University Press, 2003.

———. "Medieval Multilingualism and Gower's Literary Practice." *Studies in Philology* 103.1 (Winter 2006): 1–25.

MacQueen, John. "The Literature of Fifteenth-Century Scotland." In *Scottish Society in the Fifteenth Century,* edited by Jennifer M. Brown, 184–208. New York: St. Martin's Press, 1977.

———. "Poetry—James I to Henryson." In *The History of Scottish Literature, Volume 1: Origins to 1660 (Medieval and Renaissance),* edited by R. D. S. Jack, 55–72. Aberdeen, UK: Aberdeen University Press, 1988.

Mann, Jill. *Feminizing Chaucer.* Cambridge: D. S. Brewer, 2002; originally published as *Geoffrey Chaucer,* 1991.

Margherita, Gayle. *The Romance of Origins: Language and Sexual Difference in Middle English Literature.* Philadelphia: University of Pennsylvania Press, 1994.

Maurer, Helen. *Margaret of Anjou: Queenship and Power in Late Medieval England.* Woodbridge, UK: Boydell Press, 2003.

McAvoy, Liz Herbert. *Authority and the Female Body in the Writings of Julian of Norwich and Margery Kempe.* Cambridge: Boydell Press, 2004.

———. "'For We Be Doubel of God's Making': Writing, Gender and the Body in Julian of Norwich." In *A Companion to Julian of Norwich,* edited by McAvoy, 166–80. Cambridge: D. S. Brewer, 2008.

McCarthy, Conor. "Love and Marriage in the *Confessio Amantis.*" *Neophilologus* 84 (2000): 485–99.

McDonald, Nicola F. "Avarice and the Economics of the Erotic in Gower." In *Treasure in the Medieval West,* edited by Elizabeth M. Tyler, 135–56. York, UK: York Medieval Press, 2000.

McInerney, Maud Burnett. "'In the Meydens Womb': Julian of Norwich and the Poetics of Enclosure." In *Medieval Mothering,* edited by John Carmi Parsons and Bonnie Wheeler, 157–82. New York: Garland, 1996.

McSheffrey, Shannon. *Gender and Heresy: Women and Men in Lollard Communities, 1420–1530.* Philadelphia: University of Pennsylvania Press, 1995.

Meyer-Lee, Robert. *Poets and Power from Chaucer to Wyatt.* Cambridge: Cambridge University Press, 2007.

Middle English Dictionary (Middle English Compendium). February 2006. <http://ets.umdl.umich.edu/m/med>

Miller, Mark. *Philosophical Chaucer: Love, Sex, and Agency in the* Canterbury Tales. Cambridge: Cambridge University Press, 2004.

Mitchell, J. Allan. *Ethics and Exemplary Narrative in Chaucer and Gower.* Chaucer Studies XXXIII. Rochester, NY: D. S. Brewer, 2004.

———. "Chaucer's *Clerk's Tale* and the Question of Ethical Monstrosity." *Studies in Philology* 102.1 (Winter 2005): 1–26.

———. "Queen Katherine and the Secret of Lydgate's *Temple of Glas*." *Medium Aevum* 77.1 (2008): 54–76.

Mitchell, Marea. *The Book of Margery Kempe: Scholarship, Community, and Criticism.* New York: Peter Lang, 2005.

Morse, Charlotte C. "The Exemplary Griselda." *Studies in the Age of Chaucer* 7 (1985): 51–86.

———. "Griselda Reads Philippa de Coucy." In *Speaking Images: Essays in Honor of V. A. Kolve,* edited by R. F. Yeager and Charlotte C. Morse, 347-92. Asheville, NC: Pegasus, 2001.

Mortimer, Nigel. *John Lydgate's Fall of Princes: Narrative Tragedy in Its Literary and Political Contexts.* Oxford: Oxford University Press, 2005.

Mulder-Bakker, Anneke B., ed. *Sanctity and Motherhood: Essays on Holy Mothers in the Middle Ages.* New York: Garland, 1995.

Muscatine, Charles. *Chaucer and the French Tradition: A Study in Style and Meaning.* Berkeley: University of California Press, 1957.

Neal, Derek G. *The Masculine Self in Late Medieval England.* Chicago: University of Chicago Press, 2008.

Newman, Barbara. *From Virile Woman to WomanChrist: Studies in Medieval Religion and Literature.* Philadelphia: University of Pennsylvania Press, 1997.

Nolan, Maura. *John Lydgate and the Making of Public Culture.* Cambridge: Cambridge University Press, 2005.

Olsson, Kurt. "Aspects of *Gentilesse* in John Gower's *Confessio Amantis,* Books III–V." In *John Gower: Recent Readings,* edited by R. F. Yeager, 225–73. Kalamazoo, MI: Medieval Institute Publications, 1989.

Oxford English Dictionary Online. 2006. <http://dictionary.oed.com>

Paden, William D. "Introduction." In *Medieval Lyric: Genres in Historical Context,* edited by Paden, 1–17. Urbana: University of Illinois Press, 2000.

Parsons, John Carmi, and Bonnie Wheeler. "Introduction: Medieval Mothering, Medieval Motherers." In *Medieval Mothering,* edited by Parsons and Wheeler, ix–xvii. New York: Garland, 1996.

Partner, Nancy F. "Reading *The Book of Margery Kempe*." *Exemplaria* 3.1 (1991): 29–66.

Patterson, Lee. "Christian and Pagan in *The Testament of Cresseid*." *Philological Quarterly* 52 (1973): 696–714.

———. *Chaucer and the Subject of History.* Madison: University of Wisconsin Press, 1991.

Payne, Robert O. *The Key of Remembrance: A Study of Chaucer's Poetics.* New Haven: Yale University Press, 1963.

Pearsall, Derek. *John Lydgate.* Charlottesville: University Press of Virginia, 1970.

———. "'Quha Wait Gif All That Chauceir Wrait Was Trew?': Henryson's *Testament of Cresseid*." In *New Perspectives on Middle English Texts: A Festschrift for R. A. Waldron,* edited by Susan Powell and Jeremy J. Smith, 169–82. Cambridge: D. S. Brewer, 2000.

Pelikan, Jaroslav. *Mary through the Centuries: Her Place in the History of Culture.* New Haven: Yale University Press, 1996.

Phillips, Susan. *Transforming Talk: The Problem with Gossip in Late Medieval England.* University Park: Pennsylvania State University Press, 2007.

Price, Paul. "I Want to Be Alone: The Single Woman in Fifteenth-Century Legends of St. Katherine of Alexandria." In *The Single Woman in Medieval and Early Modern England: Her Life and Representation,* edited by Laurel Amtower and Dorothea Kehler, 21–39. Tempe: Arizona Center for Medieval and Renaissance Studies, 2003.

Pugh, Tison, and Marcia Smith Marzec, eds. *Men and Masculinities in Chaucer's* Troilus and Criseyde. Rochester, NY: D. S. Brewer, 2008.

Reames, Sherry L. "The Second Nun's Prologue and Tale." In *Sources and Analogues of the* Canterbury Tales, vol. 1, edited by Robert M. Correale and Mary Hamel, 491-527. Rochester, NY: D. S. Brewer, 2002.

Reed, Teresa P. *Shadows of Mary: Reading the Virgin Mary in Medieval Texts.* Cardiff: University of Wales Press, 2003.

Renoir, Alain. *The Poetry of John Lydgate.* London: Routledge, 1967.

Rice, Nicole. *Lay Piety and Religious Discipline in Middle English Literature.* Cambridge: Cambridge University Press, 2008.

Riddy, Felicity. "'Abject Odious': Feminine and Masculine in Henryson's *Testament of Cresseid.*" In *The Long Fifteenth Century,* edited by Helen Cooper, Sally Mapstone, and Joerg O. Fichte, 229–48. Oxford: Clarendon, 1997.

———. "Julian of Norwich and Self-Textualization." In *Editing Women,* edited by Ann Hutchison, 101–24. Toronto, Canada: University of Toronto Press, 1998.

———. "'Publication' before Print: The Case of Julian of Norwich." In *The Uses of Script and Print, 1300–1700,* edited by Julia Crick and Alexandra Walsham, 29–49. Cambridge: Cambridge University Press, 2004.

———. "Text and Self in *The Book of Margery Kempe.*" In *Voices in Dialogue: Reading Women in the Middle Ages,* edited by Linda Olson and Kathryn Kerby-Fulton, 435–53. Notre Dame, IN: University of Notre Dame Press, 2005.

Riehle, Wolfgang. *The Middle English Mystics.* Translated by Bernard Standring. Boston: Routledge & Kegan Paul, 1981.

Rigby, S. H. *English Society in the Later Middle Ages: Class, Status, and Gender.* New York: St. Martin's Press, 1995.

Robertson, Elizabeth. *Early English Devotional Prose and the Female Audience.* Knoxville: University of Tennessee Press, 1990.

———. "Marriage, Mutual Consent, and the Affirmation of the Female Subject in the *Knight's Tale,* the *Wife of Bath's Tale,* and the *Franklin's Tale.*" In *Drama, Narrative, and Poetry in the* Canterbury Tales, edited by Wendy Harding, 175–93. Toulouse, France: Presses Universitaires du Mirail, 2003.

Rytting, Jenny Rebecca. "In Search of the Perfect Spouse: John Gower's *Confessio Amantis* as a Marriage Manual." *Dalhousie Review* 82.1 (2002): 113–26.

Sahlin, Claire L. "Gender and Prophetic Authority in Birgitta of Sweden's *Revelations.*" In *Gender and Text in the Later Middle Ages,* edited by Jane Chance, 69–95. Gainesville: University Press of Florida, 1996.

Salih, Sarah. *Versions of Virginity in Late Medieval England.* Cambridge: D. S. Brewer, 2001.

——— and Denise N. Baker, eds. *Julian of Norwich's Legacy: Medieval Mysticism and Post-Medieval Reception.* New York: Palgrave Macmillan, 2009.

Sanok, Catherine. *Her Life Historical: Exemplarity and Female Saints' Lives in Late Medieval England.* Philadelphia: University of Pennsylvania Press, 2007.

Scala, Elizabeth. "The Gender of Historicism." In *The Post-Historical Middle Ages,* edited by Scala and Sylvia Federico, 191–214. New York: Palgrave Macmillan, 2009.

Scanlon, Larry. *Narrative, Authority, and Power: The Medieval Exemplum and the Chaucerian Tradition.* Cambridge: Cambridge University Press, 1996.

———. "Lydgate's Poetics: Laureation and Domesticity in the *Temple of Glass.*" In *John Lydgate,* edited by Scanlon and James Simpson, 61–97.

——— and James Simpson, eds. *John Lydgate: Poetry, Culture, and Lancastrian England.* Notre Dame, IN: University of Notre Dame Press, 2006.

Scase, Wendy. "Tolkien, Philology, and *The Reeve's Tale:* Towards the Cultural Move in Middle

English Studies." *Studies in the Age of Chaucer* 24 (2002): 325–34.

Schmitz, Götz. "Rhetoric and Fiction: Gower's Comments on Eloquence and Courtly Poetry." In *Gower's* Confessio Amantis: *A Critical Anthology,* edited by Peter Nicholson, 117–42. Cambridge: D. S. Brewer, 1991.

Severs, J. Burke. *The Literary Relationships of Chaucer's* Clerkes Tale. New Haven: Yale University Press, 1942; Hamden, CT: Archon Books, 1972.

Shahar, Shulamith. *Childhood in the Middle Ages.* Translated by Chaya Galai. London: Routledge, 1990.

Sherman, Mark A. "The Politics of Discourse in Chaucer's *Knight's Tale.*" *Exemplaria* 6.1 (1994): 87–114.

Shuger, Deborah Kuller. *The Renaissance Bible: Scholarship, Sacrifice, and Subjectivity.* Berkeley: University of California Press, 1994.

Simpson, James. *Oxford English Literary History, Volume 2: 1350–1457: Reform and Cultural Revolution.* Oxford: Oxford University Press, 2004.

Smith, Jeremy J. "John Gower and London English." In *A Companion to Gower,* edited by Sian Echard, 61–72. Rochester, NY: D. S. Brewer, 2004.

Spearing, A. C. *Medieval Dream Poetry.* Cambridge: Cambridge University Press, 1976.

———. "*The Book of Margery Kempe;* or, The Diary of a Nobody." *The Southern Review* 38.3 (Summer 2002): 625–35.

Sprung, Andrew. "'If It Youre Wille Be': Coercion and Compliance in Chaucer's *Clerk's Tale.*" *Exemplaria* 7.2 (1995): 345–69.

———. "The Inverted Metaphor: Earthly Mothering as Figura of Divine Love in Julian of Norwich's *Book of Showings.*" In *Medieval Mothering,* edited by John Carmi Parsons and Bonnie Wheeler, 183–99. New York: Garland, 1996.

Staley, Lynn. *Margery Kempe's Dissenting Fictions.* University Park: Pennsylvania State University Press, 1994.

———. "Chaucer and the Postures of Sanctity." In *The Powers of the Holy: Religion, Politics, and Gender in Late Medieval Culture,* edited by David Aers and Staley, 233–57. University Park: Pennsylvania State University Press, 1996.

———. *Languages of Power in the Age of Richard II.* University Park: Pennsylvania State University Press, 2005.

Stargardt, Ute. "The Beguines of Belgium, the Dominican Nuns of Germany, and Margery Kempe." In *The Popular Literature of Medieval England,* edited by Thomas Heffernan, 277–313. Knoxville: University of Tennessee Press, 1985.

Stein, Robert M. "The Conquest of Femenye: Desire, Power, and Narrative in Chaucer's *Knight's Tale.*" In *Desiring Discourse: The Literature of Love, Ovid through Chaucer,* edited by James J. Paxson and Cynthia A. Gravlee, 188–205. Selinsgrove, PA: Susquehanna University Press, 1998.

Stone, Robert. *Middle English Prose Style: Margery Kempe and Julian of Norwich.* The Hague: Mouton, 1970.

Straus, Barrie Ruth. "Freedom through Renunciation?: Women's Voices, Women's Bodies, and the Phallic Order." In *Desire and Discipline: Sex and Sexuality in the Premodern West,* edited by Jacqueline Murray and Konrad Eisenbichler, 245–64. Toronto, Canada: University of Toronto Press, 1996.

Strohm, Paul. *Hochon's Arrow: The Social Imagination of Fourteenth-Century Texts.* Princeton: Princeton University Press, 1992.

———. *Politique: Languages of Statecraft between Chaucer and Shakespeare.* Notre Dame, IN:

University of Notre Dame Press, 2005.

Summit, Jennifer. *Lost Property: The Woman Writer and English Literary History, 1380–1589.* Chicago: University of Chicago Press, 2000.

———. "*Troilus and Criseyde.*" In *The Yale Companion to Chaucer,* edited by Seth Lerer, 213–42. New Haven: Yale University Press, 2006.

Swanson, R. N. *Church and Society in Late Medieval England.* Oxford: Basil Blackwell, 1989.

Taylor, Karla. "Language in Use." In *Chaucer: Contemporary Approaches,* edited by Susanna Fein and David Raybin, 99–115. University Park: Pennsylvania State University Press, 2009.

Tinkle, Theresa. *Medieval Venuses and Cupids: Sexuality, Hermeneutics, and English Poetry.* Stanford, CA: Stanford University Press, 1996.

Torti, Anna. "John Lydgate's *Temple of Glas:* 'Atwixen Two so Hang I in Balaunce.'" In *Intellectuals and Writers in Fourteenth-Century Europe,* edited by Piero Boitani and Torti, 226–43. Cambridge: D. S. Brewer, 1986.

Van, Thomas A. "Walter at the Stake: A Reading of Chaucer's *Clerk's Tale.*" *Chaucer Review* 22.3 (1988): 214–24.

Van Dyke, Carolynn. "The Clerk's and the Franklin's Subjected Subjects." *Studies in the Age of Chaucer* 17 (1995): 45–68.

Voaden, Rosalynn. *God's Words, Women's Voices: The Discernment of Spirits in the Writing of Late-Medieval Women Visionaries.* Suffolk, UK: York Medieval Press, 1999.

Wallace, David. *Chaucerian Polity: Absolutist Lineages and Associational Forms in England and Italy.* Stanford, CA: Stanford University Press, 1997.

[Ward], Sister Benedicta. "Julian the Solitary." In *Julian Reconsidered,* by Kenneth Leech and Sister Benedicta, 11–35. Oxford: SLG Press, 1988.

Warner, Marina. *Alone of All Her Sex: The Myth and Cult of the Virgin Mary.* New York: Vintage Books, 1976.

Warren, Nancy Bradley. *Spiritual Economies: Female Monasticism in Later Medieval England.* Philadelphia: University of Pennsylvania Press, 2001.

———. *Women of God and Arms: Female Spirituality and Political Conflict, 1380–1600.* Philadelphia: University of Pennsylvania Press, 2005.

Waters, Claire. *Angels and Earthly Creatures: Preaching, Performance, and Gender in the Later Middle Ages.* Philadelphia: University of Pennsylvania Press, 2004.

Watson, Nicholas. "The Composition of Julian of Norwich's *Revelation of Love.*" *Speculum* 68.3 (1993): 637–84.

———. "Censorship and Cultural Change in Late Medieval England: Vernacular Theology, the Oxford Translation Debate, and Arundel's Constitutions of 1409." *Speculum* 70.4 (1995): 822–64.

———. "'Yf Women Be Double Naturelly': Remaking 'Woman' in Julian of Norwich's *Revelation of Love.*" *Exemplaria* 8.1 (Spring 1996): 1–34.

———. "The Middle English Mystics." In *The Cambridge History of Medieval English Literature,* edited by David Wallace, 539–65. New York: Cambridge University Press, 2002.

———. "The Making of *The Book of Margery Kempe.*" In *Voices in Dialogue: Reading Women in the Middle Ages,* edited by Linda Olson and Kathryn Kerby-Fulton, 395–434. Notre Dame, IN: University of Notre Dame Press, 2005.

Watt, Diane. *Amoral Gower: Language, Sex, and Politics.* Minneapolis: University of Minnesota Press, 2003.

———. "Gender and Sexuality in *Confessio Amantis.*" In *A Companion to Gower,* edited by Sian Echard, 197–214. Rochester, NY: D. S. Brewer, 2004.

———. "Saint Julian of the Apocalypse." In *A Companion to Julian of Norwich,* edited by Liz Herbert McAvoy, 64–74. Cambridge: D. S. Brewer, 2008.

Weinbaum, Batya. *Islands of Women and Amazons: Representations and Realities.* Austin: University of Texas Press, 1999.

Weissman, Hope Phyllis. "Margery Kempe in Jerusalem: *Hysterica Compassio* in the Late Middle Ages." In *Acts of Interpretation: The Text in Its Contexts, 700–1600,* edited by Mary J. Carruthers and Elizabeth D. Kirk, 201–17. Norman, OK: Pilgrim Books, 1982.

Wetherbee, Winthrop. "Romance and Epic in Chaucer's *Knight's Tale.*" *Exemplaria* 11.1 (1990): 303–28.

———. "John Gower." In *The Cambridge History of Medieval English Literature,* edited by David Wallace, 589–609. New York: Cambridge University Press, 2002.

Williams, Steven J. *The Secret of Secrets: The Scholarly Career of a Pseudo-Aristotelian Text in the Latin Middle Ages.* Ann Arbor: University of Michigan Press, 2003.

Williams, Tara. "Fragments and Foundations: Medieval Texts and the Future of Feminism." *Literature Compass* 4 (May 2007): 1003–16.

———. "'As Thu Wer a Wedow': Margery Kempe's Wifehood and Widowhood." *Exemplaria* 21.4 (Winter 2009): 345–62.

Windeatt, Barry. "Julian of Norwich and Her Audience." *Review of English Studies* 28 (1977): 1–17.

Winstead, Karen. "Capgrave's Saint Katherine and the Perils of Gynecocracy." *Viator* 25 (1994): 361–76.

———. *Virgin Martyrs: Legends of Sainthood in Late Medieval England.* Ithaca, NY: Cornell University Press, 1997.

———, ed. and trans. *Chaste Passions: Medieval English Virgin Martyr Legends.* Ithaca, NY: Cornell University Press, 2000.

———. *John Capgrave's Fifteenth Century.* Philadelphia: University of Pennsylvania Press, 2007.

Woods, William F. "'My Sweete Foo': Emelye's Role in the *Knight's Tale.*" *Studies in Philology* 88.3 (1991): 276–306.

Woolf, Rosemary. *The English Religious Lyric in the Middle Ages.* Oxford: Oxford University Press, 1968.

———. "Moral Chaucer and Kindly Gower." In *J. R. R. Tolkien, Scholar and Storyteller,* edited by Mary Salu and Robert T. Farrell, 221–45. Ithaca, NY: Cornell University Press, 1979.

Yeager, R. F. *John Gower's Poetic: The Search for a New Arion.* Cambridge: D. S. Brewer, 1990.

INDEX

www.ingramcontent.com/pod-product-compliance
Lightning Source LLC
Chambersburg PA
CBHW031251090426
42742CB00007B/411